100 GREAT DETECTIVES

DETECTIVES

or
THE DETECTIVE DIRECTORY

EDITED, WITH AN
INTRODUCTION AND NOTES

by

MAXIM JAKUBOWSKY

Xanadu

British Library Cataloguing in Publication Data

100 great detectives
 1. Detective stories
 1. Jakubowski, Maxim
 809.387209

ISBN 1–85480–025–6

First published 1991 by Xanadu Publications Limited
19 Cornwall Road, London N4 4PH.

Typeset by Selectmove Ltd.
Printed and bound in Great Britain by
The Bath Press.

CONTENTS

Introduction by Maxim Jakubowski   11

1. Margaret Lewis on Ngaio Marsh's RODERICK
   ALLEYN   17
2. Mark Timlin on William Hjortsberg's HARRY
   ANGEL   20
3. Aaron Elkins on Michael Innes' SIR JOHN
   APPLEBY   21
4. Douglas Wynn on Ross MacDonald's
   LEW ARCHER   24
5. Ion Mills on Arthur Lyons' JACOB ASCH   26
6. Robert Adey on Joseph Commings' SENATOR
   BROOKS U. BANNER   28
7. Philip Kerr on Friedrich Dürrenmatt's INSPECTOR
   BARLACH   31
8. P.C. Doherty on Umberto Eco's BROTHER
   WILLIAM BASKERVILLE   33
9. Scott Herbertson on Sjowall and Wahloo's
   MARTIN BECK   35
10. Philip Harbottle on John Russell Fearn's
    'BLACK MARIA'   37
11. Colin Greenland on Charles Burns' EL BORBAH   40
12. Victoria Nichols & Susan Thompson on Gladys
    Mitchell's DAME BEATRICE ADELA LESTRANGE
    BRADLEY   42
13. Neil Gaiman on G.K. Chesterton's FATHER
    BROWN   45
14. Wayne D. Dundee on Andrew Vachss' BURKE   47
15. Iain Sinclair on WILLIAM S. BURROUGHS   50
16. Joe Gores on Michael Gilbert's MR CALDER
    and MR BEHRENS   53
17. Michael Moorcock on Margery Allingham's
    ALBERT CAMPION   55

18. Mike Phillips on Ed McBain's STEVE CARELLA   57
19. Jonathan Main on Nicolas Freeling's CASTANG   60
20. Russell James on Peter Cheyney's LEMMY
     CAUTION   62
21. Anthony Lejeune on Earl Derr Biggers'
     CHARLIE CHAN   64
22. Soeur Van Folly on Simon Smith's
     THE CLEWSEYS   66
23. Richard A. Lupoff on Dashiell Hammett's
     THE CONTINENTAL OP   70
24. Eric Wright on Howard Engel's BENNY
     COOPERMAN   72
25. Paul Buck on Jonathan Latimer's BILL CRANE   74
26. Mark Schorr on Thomas Harris' JACK
     CRAWFORD   76
27. Barry Fantoni on Raymond Chandler's JOHN
     DALMAS   78
28. John Malcolm on Reginald Hill's DALZIEL
     and PASCOE   80
29. Ralph H. Peck on Brian Garfield's CHARLIE
     DARK   82
30. Susan Dunlap on Joyce Porter's CHIEF
     INSPECTOR WILFRED DOVER   84
31. Michael Eaton on Edgar Allan Poe's
     C. AUGUSTE DUPIN   86
32. Michael Gilbert on Dorothy L. Sayers'
     MONTAGUE EGG   88
33. Patricia Moyes on Elizabeth Peters' AMELIA
     PEABODY EMERSON   90
34. Maxim Jakubowski on Marc Behm's THE EYE   92
35. David Langford on John Dickson Carr's
     DR FELL   94
36. Susan Moody on Edmund Crispin's GERVASE
     FEN   97
37. David Williams on Haughton Murphy's
     REUBEN FROST   98
38. Gwendoline Butler on Elizabeth Daly's
     HENRY GAMADGE   101
39. James Melville on H.R.F. Keating's INSPECTOR
     GHOTE   103
40. Jill McGown on Josephine Tey's ALAN GRANT   105

41. Deborah Valentine on P.D. James' CORDELIA
    GREY   107
42. Philip L. Scowcroft on A.E.W. Mason's
    INSPECTOR HANAUD   109
43. John Conquest on P.B. Yuill's HAZELL   111
44. H.R.F. Keating on Sir Arthur Conan
    Doyle's SHERLOCK HOLMES   114
45. Scott A. Cupp on Fredric Brown's
    ED and AM HUNTER   116
46. Margaret Maron on Dorothy Dunnett's
    JOHNSON JOHNSON   118
47. Cay Van Ash on Sax Rohmer's MORIS
    KLAW   120
48. Benjamin M. Schutz on William McIlvanney's
    LAIDLAW   122
49. Jim Huang on Sarah Caudwell's JULIA
    LARWOOD   124
50. Harold Adams on Seymour Shubin's
    LIEUTENANT LaSALA   126
51. Bob Biderman on Tony Hillerman's JOE
    LEAPHORN and JIM CHEE   128
52. Michael Z. Lewin on Liza Cody's ANNA
    LEE   130
53. Reginald Hill on Anthony Trollope's
    MACKINTOSH, BUNFIT and GAGER   132
54. Peter Robinson on Georges Simenon's
    INSPECTOR MAIGRET   134
55. Loren D. Estleman on Raymond Chandler's
    PHILIP MARLOWE   136
56. Wendy M. Grossman on Agatha Christie's
    MISS MARPLE   139
57. Celia Dale on Magdalen Nabb's 'THE
    MARSHAL'   142
58. Bill Pronzini on Marcia Muller's SHARON
    McCONE   144
59. Sharyn McCrumb on Carter Dickson's
    SIR HENRY MERRIVALE   146
60. Adrian Wootton on James Crumley's MILO
    MILODRAGOVITCH   149
61. Simon Brett on Sue Grafton's KINSEY
    MILLHONE   151

8

62. John Williams on Ed Lacy's TOUSSAINT
    MARCUS MOORE   153
63. Ralph Spurrier on Colin Dexter's INSPECTOR
    MORSE   155
64. Mike Ripley on Charles Willeford's HOKE
    MOSELEY   157
65. Ed Gorman on Bill Pronzini's NAMELESS
    DETECTIVE   158
66. Peter Lovesey on Michael Kenyon's DETECTIVE
    CHIEF INSPECTOR HENRY PECKOVER   161
67. Martin Edwards on Cyril Hare's FRANCIS
    PETTIGREW   163
68. Anne Hart on Agatha Christie's HERCULE
    POIROT   165
69. Barbara Wilson on Dorothy Gilman's
    MRS POLLIFAX   168
70. Nigel Algar on Loren D. Estleman's
    RALPH POTEET   170
71. Daniel P. King on Nigel Morland's MRS PYM   172
72. Edward D. Hoch on Ellery Queen's
    ELLERY QUEEN   174
73. Jerry Raine on James Lee Burke's DAVE
    ROBICHEAUX   177
74. Jerry Kennealy on Edward Mathis' DAN
    ROMAN   179
75. Stephen Gallagher on Leslie Charteris'
    THE SAINT   181
76. Lesley Grant-Adamson on Julie Smith's
    REBECCA SCHWARTZ   183
77. Barbara Mertz, Barbara Michaels & Elizabeth Peters
    on Charlotte MacLeod's PETER SHANDY   185
78,79. Duncan Torrens on Anthony Berkeley's ROGER
    SHERINGHAM and Philip MacDonald's
    ANTHONY GETHRYN   187
80. Adam Barnett-Foster on Jerome Charyn's
    ISAAC SIDEL   190
81. Marcel Berlins on Sarah Caudwell's PROFESSOR
    HILARY TAMAR   192
82. B.J. Rahn on Patricia Wentworth's
    MISS SILVER   194
83. Robert Wallace on John le Carré's GEORGE
    SMILEY   198

84. Kim Newman on James Ellroy's DUDLEY SMITH   200
85. Jack Adrian on Edgar Wallace's THE SOOPER   202
86. Julian Symons on Dashiell Hammett's
     SAM SPADE   205
87. Frederick Nolan on Robert B. Parker's SPENSER   206
88. Catherine Aird on Emma Lathen's JOHN
     PUTNAM THATCHER   209
89. Sarah Caudwell on Patricia Moyes' HENRY
     AND EMMY TIBBETT   211
90. Robert Campbell on Robert Irvine's MORONI
     TRAVELER   213
91. Alex Auswaks on David Williams' MARK
     TREASURE   216
92. Haughton Murphy on Robert Barnard's
     PERRY TRETHOWAN   217
93. Jan Bitsch Steffensen on Nicolas Freeling's
     VAN DER VALK   219
94. Helen Esper Olmsted on Loren D. Estleman's
     AMOS WALKER   222
95. Linda Semple on Sara Paretsky's
     V.I. WARSHAWSKI   224
96. Melodie Johnson Howe & Catherine Kenney
     on Dorothy L. Sayers' LORD PETER WIMSEY   227
97. Carolyn G. Hart on Phoebe Atwood
     Taylor's LEONIDAS WITHERALL   231
98. Paula Gosling on Rex Stout's
     NERO WOLFE   233
99. Brian Stableford on M.P. Shiel's PRINCE
     ZALESKI   236
100. Frances Fyfield on Michael Dibdin's AURELIO
     ZEN   238
     Notes on the Contributors   240
     Acknowledgements   256

INTRODUCTION

KNIGHTS IN RUSTY ARMOUR AND OTHER JOURNEYMEN OF JUSTICE

D etectives. Private Eyes. Sleuths. Investigators. Cops. Dicks. They come in all shapes, sizes, sexes and historical periods. Why do they fascinate and attract us so?

One might mischievously argue that God was in fact the very first detective, when he solved the mystery of who bit into the apple, before moving on to more serious business in his second case, when Cain and Abel had a somewhat fatal argument. But this is no work of historical research to pinpoint precursors and pioneers of the investigative arts, although several contributors to this volume do come up with fascinating early day detectives.

Detectives. They've been around since time immemorial, then, as the recent commercial trend for sleuths acting in an historical setting ably demonstrates (Brother Cadfael in medieval times, as are characters by Umberto Eco and P.C. Doherty; Lindsey Davis' centurion Falco in Ancient Rome; Margaret Doody's Aristotle in Athens' golden age; Anton Gill's Ancient Egypt 'tec and, no doubt soon, some clever writer will get around to creating the first prehistoric detective, unless I get there first: who killed the dinosaurs, who made cro-magnon man vanish, no minor cases down those mean ice ages. . .). But they weren't always called detectives: they were soldiers (of fortune), nosy clerics, knights, sometimes even thieves with honour (a great tradition which culminated in the early 20th century streak of debonair rakes like Raffles, Arsene Lupin, Fantomas, the Saint and others), priests and scholars, and only later actual policemen (Vidocq of the French Sûreté being the first of his modern kind on the scene of the crime), until the final coming of

11

the private investigator in the pages of the American pulps between the two world wars.

Since there has been life, there has also been evil and transgression. Whether minor thieving or wife-snatching (or involuntary swapping, ie adultery) or in the major mode: murder. In the battle of good versus evil, order against chaos, nothing is as straightforward as it should be, and the fascinated reader delights in the ambiguities that litter the crime and mystery genre like a minefield and seeks identification with the hero or heroine, the character who will carry him along on the quest for truth, will unravel the dastardly mystery, explain the whys and wherefores and royally entertain in the process.

Whether the crime or the enigma is solved by gentle and often eccentric intellectuals or by men of action who take it in turn to get hit over the head and bed the blonde (or the local hunk, in the fashion of the current trend for feisty female private eyes), the detective has always been at the very center of the crime novel, and it is the triumphant sleuth we remember long after the nasty criminal is locked away or dutifully buried with few wreaths and flowers.

The detective is the body and soul of crime and mystery fiction. And quite rightly so. And this book is dedicated to all these fictional toilers in the darkness of the world and the soul. Long may they investigate, and provide us readers with the very best form of wish fulfillment.

Knowing my love of detective fiction, my publishers contacted me some years back with the idea of selecting my one hundred favourite sleuths of all time, writing up short appreciations and bibliographies, and sharing my enthusiasms with others. I naturally leapt at the idea.

A few months later, having written my first ten paeans to the not quite unknown soldiers of the crime wars in a red hot burst of creativity, I sadly realised that my choices were somewhat one-sided. If I were to complete the book in this way, the emphasis on the hardboiled tradition and 'noir' atmosphere would prove totally dominant to the wrongful detriment of so many wonderful but more classic sleuths of the classic tradition. Yes, all those wonderfully old-fashioned but oh so clever detectives who would solve their cases with little or no recall to violence, chases or sex, and would call all the suspects into the drawing-room of the country house at the end of the book and fiendishly expose the culprit.

So, the concept of the book was rethought, and we came up with, what I feel is a much more exciting idea of asking some of the major British and American writers and critics to make up their own selection.

Every author was asked to submit a list of two or three of their favourite characters, and I then assigned a detective to each. I think the result is wonderfully idiosyncratic and makes for compulsive reading. Some of the individual choices are predictable, but so many others much less so, and betray fascinating guilty pleasures. And yes, I am aware that a certain Golden Age gentleman detective appears twice; blame it on my lack of coordination. It could have been worse, I could have mistakenly commissioned a dozen essays on Chandler's Philip Marlowe (there were that many requests). But to make up the round hundred, another contributor actually delivered a piece incorporating two characters for the price of one. Naturally, a book on detectives could not cheat its readers!

Compiling the book the way we have has meant throwing ourselves at the mercy of our contributors and, as expected, because of the variety of choices, a great many major characters are missing from this book. Which does not mean they are unworthy or lacking in investigative prowess. Having now compiled a hundred appreciations, one could easily put volumes 2 and 3 of this endeavour in the pipeline, with so many fascinating detectives still waiting in limbo. . .

So, these are some our missing sleuths (and, no, we're not hiring anyone to investigate their strange disappearance) and a mighty fine bunch they could have been too, but mice, men and fate decreed otherwise.

First of all, characters actually created by some of our eminent contributors. The order is totally random as we all know that crime does not respect the sanctity of the alphabet.

Joe Hannibal (Wayne D. Dundee) – Spt Tetsuo Otani (James Melville) – Insp. Luke Abbott (Paula Gosling) – Lt. Jack Stryker (Paula Gosling) – John Coffin (Gwendoline Butler) – Charmian Daniels (Jennie Melville) – Annie Laurance and Max Darling (Carolyn G. Hart) – Charlie Salter (Eric Wright) – Inspector Banks (Peter Robinson) – Kiernan O'Shaughnessy (Susan Dunlap) – Jill Smith (Susan Dunlap) – Vejay Haskell (Susan Dunlap) – Lt Alfredo Raconni (Helen Esper Olmsted) – Joseph Radkin (Bob Biderman) – Dan Kearny (Joe Gores) – Albert Samson (Michael Z. Lewin) – Lt. Leroy Powder (Michael Z. Lewin) – Sergeant

Cribb (Peter Lovesey) – Lt. Sigrid Harald (Margaret Maron) – Leo Haggerty (Benjamin Schutz) – Angel (Mike Ripley) – Red Diamond (Mark Schorr) – Mrs. Pargeter (Simon Brett) – Charles Paris (Simon Brett) – Vicky Bliss (Elizabeth Peters) – Sam Dean (Mike Phillips) – Bernie Gunther (Philip Kerr) – Amelia Peabody (Elizabeth Peters) – James Glowrey (Anthony Lejeune) – Carl Wilcox (Harold Adams) – Jimmy Flannery (Robert Campbell) – Gideon Oliver (Aaron Elkins) – Polo (Jerry Kenneally) – Macklin (Loren D. Estleman) – Penny Wanawake (Susan Moody) – Rain Morgan (Lesley Grant–Adamson) – Det. Insp. Sloan (Catherine Aird) – Whistler (Robert Campbell) – Hugh Corbett (P.C. Doherty) – Petrella (Michael Gilbert) – Jacqueline Kirby (Elizabeth Peters) – Nick Sharman (Mark Timlin) – Helen West and Geoff Bailey (Frances Fyfield) – Essington Holt (Robert Wallace).

And these are only some of the popular series characters created out of typewriter and thin air by our crème de la crème of crime writing contributors. If this were a book of lists, I might also detail all the valiant detectives who only make single appearances in their books. This, you shall be spared, but it's still no reason not to pick up their books in shops and libraries. . .

As prestigious is a massive list of memorable characters by other authors who somehow didn't make it into these pages. Look out for them, too:

Travis McGee – Inspector Wexford – Adam Dalgleish – Dale Cooper – Fletch – Inspector Moto – Jemima Shore – Lovejoy – Nick Carter – Fantomas – Richard Hannay – J.G. Reeder – Reggie Fortune – Philo Vance – Nigel Strangeways – Asey Mayo – Bony – Perry Mason – Solar Pons – Mike Hammer – the Great Merlini – Miss Seeton – Mike Shayne – The Toff – Gideon – Paul Temple – Judge Dee – Donald Lam and Bertha Cool – Ed Noon – Carolus Deene – Luis Mendoza – Gravedigger and Coffin – Rabbi Small – Virgil Tibbs – Mike Faraday – Mitch Tobin – Dan Fortune – Matthew Hope – Wycliffe – Grijpstra and De Gier – Kojak – Sarah Kelling – Dave Brandstetter – Brother Cadfael – Melrose Plant and Richard Jury – Poppy Ott – Nancy Drew – Jeff and Harla Troy – Carlotta Carlyle – Pam Nilsen – Miriam Birdseye – Emma Victor – Kate Delafield – Kate Fansler – Nick and Nora Charles – Ned Beaumont – Jules de Grandin – The Shadow – Fred Fellows – Mr. Fortune – Mongo – Honey West – Mac – Ben Gates – Jake and Helene Justus – Jim Hardman – Pete Schofield – the

Nameless Detective (no, not Bill Pronzini's, but Derek Raymond's harrowing protagonist) – Dan Turner – Jack Dwyer – C W Sugrue – Mac Slade – Peter McGarr – Sexton Blake – Sam Birkett – Trent – Lucas Davenport – Nurse Hilda Adams – Janice Cameron – Jim Sader – Grace Latham – Laura DiPalma – Stanley Hastings – Drury Lane – Basil Willing – Kramer and Zondi – Erik Lonnrot – Parker – the Grub and Stakers – Murdoch – Insp. Lynley – Tony Rome – Pete Sawyer – Jacob Lomax – Qwilleran, Koko and Yum Yum – Matt Scudder – Doc Adams – Monsieur Pamplemousse – Hamish Macbeth – Paul Pine – Gabe Wager – Ellie Simons – Maggie Ryan – Nate Heller – Mallory – Holly Winter – Frank Clemons – Cliff Hardy – Sheriff Dan Rhodes – Race Williams – Satan Hall – Dr Sam Johnson – Thomas Black – Mark Renzler – Kinky Friedman – Peter Decker – Alex Delaware – Sergeant Bragg and Constable Morton – Doran Fairweather – Aaron Gunner – Sam Hunter – Claire Aldington – Achille Peroni – J.P. Beaumont – C.B. Greenfield – Rostnikov – Toby Peters – Father Koesler – Stuart Haydon – Leo Bloodworth and Serendipity Dahlquist – Fred Carver – Alo Nudger – the Yellowthread Street gang – Thomas and Charlotte Pitt – Insp. Felse – Jenny Cain – Peter Duluth – Augustus Maltravers – T.D. Stash – Eleanor Roosevelt – Celia Grant – Insp. Luke Thanet – Moses Wine – Miss Melville – Paul McDonald – Det. Stanley Moodrow – Falco – Johnny Ortiz – Insp. Finch – Insp. Frost – Harry Stoner and Insp. Pinbright.

And yes, I know there are a few missing still. . .

A useful bit of investigation for idle minds might wish to marry up the names of the characters with the name of their creators!

The crime and mystery field lends itself like no other genres to the creation of full-blooded, well-developed and, often, unforgettable characters. One hundred writers provide their quirky and loving choices. May a thousand more detectives flower in future years.

1

MARGARET LEWIS

on

Roderick Alleyn

Who could resist the urbane and handsome Roderick Alleyn? Certainly not his creator, Dame Ngaio Marsh, who first tailored his elegant shape to fit the pages of her novel *A Man Lay Dead* in 1934 and kept him young and svelte, with not even a suspicion of grey hair, until her final novel in 1982. And certainly not thousands of readers from Tokyo to Tunbridge Wells who continue to be charmed by his good manners and good looks.

Yet Alleyn is far from being just a piece of expensively-suited crumpet. An Oxford graduate, whose mother is Lady Alleyn of Danes Lodge, he fled from the diplomatic service to the ranks of the police force, and plodded the beat on rainy nights with all the other recruits. He is equally at home munching cheese and pickles and drinking best bitter in the village pub with his faithful assistant, Inspector Fox, as he is sipping fine wines with the local gentry. He speaks French like a native and can quote Shakespeare like the devil, for his own purposes.

When Roderick Alleyn entered the ranks of the gentlemen detectives his aristocratic background made a comparison to Lord Peter Wimsey inevitable. Yet as Marsh became more confident as a writer of detective fiction, Alleyn swiftly developed into a much more interesting character than that pampered and self-assured Lord. He is, after all, a salaried policeman, and he takes orders from above like any other member of his profession. It is convenient that in the mid-1930s he is travelling in New Zealand, home of Ngaio Marsh, where his talents allow the solution of a very nasty murder with a Maori connection, and that he should spend some time there during the Second World War, hunting down traitors. He is a much sought-after bachelor, an acceptable house-party guest and 'although responsive to the opposite sex, did not bounce in and out of irresponsible beds when going about his job.'

Although attractive to women, Alleyn does not fall in love until a trip to the Antipodes introduces him to the painter Agatha Troy, whom he first sees scruffy, bad-tempered and flecked with paint on the top deck of a liner moving out of Suva Harbour. Why should he be irresistibly drawn to a painter? Surely it is not unreasonable to suggest that Ngaio Marsh, who trained as a painter and in her twenties regarded herself primarily as an artist, was here indulging in a little translated romance. Alleyn has to put up a fairly spirited assault on Agatha Troy, who is initially one of the suspects in a murder enquiry (*Artists in Crime*, 1938) reducing the detective to a state of agitated hyper-apology as he inspects her under-garments and rifles her pockets during the investigation.

Troy keeps Alleyn firmly at a distance for some time, and although she eventually agrees to become his wife at the end of *Death in a White Tie* (1938), she always remains a distant, faun-like figure whom the authoritative detective can never quite take for granted. Alleyn's relationship with Troy enhances his character considerably, and his uncertainties in love make him into a much more attractive person than if he were presented as an irresistible lady-killer. Marriage to Troy is not just a cunning plot device to allow access to the rich and famous (the subjects of many of Troy's portraits have a habit of reaching a violent demise before the paint is even dry); it also allows Alleyn to unfold as a highly astute observer of the upper classes, and, occasionally, as a concerned and vulnerable victim of crime. This can strike at those he holds most dear, as when his son Ricky is twice kidnapped (*Spinsters in Jeopardy*, 1953, and *Last Ditch*, 1977), and Troy is closeted with a murderer in a canal boat (*Clutch of Constables*, 1968).

The problem of the ageing serial character which affects Roderick Alleyn and several other long-running detective heroes undoubtedly concerned his creator, but many of the later novels are set in a kind of convenient time-warp that allows Alleyn and Fox to remain vaguely suspended in the 1950s, where Chief Constables were still retired officers from the Indian Army and computers were unknown.

Alleyn's compassion and his sense of justice, his ability to see through pretensions and to look kindly on the eccentricities of the people that he meets, recognising with sympathy all the little defence mechanisms that they erect to allow them to cope with life, perhaps lead to another knight in shining armour, Philip Marlowe. Indeed, they both share a connection with Dulwich College, where Raymond Chandler went to school as did Ngaio's father, Henry

Marsh. Alleyn takes his name from the founder of this school, Edward Alleyn, the Elizabethan actor. Alleyn's 'mean streets' are found in English country villages and at fashionable London addresses, but the evils they deal with are the same: murder, blackmail, adultery, concealment of the truth. Alleyn very rarely goes on the defensive about his profession but occasionally he has been known to lose his temper and sharply to remind his high-society friends that their comfortable lives are protected by the system of law he defends.

Nothing that emerges in the thirty-two novels of Ngaio Marsh alters her initial description of her detective as being 'an attractive, civilized man with whom it would be pleasant to talk but much less pleasant to fall out'. It is not surprising that his creator, as well the readers who share his company through his many cases, 'have never got tired of the old boy'.

THE CASES OF RODERICK ALLEYN, BY NGAIO MARSH

Novels

A Man Lay Dead, 1934. *Enter A Murderer*, 1935. *The Nursing-Home Murder*, 1935. *Death in Ecstasy*, 1936. *Vintage Murder*, 1937. *Artists in Crime*, 1938. *Death in a White Tie*, 1938. *Overture to Death*, 1939. *Death at the Bar*, 1940. *Death of a Peer*, 1940. *Death and the Dancing Footman*, 1941. *Colour Scheme*, 1943. *Died in the Wool*, 1945. *Final Curtain*, 1947. *Swing, Brother, Swing*, 1949. *Opening Night*, 1951. *Spinsters in Jeopardy*, 1953. *Scales of Justice*, 1955. *Death of a Fool*, 1956. *Singing in the Shrouds*, 1958. *False Scent*, 1959. *Hand in Glove*, 1962. *Dead Water*, 1963. *Killer Dolphin*, 1966. *Clutch of Constables*, 1968. *When in Rome*, 1970. *Tied up in Tinsel*, 1972. *Black As He's Painted*, 1974. *Last Ditch*, 1977. *Grave Mistake*, 1978. *Photo-Finish*, 1980. *Light Thickens*, 1982.

Story collection

The Collected Short Fiction of Ngaio Marsh, 1989.

2

MARK TIMLIN

on

Harry Angel

When writing about the New York private-eye hero of William Hjortsberg's novel *Falling Angel*, it is almost impossible to separate the book from the character. I offer no apologies for this, as they are more closely linked than most fictional detectives to the cases they find themselves investigating. Harry Angel is an ex-cop, WW2 vet and victim of severe facial injuries that necessitated extreme plastic surgery, which at the time (1943) was in its infancy, and used ordinary wax to re-model the features. The surgery went badly wrong when Harry fell asleep in the sun some years later and the heat melted the wax. The reader gets the impression that Harry is not the most handsome of fellows, with a face resembling a potato, bringing to mind Karl Malden in *The Streets of San Francisco*.

Harry is a classic low-life, wise cracking, smart arse P.I., with a natty line in similes, a poor taste in suits and a dab hand at opening locked doors when no one's around. He runs a one-man show, *THE CROSSROADS DETECTIVE AGENCY* out of a couple of rooms in a cheesy building on 7th Avenue, which he inherited off his boss when he died. Harry lives in the Chelsea Hotel, which later became a hangout for junkies, pimps and rock musicians. The hotel gained particular notoriety when Andy Warhol was shot in one of the rooms and Sid Vicious was alleged to have stabbed his girlfriend Nancy Spungen in another. Not the most salubrious crib in town.

The book starts on Friday the thirteenth of March, 1959. Harry is hired by the suave and mysterious Louis Cyphre to find ex-crooner Johnny Favorite, né Jonathan Leibling, who owes Cyphre on an unexplained contract. Favorite has gone missing from a nursing-home where he had lived since being wounded, shell-shocked and suffered loss of memory whilst entertaining the US troops in Tunisia during the war, and Cyphre wants him found. Angel and Cyphre first meet at the *Top of the 6's* restaurant at 666 5th Avenue. Amongst other sartorial details, Harry notices that Cyphre wears an inverted gold star on his tie-pin.

CROSSROADS; Friday the 13th: The Ides of March: Inverted stars: Angel; Leibling; Favorite; Cyphre (or cipher); 666. Shades of Robert Johnson and Aleister Crowley.

By this time, students of the diabolical are rubbing their hands in anticipation. Unfortunately, Harry, not being the brightest of individuals, doesn't get the connection, and starts off on a routine missing person investigation.

Angel follows the trail of Favorite through a maze of eccentric characters, puzzling clues and horrifying murders.

Bright he may not be, but Harry is tenacious, and in one of the best plot twists in the genre, Harry finally comes face to face with Favorite.

Sadly, Alan Parker's film of the book is a great disappointment. It fiddles with locations, misunderstands and never fully explains the *dénouement*. Chucks in all kinds of cheap horror effects. And, I might add, Mickey Rourke is no Harry Angel.

No, Harry Angel is Harry Angel, and the saddest thing is that he never appears in a another book, and the hardboiled detective novel loses a fine hero.

THE CASES OF HARRY ANGEL, BY WILLIAM HJORTSBERG
Falling Angel, 1978.

3

AARON ELKINS

on

Sir John Appleby

When Maxim Jakubowski kindly invited me to write a piece on a favorite fictional detective, I chose Michael Innes' John Appleby. Something tells me that, being an American, I was expected to have the good sense to select Sam Spade, or Philip Marlowe, or Nero Wolfe, or somebody equally close to home. And possibly I could have written more confidently about someone from my own culture. But the fact of the matter is that I've had more hours of pleasure following Sir John's adventures than than those of almost anyone else I can think of.

One reason, of course, is that there are more of them. Appleby first appeared in 1935 in *Death at the President's Lodging*, and has been at it virtually ever since. Only Hercule Poirot matches his extraordinary achievement in solving crimes in six successive decades. And while there is room for argument as to which of the two has the greater quality and quantity of little gray cells, there can be no doubt that Appleby has made a better career of it. He has gone from Inspector, to Detective Inspector, to Commissioner of the London Metropolitan Police, acquiring a knighthood, a wife, and a son along the way. In the end—like Poirot from the beginning—he continued his sleuthing from a comfortable retirement.

Any detective hero who can claim a large and enthusiastic readership for so long obviously has something going for him, and in Appleby's case it is surely the man's style—witty, quirky, stunningly erudite, impeccably courteous (but not notably patient with lesser intellects), and quick with the apposite quotation or the classical allusion. 'Donnish' is the word that comes to mind, and H.R.F. Keating and Michelle Slung, in excellent critical essays, have pointed out that Appleby is not merely the most donnish of donnish detectives, but the first of them. To all intents and purposes, Michael Innes invented the breed. And Michael Innes, as almost everyone knows, is a pseudonym of J.I.M. Stewart, who is himself (what else?) an Oxford don.

What makes donnish detectives fun for those who like them (and exasperating for those who don't) is their frequently cavalier treatment of such dull things as fingerprints, bloodstains, etc., so that the author can get on with the book's main business: i.e., the academic in-jokes, the asides, and the obscure but fascinating facts on obscure but fascinating subjects. Oh, Appleby solves his cases, all right, and does it with cleverness and dash, but he doesn't usually like to be bothered with the examination of corpses, the gathering of physical evidence, and other inessential drudgery.

In *Appleby and the Ospreys* there is this exchange involving the now-retired commissioner:

> 'We'll go to the library, Sir John,' Ringwood said. 'You'll want to view the body.'
>
> Appleby, in fact, didn't want to view the body. He had viewed

plenty of bodies in his time, and had no inclination to add that of the late Lord Osprey to the list.

'I think not,' he said. 'If the thing came to a murder trial, and it became known that I'd had a sniff at the corpse, I might find myself under subpoena as a witness for the defence, or something of that kind. It wouldn't do, Mr Ringwood. It wouldn't do at all.'

Talk about lame excuses. A passage like that is enough to bring on a heart-attack in a dyed-in-the-wool fan of the police procedural novel.

But of course Appleby isn't there to enlighten us on the latest in forensic technology. He's there to amuse us with his wit and his scholarship, and the crime at hand is simply the vehicle he uses to do it. We read him for fun, not for down-and-dirty police details.

In the autobiographical *Myself and Michael Innes*, Stewart sums up his approach:

> Detective stories are purely recreational reading after all, and needn't scorn the ambition to amuse as well as puzzle.

And amuse is precisely what the urbane, reflective, and polymathic Sir John Appleby has done for well over fifty years.

THE CASES OF SIR JOHN APPLEBY, BY MICHAEL INNES

Novels

Death at the President's Lodging, 1936. *Hamlet, Revenge*, 1937. *Lament for a Maker*, 1938. *Stop Press*, 1939. *The Secret Vanguard*, 1940. *There Came Both Mist and Snow*, 1940. *Appleby on Ararat*, 1941. *The Daffodil Affair*, 1942. *The Weight of the Evidence*, 1943. *Appleby's End*, 1945. *A Night of Errors*, 1947. *Operation Pax*, 1951. *A Private View*, 1952. *Appleby Plays Chicken*, 1957. *The Long Farewell*, 1958. *Hare Sitting Up*, 1959. *Silence Observed*, 1961. *A Connoisseur's Case*, 1962. *The Bloody Wood*, 1966. *Appleby at Allington*, 1968. *A Family Affair*, 1969. *Death at the Chase*, 1970. *An Awkward Lie*, 1971. *The Open House*, 1972. *Appleby's Answer*, 1973. *Appleby's Other Story*, 1974. *The 'Gay Phoenix'*, 1976. *The Ampersand Papers*, 1978. *Sheiks and Adders*, 1982. *Appleby and Honeybath*, 1983. *Appleby and the Ospreys*, 1986.

Short Story collections

Appleby Talking, 1954 (23 stories). *Appleby Talks Again*, 1956 (18 stories). *The Appleby File*, 1975 (15 stories).

Uncollected stories
'The Scattergood Emeralds', 1954. 'A Small Peter Pry', 1954. 'The Impressionist', 1955. 'The Perfect Murder', 1955. 'The General's Wife is Blackmailed', 1957. 'The Left-handed Barber', 1957. 'A Change of Face', 1957. 'The Theft of the Downing Street Letter', 1957. 'The Tinted Diamonds', 1957. 'Jerry Does a Good Turn for the DJAM', 1958. 'The Mystery of Paul's "Posthumous" Portrait', 1958. 'Who Suspects the Postman?', 1958. 'The Inspector Feels the Draught', 1958. 'The Author Changes His Style', 1958. 'The Party That Never Got Going', 1959. 'The Secret in the Woodpile', 1975. 'Pelly and Cullis', 1979.

4

DOUGLAS WYNN

on

Lew Archer

'The light-blue haze in the lower canyon was like a thin smoke from slowly burning money. Even the sea looked precious through it, a solid wedge held in the canyon's mouth, bright blue and polished like a stone. Private property: colour guaranteed fast; will not shrink egos. I had never seen the Pacific look so small.'

This could have been written by Raymond Chandler or possibly even Dashiell Hammett. In fact it is Ross Macdonald, or rather his detective Lew Archer, who starred in his American detective novels which came out between 1949 and the middle 1970s. Some American reviewers have claimed that Ross Macdonald is a better novelist than either Chandler or Hammett.

Macdonald has admitted that Archer is based on himself. He isn't Archer exactly, but Archer is him.

In fictional terms, Archer was born in 1913 and until his teens ran with an undesirable crowd. But a friendly detective on the Long

Beach Police Force, who caught him stealing, straightened him out instead of sending him to Juvenile Hall, and he later served for five years on the same force. He resigned, however, because he wouldn't work for a corrupt police administration and became a private detective, licence number 6345, operating mainly in the State of California.

Since he became a private detective his wife Sue has divorced him. According to Archer: 'because she didn't like the company I kept.'

Sex is not an important element in the books. In the early ones Archer is usually attracted to a lady in each story. Often this is the motive for continuing his investigation. But it never goes further than a discreet kiss, and by the end of the story the romance usually seems to have been forgotten. In the later books Archer has a more definite relationship with his lovers. He sometimes sleeps with them, but even this is only incidental to the main story and he is often upbraided by his ladies for not being around when needed.

In the early books: *The Moving Target* (1949), *The Drowning Pool* (1950), *The Way Some People Die* (1951) and *Find a Victim* (1954), Archer is in some ways a typical detective of the hardboiled school. A man of action, he uses his fists and his gun. In *The Moving Target* he actually kills a man, although it is in self-defence.

In the later books, notably, *The Far Side Of The Dollar* (1965), *The Goodbye Look* (1969), and *The Underground Man* (1971), Archer becomes less a doer than a questioner, a kind of consciousness in which other lives emerge and a not-unwilling catalyst for trouble. In these he solves mysteries of impenetrable complexity, often concerning family relationships which have their origin in events which happened twenty or more years ago. But, as in all of Macdonald's best books, the solution to the problem is carefully built up until at the end, often on the last page, the whole thing is suddenly turned on its head. Archer demonstrates that what we all thought was the logical explanation of the events can be looked at in another way and the true explanation is something we had never suspected.

THE CASES OF LEW ARCHER, BY ROSS MACDONALD

Novels

The Moving Target, 1949. *The Drowning Pool*, 1950. *The Way Some People Die*, 1951. *The Ivory Grin*, 1952. *Find a Victim*, 1954. *The Barbarous Coast*, 1956. *The Doomsters*, 1958. *The Galton Case*, 1959. *The Zebra-Striped Hearse*, 1962. *The Wycherly Woman*, 1961.

The Chill, 1964. *The Far Side of the Dollar*, 1965. *Black Money*, 1966. *The Instant Enemy*, 1968. *The Goodbye Look*, 1969. *The Underground Man*, 1971. *Sleeping Beauty*, 1973. *The Blue Hammer*, 1976.

Story collections
The Name is Archer, 1955. *Lew Archer, Private Investigator*, 1977.

5
ION MILLS
on
Jacob Asch

I have to declare an interest here: not only have I read with pleasure the Jacob Asch private eye novels of Arthur Lyons, I publish them under our No Exit Press imprint—so don't expect objectivity!

Arthur Lyons was born in L.A. in 1946 and he now resides in Palm Springs, (Chandler's Poodle Springs), where he spends a good deal of his time running The English Grille restaurant. Over a period of some 15 years he has written ten first-class crime novels.

Lyons' detective, Jacob Asch, is probably the best known Jewish P.I. around, along with Roger Simon's Moses Wine. He makes his first appearance in *The Dead Are Discreet* after release from jail where he was sent for contempt for refusing to name a source in his erstwhile career as a Los Angeles reporter.

All his novels are based in the LA/Southern California region and he has often evoked comparison with Ross Macdonald—'his less pretentious heir' (*Trouble is their Business* by John Conquest) and his earlier work with Chandler. He covers a variety of subjects and he is able over the series to bring out different aspects of Asch's character and his past making him a reasonably well-rounded figure.

In fact Lyons' most popular book in terms of sales has been a non-fiction title on the concepts of devil worship called the *Second Coming* and this interest is reflected in the first two Asch titles, *The Dead Are Discreet* (1974) and *All God's Children* (1975). *The Killing Floor* (1976) covers the meat packing industry, while *Dead Ringer* (1977) is an 'evocative depiction of professional boxing' (*Private Eyes: 101 Knights* by Baker & Nietzel) and *At The Hands Of Another* (1983) covers insurance scams, while *Three With A Bullet* (1984) turns the spotlight on the rock music business. In his later books he turns on the film industry in *Fast Fade* (1987) and his most recent book, *Other People's Money* (1989) deals with art smuggling.

My own personal favourite by some way is *Hard Trade* (1982) which is an excellent novel about political power and corruption and 'exploitative and idealistic homosexuals' and is described in Reilly's *20th Century Crime and Mystery Writers* as 'the best political study in detective fiction since Hammett's *The Glass Key*'. In fact this mid-period probably produced the second-best Asch novel as well, *Castles Burning* (1980) set amongst the plush, sybaritic world of Palm Springs.

It is interesting to note that Lyons does not think much of Ross Macdonald because he tends to over-elaborate on the reasons for murder—as far as Lyons is concerned people murder for revenge, money, jealousy or because they are not the full shilling! This makes sense to me. Lyons feels more at home with Chandler and Hammett and, interestingly, Nelson Algren, whose books are once again fashionable.

When it comes down to it you have to put Lyons close to the top of the first division of modern 'hardboiled' crime writers. You can forgive him the apparent lapses into sexism and ambiguous attitude to homosexuality because you always want to turn the page to see what happens next and the quality of books like *Hard Trade* is undeniable. David Geherin in *The American Private Eye* (1985) summed his writing up as 'lean yet sharply descriptive prose, crisply paced narratives, pungently realistic dialogue, a scrupulous avoidance of clichés and unfailingly credible characters all combine to produce fiction of the highest order'.

Go on treat yourself to *The Dead Are Discreet* . . . you'll be back for more!

THE CASES OF JOCOB ASCH, BY ARTHUR LYONS

Novels

The Dead Are Discreet, 1974. *All God's Children*, 1975. *The Killing Floor*, 1976. *Dead Ringer*, 1977. *Castles Burning*, 1980. *Hard Trade*, 1982. *At The Hands Of Another*, 1983. *Three With A Bullet*, 1984. *Fast Fade*, 1987. *Other People's Money*, 1989.

Uncollected stories

Missing in Miami, 1986. '*Dead Copy*', 1988.

6
ROBERT ADEY
on
Senator Brooks U. Banner

T hose who have met Senator Brooks Urban Banner (Dem) are unlikely ever to forget him. At 6 foot 3 inches tall, and 270 lbs, anyone might expect to make an impact, but top it off with a massive bison head, a mane of grizzled white hair, a ruddy jowled face and a big red W.C. Fields nose, and there's someone who'll live in the memory.

As for his clothing—well, no one could accuse the Senator of being a conservative dresser. He delights in voluminous shirts striped like a peppermint stick, red braces (suspenders, if you're American) holding up sagging grey britches, a moth-eaten frock coat, a range of headgear that runs from a soiled but much beloved campaign Panama to a tall but rather dilapidated silk hat, and a range of footwear that takes in grubby tennis shoes, scuffed moccasins and huge storm rubbers with red ridged soles. Not to mention a greasy string tie.

And if Banner appears to have a mode of speech as outlandish as his dress—'Meetcha, cheesecake' is his regular greeting to the ladies—don't be fooled for a minute by this purposely ungrammatical approach. Behind those frosty blue eyes and the chewed and often unlit 75 cent Pittsburgh stogies is a brain as sharp as a tack. Banner may have been brought up in an orphanage, but he has studied widely at the University of Life and sports a *curriculum vitae* which includes infantry lieutenant, hobo, auctioneer, furniture salesman, sideshow barker and county sheriff—and he graduated with honours from Cornell University and Albany law-school.

Add to this multifarious career background membership of the Idle Hour Club, the Adventurers' Club and the Sphinx Club (for magicians only, that one) a consuming interest in locks and clockwork toys, magic tricks and comic books, and it comes as no surprise to learn that, in pretty near all the murder cases that Banner is called upon to solve, death has occurred in that most bizarre and theatrical of circumstances—the Impossible Murder.

Viz.:

Death by stabbing in a sealed glass cell (his first published adventure but not his first case, as reference is made therein to an earlier problem of 'the luminous murderer', which was not in fact published until some time later); or

Death from strangulation by a vampire emerging from a mausoleum locked for 150 years; or

Death by shooting when seconds later the smoking murder weapon is produced from a sealed envelope in an adjacent room; or

Death by stabbing in a guarded seance-room where all witnesses are strait-jacketed (yes, literally!) and the murderer's prints on the weapon cannot be matched with those of anyone present; or

Death by shooting where the killer's footprints lead one way only, to a scarecrow in the middle of a ploughed field;

—and there are many more equally strange problems to which Banner effortlessly provides, give or take the odd corpse, equally neat solutions.

Banner has no Watson in tow to record his cases and, of the police authorities who feature from time to time in the tales, only the counter-intelligence man, Colonel Walter Seven, makes more than one appearance.

Most of the settings are New York City and New York State, and Banner is never more at home than when he is prowling around empty vaudeville theatres or off-season amusement parks: perfect backdrops for the kind of problems he investigates.

He also has, however, a globe-trotting side to his nature (and is not above a bit of counter-intelligence work himself), and has been found in pursuit of the bizarre as far afield as London (New Scotland Yard assisting), Paris (chasing vampires) and even Tokyo, Hong Kong and Cuba.

While most of the Banner tales have been told there are still a handful that his amanuensis, Joe Commings, has not yet had published, and a few more—we might speak of Jack Horner, the poisoner, or the Armenian stabbing case, or the steamer-trunk mystery—that have been mentioned but of which no written record is known.

So there's every hope that Banner, clearing his throat with a mighty 'Haak!', and a glass of Haig and Haig at the ready, will entertain us yet again.

THE CASES OF BROOKS BANNER, BY JOSEPH COMMINGS

'Murder Under Glass'—*10-Story Detective*, March 1947
'Fingerprint Ghost'—*10-Story Detective*, May 1947
'The Spectre on the Lake'—*10-Story Detective*, July 1947
'The Black Friar Murders'—*Ten Detective Aces*, January 1948*
'The Scarecrow Murders'—*10-Story Detective*, April 1948
'Death By Black Magic'—*Ten Detective Aces*, November 1948
'Ghost in the Gallery'—*Ten Detective Aces*, July 1949; as 'The Devil's Cousin', Mystery Digest, July/August 1959
'The Invisible Clue'—*Hollywood Detective*, April 1950
'Serenade to a Killer'—*Mystery Digest*, July 1957
'The Female Animal'—*Mystery Digest*, January 1958
'The Bewitched Terrace'—*Mystery Digest*, July 1958; as 'The Fraudulent Spirit', *Mystery Digest*, September/October 1959 (as by 'Monte Craven')
'Through the Looking Glass'—*Big Time Mysteries* (Dodd Mead, 1958)
'Three Chamberpots'—*Mystery Digest*, November/December 1959
'Murderer's Progress'—*Mystery Digest*, November/December 1960
'A Lady of Quality'—*Mystery Digest*, September/October 1961
'Castanets, Canaries and Murder'—*Mystery Digest*, January/February 1962
'The X-Street Murders'—*Mystery Digest*, March/April 1962
'Open To Danger'—*Mystery Digest*, July/August 1962
'Hangman's House'—*Mystery Digest*, November/December 1962
'Betrayal in the Night'—*Mystery Digest*, January/February 1963

'The Giant's Sword'—*Mystery Digest*, May/June 1963
'The Last Samurai'—*The Saint Mystery Magazine*, July 1963
'The Cuban Blonde'—*The Saint Mystery Magazine*, January 1965
'The Glass Gravestone'—*The Saint Mystery Magazine*, October 1966
'The Moving Finger'—*Mike Shayne Mystery Magazine*, April 1968
'Stairway to Nowhere'—*Mike Shayne Mystery Magazine*, November 1979**
'Nobody Loves A Fat Man'—*Mike Shayne Mystery Magazine*, June 1980
'Assassination-Middle East'—*Mike Shayne Mystery Magazine*, May 1981
'Dressed To Kill'—*Mike Shayne Mystery Magazine*, March 1982
'Murder of a Mermaid'—*Mike Shayne Mystery Magazine*, August 1982
'The Fire-Dragon Caper'—*Mike Shayne Mystery Magazine*, May 1984
'The Grand Guignol Caper'—*Mike Shayne Mystery Magazine*, November 1984

*Originally written, and submitted, as a Banner story, but for some strange reason changed editorially so that the protagonist became one 'Mayor Thomas Landin'.
**Co-written with Edward D. Hoch.

7

PHILIP KERR

on

Inspector Barlach

The detective creation of the noted Swiss dramatist Friedrich Dürrenmatt, Hans Barlach of the Berne City Police, makes only two fictional appearances: as an Inspector in *The Judge and his Hangman*, and then as a newly-promoted Police Commissioner in *The Quarry*. And yet these two stories, set in the immediate post-war years are so distinctive, so unusual, that their impact (and as a corollary that of Barlach himself) is quite out of proportion to their comparative exiguity.

It is not just the unfortunate Barlach's terminal stomach cancer that makes him a character of considerable sympathy. Nor is it merely Barlach's sense of his own expendability in the pursuit of evil. Barlach himself counts these considerations as of very little consequence beside the prospect of capturing a murderer. In his own words, 'We all ought to be Don Quixotes'. No, what distinguishes Barlach above all else is his unfailing humanity and idealism in a grotesque and often nihilistic world.

There was an early indicator of Barlach's unswerving devotion to principle during the early Nazi days when, as the head of the Criminal Investigation Department in Frankfurt on Main, he slapped the face of a high official of the new German Government. This necessitated his immediate return to the neutral safety of Berne, where his action 'was assessed progressively in accordance with the European political situation: first as disgraceful, later as regrettable but understandable, and finally as the only possible thing a Swiss could have done.'

Barlach is not likely to find much favour with those who prefer their detective-heroes always to act in accordance with the book. With only twelve months to live it is understandable that he should care little for police procedure where the elimination of a master-criminal like Gastmann is concerned. It is this medical condition which not unnaturally tends to isolate Barlach as an individual, adding to the danger in which he finds himself, and thereby evoking a rather uneasy response in the reader, which helps make the Berne policeman one of the most Kafkaesque creations in detective fiction.

Indeed his methods are so unorthodox as to be hardly worthy of the description. He acts viscerally (literally so in the case concerning the Nazi war criminal Emmenburger), instinctively, like 'an old cat who cannot give up chasing mice'. Even on what ought to be his deathbed he still feels impelled to try and tidy up a world that 'was bad by slovenliness'. And if he can use his own sick body as the bait to catch an SS doctor who once performed operations without anaesthetics on concentration camp inmates, and now performs them on the rich Swiss who come to his private Zurich clinic, then this is as much because of Barlach's own very Swiss sense of neatness as it is because of his own particular faith in justice.

In another of Dürrenmatt's detective stories (this time not featuring Barlach but the obsessive policeman Matthias) a crime writer is treated to a lecture by a former Zurich police chief which illustrates well the spirit of Inspector Barlach. In lamenting the fraud of many detective stories, the police chief says: 'You set up a world that you can manage. That world may be perfect—who knows?—but it is also a lie. Drop the perfection if you want to get anywhere, if you want to get at things, at reality, which is what a man ought to be doing.'

I see nothing here with which I can disagree. Even so, for a perfect imitation of a plausible detective in an imperfect world, it would be hard to outdo the all-too-brief fictional career of Inspector Hans Barlach.

THE CASES OF INSPECTOR BARLACH, BY FRIEDRICH DÜRRENMATT
The Judge and his Hangman, 1954. The Quarry, 1961.

8

P.C. DOHERTY

on

Brother William Baskerville

The Name of the Rose is set in an unnamed Italian monastery in the year 1327 and the events portrayed there are played out against a background of political and religious turmoil in Europe. The novel centres around the murder of four monks, all of whom have had access to a forbidden manuscript in the abbey's labyrinthine library. The actual cause of death as well as the true identity of the murderer are subtly hidden beneath a vivid evocation of medieval life and religious turmoil. The novel is comprised of interlocking puzzles: secret passageways, forbidden manuscripts, monks with a great deal to hide, the presence of the dreaded Inquisition and the bitter rivalry between different medieval schools of political thought.

Brother William Baskerville is the sardonic, but not cynical, English Franciscan who imposes order on this chaos even though it leads to the destruction of the abbey, the death of his rival and the burning of what Brother Baskerville loves best, those great works of literature of which the Medieval Church was so suspicious. The story is told by Brother Baskerville's young assistant, Adso of Melk, and, in the first few pages of the novel, Adso gives a thumbnail sketch of his master and mentor. I found this and the development of Brother Baskerville's character fascinating in its constant echo of Conan Doyle's Sherlock Holmes. First, like Holmes, Brother Baskerville's exploits are accurately described by a faithful 'Watson', the young Benedictine novice. Secondly, Adso's attitude to Brother Baskerville is very similar to that of Watson to Holmes, a mixture of deep admiration and superficial criticism. Thirdly, there is a strong physical likeness between Holmes and Baskerville. They are both taller than the average man, thin, rather ascetic with sharp, hawkish features. They also share the same personality traits; both are keen observers of human nature, detached but not too cynical, have a passion for logic and a deep admiration for what is best in the human spirit. They are both middle-aged bachelors with a gentle, mocking, yet compassionate view of human sexuality. Their method of detection is also similar: Holmes spends long periods of time in reflection on a certain problem before galvanising both himself and Watson into frantic action. Brother William Baskerville is the same: indeed, some of his phrases and modes of expression are highly reminiscent of Holmes, such as 'The devil take it!' Or the use of the repetitive command like 'To the stables! To the stables!' Of course, Brother Baskerville's constant instruction to the young Adso to apply logic—'try to formulate a hypothesis'—is reminiscent of Holmes' sermonising to Watson and both Holmes and Brother Baskerville solve their cases through a mixture of sharp observation, careful detection and the application of brilliant logic.

Both Brother Baskerville and Holmes have experienced deep personal tragedy in their early years. Watson makes fleeting references to this but Adso of Melk accurately describes how Brother Baskerville had been closely interrogated by the Inquisition and only escaped its clutches due to the intervention of powerful patrons. Holmes' possible addiction to opium is reflected in Brother

Baskerville's use of certain herbs which he, too, eats to soothe the nerves. A harmless addiction? Perhaps not, for when Adso asks to try some, Brother Baskerville sardonically replies that what's good for an old Franciscan may not be so good for a young Benedictine! What is quite delightful is the Franciscan's name, so redolent of the English squirearchy. Baskerville denotes Manor houses, fields and forests and is borrowed directly from one of Conan Doyle's most popular Sherlock Holmes story, *The Hound of the Baskervilles*. Finally, the actual setting, although a 14th-century Italian monastery, conjures up sweet memories of the great English country-house murders where Holmes (as well as other fictional detectives) plied their trade. As in the greatest of these the murders are brutal, take place over a short period of time and end with their pleasant, peaceful setting being caught up in a vortex of destruction which affects everybody who lives there. William Baskerville and *The Name of the Rose* are brilliant contributions to this genre of the detective story and, in it, the author impishly pays homage to some of the outstanding hallmarks of criminal fiction.

THE CASES OF WILLIAM BASKERVILLE, BY UMBERTO ECO
The Name of the Rose, 1980.

9

SCOTT HERBERTSON

on

Martin Beck

b. August? 1922. m. Inga 1951. 2 children Ingrid b. 1955 and Rolf b.1958. Separated from wife May 1969. Started police career as a patrolman in 1944 (to avoid the call up), rose by 1970 to become head of the National Homicide Squad.

In the ten novels that Per Wahlöö and Maj Sjöwall wrote about Martin Beck and his Stockholm Homicide Squad colleagues, Beck is portrayed as a developing, organic character. Unlike most police procedural series, the Sjowall and Wahloo novels show characters who react to each other and to external pressures, and who change and grow as a result.

We first meet Martin Beck at Christmas in 1964 as a disenchanted, dyspeptic 42-year-old in the Roseanna case. He is permanently out of sorts; with his stomach, his wife and his superiors. He has a cold for six months of the year. He seems to live for nothing but his job. His only recreation is making model ships and his only friend his colleague, Lennart Kollberg. He keeps himself going by remembering his virtues as a cop—he is stubborn, logical and calm. He is also capable of perceptive and sometimes lateral thought.

In a period centring round his near death in the 'Laughing Policeman' case Martin Beck changes. He sloughs off the encumbrances of his nagging wife and his bad health. He finds a soulmate in Rhea Nielsen, a left-wing lecturer and landlady to a semi-communal block of flats. He has changed by the later cases into a tall, fit, well-built man, with a slight stoop. He has even managed to get rid of his beat cop mannerism of rocking back and forth on the balls of his feet with his hands clasped behind his back. He takes to wearing sandals, jeans and a polo neck jersey.

The change in Beck is not purely physical and sartorial; the most significant change is mental. He is loosened up by his contact with Rhea and her friends, shaken up by Kollberg's disenchantment with and ultimate resignation from the force, and eyes opened by the injustice of a social system which forces him to track down and imprison decent people who have been driven to crime by desperation and the failure of the social system. When we leave Beck after the farcical 'Terrorists' case he is having to justify to himself whether he should continue in a police force which he is seeing as an instrument of political coercion.

The best way to get under the skin of Beck and his colleagues is to read the books in sequence, though British readers should note that *The Man on the Balcony* and *The Man who went up in Smoke* were published in reverse order in Britain.

Trivia time

Beck was portrayed very well by Walter Matthau in the film of 'The Laughing Policeman'.

There is an historical Martin Beck. Houdini's manager had this name. Although Beck occasionally performs feats of prestidigitation in the solution of crimes it is unlikely that there is a connection.

THE CASES OF MARTIN BECK, BY SJOWALL AND WAHLOO

Roseanna, 1967. *The Man on the Balcony*, 1968. *The Man who went up in Smoke*, 1969. *The Laughing Policeman*, 1970. *The Fire Engine that Disappeared*, 1971. *Murder at the Savoy*, 1971. *The Abominable Man*, 1972. *The Locked Room*, 1973. *Cop Killer*, 1975. *The Terrorists*, 1976.

10

PHILIP HARBOTTLE

on

'Black Maria'

M aria Black is my favourite fictional detective because she combines several disparate and contrasting elements, each one dovetailing into place to provide a satisfying entertainment. All of the classic ingredients of the traditional English detective story are on show: a horrifying murder, baffling mystery, the locked room, cerebral detection employing both scientific methods and psychological insights into the criminal mind, liberally sprinkled with satire and dry humour.

The elderly lady detective is by no means unique, but author Fearn surrounded her with an array of contrasting supporting characters and ingenious plots. The clever storylines, often scientific, were to be expected from an author who began his career as a pioneer exponent of science fiction, appearing in all of the specialist pulp magazines of the early 1930s. In 1938 he successfully introduced a new kind of S.F. under the pseudonym of 'Thornton Ayre'. The new technique (which Fearn called 'webwork') involved connecting seemingly meaningless elements together to unravel a mystery. The method was already well known in detective fiction, the leading exponent being Harry Stephen Keeler. But by 1939, Fearn was confessing his growing boredom with the S.F. pulp story, and expressed a preference for mysteries. *Black Maria, M.A.*, a 'webwork' detective novel, was drafted by March 1940, but it was a couple of years before Fearn found time from his S.F. pulp magazine chores to complete it. He sold it to Rich and Cowan in 1943, who promptly put him under contract. In the next few years, Fearn wrote a whole flock of detective novels, most notably (outside of Black Maria) the 'Hugo Blayn' scientific mysteries for Stanley Paul, featuring 'Dr Carruthers' and 'Inspector Garth'.

However, market conditions meant that Fearn (as a full-time writer) had to continue writing S.F., and after 1950 he wrote little detective and mystery fiction. This was something to be regretted, as his published works in the detective field were generally superior to anything else he wrote.

In 1949, Fearn was commissioned by *Crime Book Magazine* to tell 'how he invented the character of his school-ma'am sleuth', and extracts from his article are reproduced below, together with a complete bibliography. Long out of print, and known only to collectors, the novels were recently rediscovered and successfully translated for an Italian readership. They still await an enterprising UK publisher.

'Miss Maria Black was conceived out of a childhood memory of a distant relative with the commanding manner of a general and the logical mind of an analyst . . . she emerged as an elderly headmistress with a fund of knowledge, of psychological insight and, above all, understanding of human nature.

'That a lady supervising a successful girls' college should also possess all the attributes of a keen student of crime seemed at first too much to expect . . . but by infusing some humour into the situation I could easily imagine Miss Maria being so human in herself as to sneak off to her favourite pastime when nobody was looking. Hence her clandestine visits to the local cinema where crime films hold sway, and her ruling that none of her pupils should go there!

'The beauty of the name "Maria Black" lies in its reversibility, especially among schoolgirls looking for an alternative to "The Beak". Then, one can hardly dissociate a "black maria" from a police van, which is suggestive of criminals brought to book.

'*Black Maria, M.A.* took her to America where she encountered that contrasting character "Pulp" Martin, a gentlemanly tough from the Bowery. I became so fond of him that he continued to act as Maria's bodyguard in her later adventures, doing for her the sort of work she cannot do herself while preserving her dignity. His flamboyance, his foul cigarettes and atrocious suits, serve to offset her straight-backed frigidity and strengthen the humour which is a dominant strain in the Maria novels.

'In *Maria Marches On*, the dirty work took place within the noble pile of Rosemary College for Young Ladies, and I sensed the danger of limiting her activities to these precincts. Then it became obvious that the nearby village had possibilities; and so a cinema and a stretch of adjacent countryside became venues for crime, while in *One Remained Seated* and *Thy Arm Alone* appeared another character who, by his almost incredible obtuseness, helped to underline Maria's perspicacity. Inspector "Eyebrows" Morgan is not, I hope, typical of a village police inspector: he is, rather, a caricature of one, deliberately overdrawn to extract all of the humour it is possible from a story of crime.

'In *Death In Silhouette*, Maria contrives to break free of both college and environs to investigate the suicide of a young man engaged to one of her former pupils.

'Scorning the elaborate paraphernalia of the professional detective, Maria is always careful to stay on her own side of the fence while assisting justice to assert itself. When she cannot prove a point by forensic methods she shames the professional into doing it and so gains her end, her strong suit being the biting sarcasm she employs when the ponderous juggernaut of the law misses the mark.'

THE CASES OF 'BLACK MARIA', BY JOHN RUSSELL FEARN

Black Maria, M.A., 1944. *Maria Marches On*, 1945. *One Remained Seated*, 1946. *Thy Arm Alone*, 1947. *Death in Silhouette*, 1950.

11
COLIN GREENLAND

on

El Borbah

El Borbah is an old-fashioned American private eye who works in an unnamed city full of freaks and weirdos, megalomaniac cults and oppressed robots. Sweating suburbanites and worried heirs beg him to find their strayed offspring and missing lovers. El Borbah's reaction to each is always much the same. 'What the hell . . . he's got the foldin' green stuff.' Adequately paid, he sets off, callous as the city, to bull his way to the black heart of the mystery. His modus operandi is simple, a combination of violence and bribery mediated by threats. It works every time. His weapons are the frog punch, the indian burn, and, in extremis, 'flying lessons'. He snaps ropes with his pectorals and sneers at the heavies' utmost. Locked in a room with a steel door, he punches his way out through the wall.

El Borbah is one of the comic-strip characters of Charles Burns, one of the new generation—in fact, the same Washington college— that includes Lynda Barry and Matt Groening, creator of TV cult family the Simpsons. Named after performance artist Jim Borbah, another of Burns's friends, he looks like a Mexican wrestler, his hefty body permanently dressed in a leotard and long lace-up boots, a superhero mask-hood over his tiny head. He has a little tattoo of a snake on his left shoulder, a skull-and-crossbones on his right. He lives on Mexican junk food, cigarettes, bourbon, tequila and beer. He drives like a maniac, laughing at scurrying elderly pedestrians. His office is in a disgusting state.

The cases of El Borbah, tales of sleazy sex and mad science, mostly published in *Heavy Metal* magazine, were collected in 1988 as *Hard-Boiled Defective Stories*. 'True hard-boiled pulp,' runs the slogan, 'but somehow . . . defective.' Burns deliberately stretches the repertoire of tough-guy mannerism to breaking point. Slouching away from the doorstep of a witness who's taken his money and then talked back, El Borbah muses, 'I should have dragged her out of there and killed her . . . but it's getting late . . .'

Like Dick Tracy, Batman and his other, more chivalric predecessors in the naïve comic books of the 1940s that Burns cites among his influences, El Borbah combats a continual stream of villains even more bizarre than himself. Precisely drawn in a flat, almost woodcut style with thick black outlines and bald composition, the grotesquerie of the character and the problems he has to deal with—cadaverous muggers, militant babies with transplanted heads—becomes banal. Looking for a runaway youngster in a bar full of people with square heads, two heads, robot masks, parasites and implanted accessories, his reaction is characteristically deadbeat: 'All these jerks look the *same!*'

Comics journalist Fiona Jerome describes the masked shamus as 'a huge, mysterious bruiser who, unlike all the messed-up people he rather desultorily aids, is completely untouched by the weird world they share.' El Borbah is a brutal, amoral, faceless thug. I admire him, and trust him completely. He is our representative, our guide, even our protector in his hideous, fascinating urban inferno. The delicious question that remains is, if El Borbah is our hero, even if only for a dozen pages of a funny-book, then what are we?

THE CASES OF EL BORBAH, BY CHARLES BURNS
Hard-Boiled Defective Stories, 1988.

12

VICTORIA NICHOLS & SUSAN THOMPSON

on

Dame Beatrice Adela Lestrange Bradley

O bservation, conversation and ratiocination are three words which most adequately describe the deductive methods of this highly unusual character. A woman of advanced years and much experience as the series opens in 1929, Dame Beatrice has earned an impressive reputation as both a practising psychiatrist and a consultant to the Home Office. Her competence is well respected by police, government officials and her colleagues. Mrs Bradley's eccentric appearance and disarming demeanor, polished techniques of interrogatory word-association, and the Freudian analytical process serve to catch suspects off their guard. An astute knowledge of human nature enables this unique detective to use her penetrating mind to recognize the deeper pattern of events leading to the ultimate human crime.

Although this woman's academic and medical training must have taken place around the turn of the century—well before education for women was easily accepted—Mrs Bradley's feminism is neither strident nor demanding. Her competence speaks for itself and she does not belabor the obvious. Her reputation for solving murders is not solely based on her professional qualifications, however. Allusions to Mrs Bradley's arcane knowledge and powers are scattered throughout the series and these abilities coupled with her slightly more acceptable Freudian credentials form the foundation for her aptitude as a sleuth.

The stories themselves are not conventional murder mysteries. Murder does take place, to be sure, and it takes place in a wide range of locales and situations. There are the occasional Roman ruins, Scottish Highland lakes and island caves as well as the expected manor house, boarding school or city flat. Morris dancers, the Green Man, several professed witches and a cousin of the Loch Ness Monster are characters not surprisingly found as allies and suspects in these novels. The detective herself shrieks, grimaces and cackles throughout her investigations. Her crone-like appearance and bizarre form of dress belie her soothing, mellifluous voice and kindly nature. Children are not at all put off by her unnerving mien. If anything, they seem to gravitate naturally toward her and are willing to accede to her every wish. The novels which feature children are some of the most compelling in the series as the innate honesty of youth is mirrored by Mrs Bradley's own integrity.

Mrs Bradley's circle of family and friends is wide and diverse. Occasionally, Ferdinand Lestrange, Dame Beatrice's son and a well-respected barrister lends an able hand. At other times, one or another of her legion of nieces or nephews is there as a partner to adventure. Laura Menzies is introduced to both Mrs Bradley and the series in 1942. Her duties encompass those of secretary, confidante, and legperson and her irreverent view of her employer—of whom she often refers as Mrs Croc or The Old Trout—adds spice to the stories.

We find striking parallels between this detective's methods and those of The Master, Sherlock Holmes. Both possess a vast store of information—both conventional and esoteric. Both know the whys and wherefores of a case at its outset and proceed to uncover the facts to fit their theories and conclude their cases to other's satisfaction. However, where Holmes detects to exercise his great intellect and keep boredom at bay, Dame Beatrice does so out of a strong sense of moral conviction. Her sense of morality does not always coincide with contemporary standards, however, and she is not above applying her own form of justice to matters in which she is involved.

Author Gladys Mitchell plays fair with readers, laying out all the clues to the case and holding nothing back. At the same time, her creation, Dame Beatrice holds the full set of keys to the case and reaches conclusions in an accurate if surprising manner. History, folklore, witchcraft and the early arts of psychiatry and forensics are deftly woven into each of these tales and make all of them truly provocative reading.

THE CASES OF MRS BRADLEY, BY GLADYS MITCHELL

Novels

Speedy Death, 1929. *The Mystery of a Butcher's Shop*, 1929. *The Longer Bodies*, 1930. *The Saltmarsh Murders*, 1932. *Death at the Opera*, 1934. *The Devil at Saxon Wall*, 1935. *Dead Man's Morris*, 1936. *Come Away, Death*, 1937. *St Peter's Finger*, 1938. *Printer's Error*, 1939. *Brazen Tongue*, 1940. *Hangman's Curfew*, 1941. *When Last I Died*, 1941. *Laurels are Poison*, 1942. *The Worsted Viper*, 1943. *Sunset over Soho*, 1943. *My Father Sleeps*, 1944. *The Rising of the Moon*, 1945. *Here Comes a Chopper*, 1946. *Death and the Maiden*, 1947. *The Dancing Druids*, 1948. *Tom Brown's Body*, 1949. *Groaning Spinney*, 1950. *The Devil's Elbow*, 1951. *The Echoing Strangers*, 1952. *Merlin's Furlong*, 1953. *Faintley Speaking*, 1954. *Watson's Choice*, 1955. *Twelve Horses and the Hangman's Noose*, 1956. *The Twenty-Third Man*, 1957. *Spotted Hemlock*, 1958. *The Man who Grew Tomatoes*, 1959. *Say it with Flowers*, 1960. *The Nodding Canaries*, 1961. *My Bones will Keep*, 1962. *Adders on the Heath*, 1963. *Death of a Delft Blue*, 1964. *Pageant of Murder*, 1965. *The Croaking Raven*, 1966. *Skeleton Island*, 1967. *Three Quick and Five Dead*, 1968. *Dance to your Daddy*, 1969. *Gory Dew*, 1970. *Lament for Leto*, 1971. *A Hearse for Mayday*, 1972. *The Murder of Busy Lizzie*, 1973. *A Javelin for Jonah*, 1974. *Winking at the Brim*, 1974. *Convent on Styx*, 1975. *Late, Late in the Evening*, 1976. *Noonday and Night*, 1977. *Fault in the Structure*, 1977. *Wraiths and Changelings*, 1978. *Mingled with Venom*, 1978. *Nest of Vipers*, 1979. *The Mudflats of the Dead*, 1979. *Uncoffin'd Clay*, 1980. *The Whispering Knights*, 1980. *The Death-Cap Dancers*, 1981. *Lovers Make Moan*, 1981. *Here Lies Gloria Mundy*, 1982. *Death of a Burrowing Mole*, 1982. *The Greenstone Griffins*, 1983. *Cold, Lone and Still*, 1983. *No Winding Sheet*, 1984. *The Crozier Pharaohs*, 1984.

Uncollected stories

'The Case of the Hundred Cats', 1936. 'Daisy Bell', 1940. 'Strangers' Hall', 1950. 'A Light on Murder', 1950. 'Rushy Glen' 1950. 'Juniper Gammon,', 1950. 'The Spell,' 1952.

13
NEIL GAIMAN

on

Father Brown

I t is not that the Father Brown stories lack colour. Chesterton was, after all, an artist, and begins almost every story by painting in light. 'The evening daylight in the streets was large and luminous, opalescent and empty.' ('The Man in the Passage'); 'It was one of those chilly and empty afternoons in early winter, when the daylight is silver rather than gold, and pewter rather than silver.' ('The God of the Gongs'); 'The sky was as Prussian a blue as Potsdam could require, but it was yet more like that lavish and glowing use of the colour which a child extracts from a shilling paint box.' ('The Fairy Tale of Father Brown')—three examples picked at random from *The Wisdom of Father Brown*, each occurring in the first paragraph.

We first meet him in 'The Blue Cross'; a bumbling Essex curate, laden down with brown paper parcels and an umbrella. Chesterton borrowed the parcels, the umbrella, and perhaps the central character from his friend Father John O'Connor—once he had discovered, with surprise, that a priest (whom society assumes to be unworldly) must by profession be on close terms with the World and its sins. 'The Blue Cross' illustrates this principle: Flambeau, the master-thief, is out-thought every step of the way by the little priest, because the priest understands theft.

He had a black clerical garb and hat; sandy hair, and grey eyes as 'empty as the North Sea'. He was Father Brown (possible initial J, possible first name Paul) one of the great colorless figures of detective fiction, who continued through another sixty-odd short stories, less concerned with hounding down criminals, relentlessly bringing them to justice, or with solving crimes, than with offering the offender a chance at forgiveness, or merely being the commonsense vehicle that illuminates a Chestertonian paradox. Other great fictional detectives receive biographies, as aficionados backfill details of their lives and exploits (where *was* Watson's wound?); but Father Brown defies attempts to round out the details of his life outside of the canon. He had no home life, no early years, no last bow. He lacked colour.

It was Chesterton himself who pointed out that his subtitle to the novel *The Man Who Was Thursday*, 'A Nightmare', tended to be overlooked. Perhaps that explains something else about the Father Brown stories: their logic is dream logic. The characters from a Father Brown story have little existence before the story starts, none after it has finished: each cast of innocents and malefactors is assembled to make the story work, and for no other reason. The tales are not exercises in deduction, for rarely is the reader presented with a set of clues and logical problems to work through. Instead they are the inspired magic tricks of a master showman, or *trompe l'oeil* paintings in which the application of a little brown suddenly turns an eastern swami into a private secretary, or a suicide into a murder and back again.

The Father Brown stories are games of masks—it is rare that an unmasking of some kind does not occur. The denouement tends less to be a summation of misdirected clues, than a revelation of who, in the story one has read, was really who.

It has been said that Chesterton was not proud of Father Brown; it is true that he wrote the stories, especially in the latter days, to fund *GK's Weekly*, the mouthpiece for his theories of Distributism (a sort of bucolic socialism, in which every right-thinking Englishman would own his own cow, and a plot of land to graze it on). It is also true that many of the Father Brown stories are repetitive; there are only so many masks, so many times a man can disguise himself as himself. But even the worst of the stories contains something magical and rare. A sunset, perhaps, or a fabulous last line.

Chesterton himself was colorful, larger than life: one would imagine that in the creation of a detective he would have opted for the flamboyant—his hero would be a Flambeau, or a Sunday. Father Brown, on the other hand, seems created less as a detective than as a reaction to detectives, in a *milieu* in which, as GKC complained, '. . . the front of the cover shows somebody shot/ And the back of the cover will tell you the plot.' ('Commercial Candour').

You cannot celebrate Father Brown, for he doesn't exist. In the Chestertonian game of masks, the detective is the McGuffin, significant by his very insignificance. A plain little goblin of a man, less disorganised and flustered the more the tales go on, but still colorless to the extreme, as he walks among the mirrors and the ever-changing lights.

'One of the wise and awful truths which this brown-paper art reveals is this,' said Chesterton, discussing his fondness for drawing with chalks on brown paper, 'that white is also a colour.' And it is also a wise and awful truth that the most colorless of all detectives was employed to reveal the most colorful of all detective stories.

THE CASES OF FATHER BROWN, BY G. K. CHESTERTON

The Innocence of Father Brown, 1911. *The Wisdom of Father Brown*, 1914. *The Incredulity of Father Brown*, 1926. *The Secret of Father Brown*, 1927. *The Sandal of Father Brown*, 1935. *The Father Brown Omnibus*, 1935 (collects above five collections, but 1951 reprint adds a Father Brown story not included in any of the five initial collections).

14
WAYNE D. DUNDEE
on
Burke

Calling Burke, the lead character in Andrew Vachss' acclaimed crime series, merely a detective or a private eye is sort of like calling Muhammad Ali a prize fighter. Such labels may work okay as a thumbnail description, but they fall far short of telling the complete story.

Burke is generally referred to, in reviews and so forth, as a private eye; and Vachss' writing is often compared—sometimes favorably, sometimes not—to that of Chandler and Hammett, the two long-standing icons of the genre. This is both unfortunate and unfair. Aside from the inherent debt any contemporary writer of first-person crime novels owes to the old masters, Vachss borrows little of their style and, while it is true Burke's actions are often private-eye-like, his motives and methods are about as far from Chandler's much-vaunted 'code' as you can get. In Burke's world, this is how it must be.

The overriding theme in the Burke books is retribution against criminal freaks—the cold sub-species that neither society at large nor the legal system seems to comprehend or know how to deal with. (In this context, Burke's influences could perhaps more accurately be traced back to Spillane's Mike Hammer and his almost psychotic hatred for hoods, especially those at an 'untouchable' level; and, stylistically, Vachss' admitted admiration for Paul Cain shows through in his stripped-down prose and lightning cuts.)

In particular, Burke's wrath is directed at the freaks who prey on the young. Adhering to some antiquated code when dealing with such monsters would be suicidal, to say nothing of ridiculous. None of which means Burke is without discipline or his own set of values. In his own way he is an intensely moral man, a man who recognizes true evil and is compelled to deal with it in the only ways left open to him. First and foremost, Burke is a survivor—a tough, savvy, ex-con outlaw with an analytical mind and a photographic memory. It is this background that gives him his unique insight into the monsters he stalks. It is something at his core that drives him to put these things to use in the manner he does. He knows the workings of the mean streets like few others we have met in the pages of popular fiction and as a matter of course takes near-paranoid measures to insulate himself from all who would harm him. He is nevertheless willing to face risks in his battle against the freaks.

Burke's detective skills demonstrate an instinct and a degree of cleverness right up there with the best of the breed. The difference is that his have been honed on the wrong side of the law. He is neither a shafted nor disillusioned former cop, he has no buddy still on the force to exasperate, no license to protect, no client (at least not in the formal sense) to worry about. When he goes against convention or breaks society's rules in the course of his pursuit, it is far more believable than with most other characters because those rules and conventions have *never* worked for Burke, are indeed totally foreign to him. That is his legacy and his options remain shaped by it.

By 'normal' standards, Burke's world at all levels is slightly skewed. He lives in New York City, operates out of an office (arrived at via a periscope-monitored hallway and a flight of stairs whose steps are electronically sensored and can be erased by a switch on Burke's desk) with Astroturf carpeting to accommodate Pansy, the 140-pound Neopolitan Mastiff dog who guards it. Burke's friends (and frequent accomplices) include: Max the Silent, a mute Mongolian giant of awesome strength and martial arts skill; Michelle, a breathtaking trans-sexual hooker; the Prof, Burke's former prison mentor, now street hustler extraordinaire who speaks in rhymes as simple as his schemes are complex; the Mole, an avowed Nazi hunter possessing genius-level mental capabilities who resides in a Bronx junkyard with a pack of feral dogs; and Mama Wong, ageless Oriental proprietor of the Poontang Gardens restaurant, who protectively overlooks the comings and goings of all, especially her two 'sons' Burke and Max. It is a purposeful irony of the Burke books that this band of misfits who would readily be viewed as 'freaks' by most straight citizens are in fact united against the truly dangerous freaks that tend to appear outwardly harmless.

This underlying 'family of choice' theme—their unity forming phoenix-like from the ashes of their individual life experiences and in hopeful contrast to the chaos and decay around them—has built steadily through the series, each book expanding and fleshing out one or more of the secondary characters (without ever getting in the way of the story being told). It is another irony that Burke, the primary factor bringing them together, remains to a large degree the most distant and unaffected by their changes. In fact, the more bonds that emerge and strengthen within the group, the more Burke becomes, in a sense, edged out. Driven by his obsession and haunted by his lost loves (Flood, the title character of the first book in the series; and Belle of the third book, *Blue Belle*), he seems destined to stay the tragic quasi-loner of classic romance, a man on a violent, fascinating (to the reader), perhaps endless quest.

THE CASES OF BURKE, BY ANDREW VACHSS

Flood, 1985. *Strega*, 1987. *Blue Belle*, 1988. *Hard Candy*, 1989. *Blossom*, 1990. *Sacrifice*, 1991.

15

IAIN SINCLAIR

on

William S. Burroughs

' **P**erhaps I have opened the wrong door and at any moment The Man In Possession, The Owner Who Got There First will rush in and scream:

"What Are You Doing Here? Who Are You?"' (*Naked Lunch*, 1959.)

Good questions. Fired into a pitiless mirror. William Seward Burroughs. Agent, criminal, or other? *Third Mind*. This desperate need to know everything, see everything, record everything. William Burroughs, prime agent of his own spectral corporation, has amassed a collection of files to rival any state-sponsored coldstore of repression, any cheap-play blackmailer. Chilled moments, photographs snatched out of time, Mayan codices. The image is pure information, required evidence or masturbatory aide-mémoire. Active mug-shots that refuse to play dead, that retain the capacity of transforming an already completed script. The script that the author has been hired to discover and to eliminate.

'I'll be walking down the street and I'll suddenly see a scene from my book and I'll photograph it and put it into a scrapbook.' (*The Third Mind*, 1978.)

The shape of the book is waiting for you, but the killer remains hidden until you stumble upon a previously unknown doorway. These crimes, especially unsolved crimes, recur eternally through all the galleries of memory. Rippers and assassins primed to complete some brutal exercise in numerology, some occult equation. Burroughs has watched it all, life after life, through the eyes of a mutating centipede.

The commonplace obsession of the detective with his prey is not enough for Burroughs. He wants to share the risk of performance, the serial strokes that attempt, futilely, to change a man's fate. But all his role-playing, his carefully cultivated gun-toting persona, does not fool the audience that matters, the old ones, the grey gods. He is an agent who can be turned at any moment. 'Inspector Lee, how can one be sure that you are a nova officer and not an imposter?' (*Nova Express*, 1964). Jekyll or Hyde? Neville St Clair or Hugh Boone? William Wilson or the other William Wilson? Writer as hitman, or writer as eavesdropping sneak?

This version of undercover man is a reality, only the invisibility is a lie: the myth that William Burroughs is one of the undead, the immortals. His face is everywhere. Anonymity, greyness, viral sickness are the products he endorses. 'A picture projected on flesh is flesh.' (*How To Be Humphrey Bogart*, 1970). Sit on a chair and allow a portrait of Jesse James to be superimposed on your face. You become Jesse James—without his history. A James without karma. You are still guilty, but you have no memory of the crimes. You are free to enact hallucinations of revenge.

From the beginning there was this element of disguise, subversion, subterfuge. Burroughs says that he did not think of himself as a writer. He was a seeker, a disbarred medic. His first book, *Junkie*, emerged under an aka from a house more familiar with what Ginsberg called 'commercial schlupp.' It was bound back-to-back with the '*True Adventures of a T-Man's War Against the Dope Menace*.' Its ironies stayed comfortably within generic parameters. Introducing the Penguin revision of 1977, Ginsberg speaks of 'invisible Inspector Lee.'

The origins of *Naked Lunch* were exilic. The text was typed by other hands: Kerouac, Ginsberg, Alan Ansen. Kerouac christened it. Where was the supposed author? Avoiding customs' shakedowns, chasing the most favourable exchange rates, feeding or kicking his demons; alone in bleak rooms, or indulging his current 'Johnny.' Some collaborator, some temporary Watson, did the business, shaped and ordered the typescript. The author remained a potent underground rumour.

And when the mercury spectre surfaces it is always in another country: another story needs to be told, another case is opening. 'We found he looked very Occidental, more Private Eye than Inspector Lee . . . bullfight posters fluttered out from under his long trench coat . . . an odd blue light flashed around under the brim of his hat.' (Brion Gysin, *The Third Mind*). An alien presence, 'cellular stoicism', constantly moving, trying to cheat death. Immortality the only goal worth striving for. In Mayfair where 'he was writing away, studying these Egyptian texts ... he constantly brought pimps, hustlers and small-time gangsters to the flat ... A novelist needs the reader in that he hopes that some of his readers will turn into his characters. He needs them as vessels on which he writes.' (Victor Bockris, *With William Burroughs*. 1981).

The only crimes worthy of Inspector Lee's attention are the ones that have not yet been committed. Suicide disguised as ritual murder. Through the fantastically flawed channel of Scientology Burroughs tracked down the rogue engrams of ancient blockages, brain clots that opposed the elegance of future lives. He cultivated the criminal fringe because he needed its coded language, its bent legends. Only when *all* the secrets are out will he achieve the absolute high of paranoid bliss. Stone silence. Junk hunger frantic for the skin pages of the junkie through which it can express itself.

Lee tries to hack his way out of the language fix. 'Cut the old lines that hold you right where you are sitting now.' Chemical jolts, cut-ups, techniques of alienation: until a visionary, non-linear scramble is achieved. *The Last Words of Dutch Schultz*. Word-soup, the celebration of a pre-emptive wake. 'They dyed my shoes. Open those shoes.' That brain-damaged pitch so enticingly captured by James Ellroy in the monologue he crafts for Davey Goldman in *L.A. Confidential*.

The circuit is completed. Once the writer drew his routines out of the heat of pulp fiction, spoke in borrowed voices. Now the hardboiled masters have made their pact with the dark places that he was first to illuminate. Charles Willeford transfers a Burroughs quote across his title-page: 'No one owns life. But anyone with a frying pan owns death.' The old man has finally made it; he even doubles as a painter, a character actor in Hollywood. Unnoticed, the virus has found its place in the culture.

THE PRINCIPAL WORKS OF WILLIAM BURROUGHES

The Naked Lunch, 1959. *The Soft Machine*, 1961. *The Ticket that Exploded*, 1962. *Nova Express*, 1964. *The Wild Boys*, 1971. *Exterminator!* 1973. *Cities of the Red Night*, 1981. *The Place of Dead Roads*, 1983. *Interzone*, 1989.

16

JOE GORES

on

Mr Calder and Mr Behrens

G *ame Without Rules*, by Michael Gilbert, is eleven adventures featuring two cultured, middle-aged, highly educated British gentleman cut-throats named Mr Calder and Mr Behrens. Samuel Behrens lives with his aunt at the Old Rectory in Lamperdown, and keeps bees; Daniel Joseph Calder lives in a cottage on a hilltop outside that same village with his 128-pound Persian deerhound named Rasselas. Despite the bucolic setting, there is a buried phone line between their homes, elaborate systems of burglar alarms and steel plates inside their window shutters, and from time to time both of these seemingly retired gentlemen disappear without warning.

Mr Calder and Mr Behrens are British spies, 'run' by Mr Fortesque, manager of the Westminster branch of the London and Home Counties Bank and a great deal more besides, and belong to the 'E' (External) Branch of the Joint Services Standing Intelligence Committee. In the best tradition of British espionage literature, 'E' Branch does not officially exist.

What makes the Calder and Behrens stories so wonderful (apart from Rasselas, about whom a doctoral dissertation should be written), is their tone. These proper British gentlemen take tea together every Tuesday afternoon, as proper British gentlemen should, but quite often plan over their Darjeeling and scones the most cold-blooded actions imaginable on behalf of their service.

> 'There's a woman, she has to be killed' . . .
> 'Anyone I know?' said Mr Behrens.
> 'I'm not sure' . . .
> 'I imagine that I am to cover you here. Fortunately my aunt is taking the waters at Harrogate.'
> 'If you would.'
> 'The same arrangements as usual.'
> 'The key will be on the ledge over the woodshed door.'

Game Without Rules ranges from rural England to Eastern Europe, from pre-war Germany to the present, dealing with vacillating scientists vital to Britain's security, intelligence community moles, Moslem middle-east rulers who must not be discredited, opposition agents using a naive charismatic minister to get a nuclear facility shut down, an East German clerk defecting with a Russian decoding machine who must be protected. The stories are told with informed intelligence, wit, humor, suspense, and the sort of derring-do one can believe of middle-aged English gentlemen.

> Mr Behrens said . . . 'If I were to lift my right hand a very well-trained dog . . . would jump for your throat.'
> The colonel smiled . . . 'What happens if you lift your left hand? Does a genie appear from a bottle and carry me off?'
> 'If I raise my left hand,' said Mr Behrens, 'you will be shot dead.'
> And so saying, he raised it.

The stories also are full of a casual authenticity. Speaking of a foreign agent who collects information piecemeal and passes it on at intervals of months or even years, instead of travelling to and from Moscow or meeting other agents clandestinely, Mr Calder remarks that she is a 'season ticket holder, not a commuter.' Gilbert compels belief in the same manner that le Carré compels belief, and for the same reason: he knows intimately and first-hand the sometimes deadly political bureaucratic labyrinths on both sides of the curtain.

When Gilbert writes of violence, he writes with a kind of poetry, as if choreographing the action; but his violence is as short and harsh and wrenching as only real violence can be.

'The door came open fast, as if kicked, and Rasselas came through in a smooth golden curve, his teeth bared, making straight for Colonel Tyschenko's throat.

'Behind the dog waddled the squat figure of Mr Calder. He shot the guard twice, at close quarters, through the chest, before he could get his hand to the trigger of his machine pistol . . . (He) crouched, steadied himself, and shot Colonel Tyschenko. The bullet went through the colonel's mouth and out the back of his head.'

In these stories, the game is afoot, the game is at once charming and deadly, and the game does not get any better than this. A critic once remarked that Maugham's *Ashenden* is the finest collection of short espionage fiction ever written. That critic is wrong. The honor goes to Michael Gilbert's *Game Without Rules*, and to its twelve-story sequel, *Mr Calder and Mr Behrens*.

THE CASES OF CALDER AND BEHRENS, BY MICHAEL GILBERT

Game without Rules, 1967. *Mr Calder and Mr Behrens*, 1982.

Uncollected story
'*Double-double*', 1967.

17

MICHAEL MOORCOCK

on

Albert Campion

I suppose if I had any honesty in the matter I'd have to admit that my actual favourite detective is Sexton Blake in the decades between 1920 and 1940 when Anthony Skene pitted him, time after time, against M. Zenith the Albino, the direct inspiration of my own fantasy character. However, if I were to be grown-up about it, I'd say that Zenith (and Blake, for that matter) had the misfortune to be serial characters for some thirty-five years and tended, therefore, to have rather short memories, making the same fundamental mistakes over and over again in order to remain ongoing adversaries, while my other favourite English detective, Albert Campion, is fairly remarkable amongst detectives of his generation in that he very evidently matures as his career progresses.

The merry Raffles-cum-Pimpernel of the earliest Allingham books became the thoughtful thirty-ish investigator of the later, immediate pre-war years and, after the war, the involved social observer of the Forties and Fifties, and the saddened, determinedly hopeful bastion against active evil of the Sixties, when his creator died. Her husband, friend, illustrator and collaborator Philip Youngman Carter completed her last book and wrote two more Campion books of his own before he, too, died. Again, unlike his contemporaries of the Christie, say, or Sayers persuasion, Campion was rarely guilty of snobbery or racialism or condescension, or the kind of hideous misanthropy those old Queens of Detection indulged in without even, it seems, a slightly squeamish sensation in the stomach. No country houses full of easily-mocked or disapproved-of fools and scavengers for Allingham's books. She appeared to like something, at least, about all her characters, to make attempts even in her earliest and most obviously schematic tales, to know and understand them.

Campion came, like Hammett's protagonists, to understand the depths of evil to which men sink in their greed for power, came to believe in the need for an active philosophy against evil. Hammett chose Communism. Allingham saw the answer in a positive, humble kind of muscular Anglicanism personified in Canon Avril who is the true hero of *Tiger in the Smoke*, as Campion gratefully acknowledges. Old-fashioned virtues, maybe, but they give Campion increasingly difficult moral problems along with the criminal ones which, in their solution, brings another piece of self-illumination for him and some sort of psychological revelation for us. The fascination of reading Campion's 22 books in chronological order is to observe a good writer maturing into a fine one—a good, but somewhat derivative character, turning into a profound original.

Campion's real development doesn't begin until around *Dancers in Mourning*. His complex involvement with Jimmy Sutane, the dancer, and his wife, Linda, their own stoically borne pain, the extraordinary courage, suddenly informing the whole story in the novel's last line are subtly reflected in the genre themes which make it a classic of its kind. Campion's marriage to a vital, younger equal, Amanda, the brilliant engineer, his responsibilities as a father, all add to his powers of detection. In some ways, I suppose, he is a great example of the old-fashioned Christian gentleman (Scott out of Mallory) but, like Philip Marlowe, none the worse for that. By being interested in the characters he, like Marlowe, begins to piece together the answers to the mystery. Neither character moralises much (and Campion lacks Marlowe's somewhat disconcerting attitudes to marijuana-imbibers and non-heterosexuals). Campion's only interested in attacking cruelty, active evil. He's convincing precisely because his change from gay romantic of the early thirties to sober idealist of the 1960s is so likely. He's a joy to live with, and so, incidentally are the many recurring characters of the series. For me, Campion's unique amongst his contemporaries. The only one whose stories I can continually enjoy.

THE CASES OF ALBERT CAMPION, BY MARGERY ALLINGHAM

Novels

The Crime at Black Dudley, 1929. *Mystery Mile*, 1930. *Look to the Lady*, 1931. *Police at the Funeral*, 1931. *Sweet Danger*, 1933. *Death of a Ghost*, 1934. *Flowers for the Judge*, 1936. *Dancers in Mourning*, 1937. *The Case of the Light Pig*, 1937. *The Fashion in Shrouds*, 1938. *Traitor's Purse*, 1941. *Coroner's Pidgin*, 1945. *More Work for the Undertaker*, 1948. *The Tiger in the Smoke*, 1952. *The Beckoning Lady*, 1955. *Hide my Eyes*, 1958. *The China Governess*, 1962. *The Mind Readers*, 1965. *Cargo of Eagles*, 1968. *Mr Campion's Farthing*, 1969 (by Youngman Carter). *Mr Campion's Falcon*, 1970 (by Youngman Carter).

Story collections

Mr Campion: Criminologist, 1937. *Mr Campion and Others*, 1939. *The Case Book of Mr Campion*, 1947. *The Allingham Casebook*, 1969 (eighteen stories, ten with Campion). *The Allingham Minibus*, 1973 (eighteen stories, three with Campion). *The Return of Mr Campion*, 1989.

18

MIKE PHILLIPS

on

Steve Carella

I first met Steve Carella in Notting Hill near the end of the sixties. I'd been dawdling past a second-hand bookshop when my attention was caught by a book with the picture of an axe on the cover. I began flipping through it and halfway down the first page I was hooked. I didn't know then that Steve was to be the hero of Ed McBain's massive series about the 87th precinct, or that I would still be reading about him more than twenty years later. The irony was that I'd only got into the book because one or two of the characters were black, and I had the feeling it was going to say something about race in the USA. This was the time of civil rights and black power, but the book didn't say anything I could predict about those matters, and surprisingly, the most interesting thing in it was the character of the detective.

Up to that time the detectives I was familiar with were completely unreal—rich eccentrics, or glamorous spies or psychotic private eyes or living in a period that was distant history to someone my age. Carella was different. A dapper man, with brown eyes which held the shadow of pain about the things he'd seen and experienced, he had a sympathy for the deprived and crazy people he encountered. Carella knew somehow that crime wasn't just a simple matter of goodies and baddies. He was dedicated to catching bad guys, and the really bad ones made him angry, but when someone was sick or lost or made desperate by circumstances he was saddened and depressed, and he was caught up himself by the coincidence of their humanity. Most important, you could read his feelings about his life and the things he had to do, and they weren't vastly different from the feelings an ordinary person might have.

He wasn't an isolated loner either. He had a wife, the deaf mute, Teddy, and a couple of children. He was also the centre of a little world in the precinct. The other policemen depended on him, specially the young, naïve ones like Bert Kling, and he offered them both a moral view of the world they lived in and a wealth of experience on which they could draw. He was the sort of adult you could imagine meeting and talking with, perhaps discussing something that was troubling you.

My identification with him wasn't total, but as I followed him through one book after another I began to feel as if he was a person whose life continued and developed in between times.

Not long after our first encounter I discovered that Ed McBain was also Evan Hunter, and the wheel came full circle, because it had been Evan Hunter who wrote *Blackboard Jungle*, the first serious book of the fifties about juvenile delinquency, and the first book I'd read by a white writer which made a convincing attempt to try and understand what was going on among young people in the American inner cities.

The hero had been a young teacher with a rebellious and delinquent class. They'd made a movie of it, starring Glenn Ford and Sidney Poitier, and we'd played the hop from school every afternoon to see it, sitting right up the front mouthing the words. Carella was the teacher from *Blackboard Jungle* grown up and turned cop. He'd become more cynical and now he locked up or shot the bad boys instead of trying to convert them, but he still had the same urgent, painful concern about the waste of life and the same indignation about the circumstances which turned them out.

Sometimes, over the years, I've grown a little tired of Steve. His constant and endless devotion to his horribly cute wife and kids is probably the most wearing aspect of his character, and over the years the man has begun to be buried inside the policeman. It's unlikely now that he'll do anything unpredictable or surprising. I even feel quite pleased when the deaf man, El Sordo, shows him up as the unimaginative twit he sometimes is, running circles round the entire precinct, while Steve sticks doggedly to his boring police routines. But there's still no one like him, and when I open one of the books, I still feel as if I going back to meet an old friend, a real man.

THE CASES OF STEVE CARELLA, BY ED McBAIN

Cop Hater, 1956. *The Mugger*, 1956. *The Pusher*, 1956. *The Con Man*, 1957. *Killer's Choice*, 1958. *Killer's Payoff*, 1958. *Lady Killer*, 1958. *Killer's Wedge*, 1959. *'Til Death*, 1959. *King's Ransom*, 1959. *Give the Boys a Great Big Hand*, 1960. *The Heckler*, 1960. *See them Die*, 1960. *Lady, Lady, I Did It!*, 1961. *Like Love*, 1962. *Ten Plus One*, 1963. *Ax*, 1964, *He Who Hesitates*, 1965. *Doll*, 1965. *Eighty Million Eyes*, 1966. *Fuzz*, 1968. *Shotgun*, 1969. *Jigsaw*, 1970. *Hail, Hail, the Gang's all Here*, 1971. *Sadie, When She Died*, 1972. *Let's Hear it for the Deaf Man*, 1972. *Hail to the Chief*, 1973. *Bread*, 1974. *Blood Relatives*, 1975. *So Long as You Both Shall Live*, 1976. *Long Time no See*, 1977. *Calypso*, 1979. *Ghosts*, 1980. *Heat*, 1981. *Ice*, 1983. *Lightning*, 1984. *Eight Black Horses*, 1985. *Poison*, 1987. *Tricks*, 1987. *Lullaby*, 1989. *Vespers*, 1990. *Widows*, 1991.

19
JONATHAN MAIN
on

Castang

In the sulphorous outskirts of a town in the French provincial hinterland, past dusk, past caring, two cafés lean together over the pavementless street. The first boasts pink linen as freshly laundered as its waiters' manners and a menu as long as the Champs Elysées. The second is a darker place with a *plat du jour* blackboard in its window and yellowed lampshades over its tables, a kinder place in which to contemplate without distraction and it is true, without the slippery pretensions of its neighbour.

If you arrive here—tourists rarely visit this town—and find yourself brave enough to prefer the *tripe maison* on the board, you may encounter Castang picking over an excellent plate of cheese.

He is not a cop for glory. This much is obvious in his disdain for the perfection next door. Offer him a car chase and he will most likely laugh at you. Give him a gun to carry and he will handle it with nervous care.

This detecting is just a job like any other and whilst he does share some of the characteristics common to his movie-bred counterparts, cigarettes, whisky, a mind like an island, the differences are as intrinsic as those between an uptown condo and an autoroute *pissoir*. This is a world where people do unspeakable harm to each other, with brutal hypocrisy.

The girl's body in the boot of a judge's roller needs to be looked at. Prodded to prod the brain. It is not glamorous. But he has never known her. Henri has no seedy, witty comment to bestow upon her blood-congealed countenance. A bomb in a nunnery. Who the fuck put that there?

A servant of a state to which he has never truly convinced himself that he belongs, Castang weaves through reality with the clumsy deftness of an injured human being and has the scars to prove it—left shoulder, arm not working as it once did. True too, obviously, that not all the scars are physical.

A pragmatist, artfully struggling to define the motives for the crimes of the creative, he absorbs petty jealousies, natural deceit, crummy wallpaper and ketchup stains with the begrudging ease of a policeman who once, maybe, imagined that in pursuing the guilty, a difference could be made. Not water into wine but a certain equanimity. Maybe.

That time is now long gone, Henri has spent too much time working in the salt mines looking for peace, attempting to figure the innocent from the guilty. What remains is an endearing pessimism, a cynicism, a whateveryouwill, but without the hard heart. And thank god for that.

He is a wilful character, often pigheaded and full of pride. Mistakes have been made, copybooks blotted, toes stepped on. Exasperated superiors answered to, and not always with the truth. Richard, his erstwhile boss, has often shown forbearance with a grim half-smile, a fact for which Henri is grateful. Others have said otherwise and shown it. The old cops tell him that he thinks too much and consider it a failing and the thought of desk sitting, pushing paper clips in the Ardèche haunts him.

Here is an oddfish who has travelled back from New York with a pricey masterpiece where his gun should be only to ask, blatantly, who am I?

Perhaps he slept with the art expert in order to find out. But his sensibility pronounces the answer in a neatly despatched report. Hum. Irritatingly, brilliantly executed. Where did this bugger learn to write? The crime, on paper, hugely simple. The mind behind the gummy typing frighteningly complex. But listen, he was born like the rest of us. Onto sheets, into hands. Who could possibly expect anyone to solve a crime without recognising that we all excrete into the palms of the midwife?

Henri is aware. He admits beauty with a shrug, acknowledges intelligence with equality. Nothing escapes him eventually. Not the general's bloody garden trowel, not the dumped car in the multi-storey, not the whore. Sure, his paymasters see that he gets rained on, shot at, forced to peel off his clothes with wry, resigned amusement on a windy beach. Passed over for promotion. We all see to that. Its his belief in *something* that compels us to follow the crime, his job, however mundane, and to gasp truly surprised around the next corner while this man, quietly quoting Peggy Lee, takes it with conserved anger. Like the spar fisted by the fat man's glove. We are stunned. He is merely inspired.

You watch him tidy the *Pont l'Evêque* cheese from his plate, amazed by his austerity. But now his mind is on the whisky his wife will pour him when he gets in. She, Vera, knows all about austerity. Being bred in Czechoslovakia, a privileged career as a gymnast crippled by a single fall. Her background is a country not to be trusted, another blot in the copybook. The veryimportants know all about communism. Passed over for promotion. Castang, passes on to another sulphorous French town.

THE CASES OF CASTANG, BY NICOLAS FREELING

A Dressing of Diamond, 1974. *What are the Bugles Blowing for?*, 1975. *Lake Isle*, 1976. *The Night Lords*, 1978. *Castang's City*, 1980. *Wolfnight*, 1982. *The Back of the North Wind*, 1983. *No Part in your Death*, 1984. *Cold Iron*, 1988. *Not as far as Velma*, 1990.

20
RUSSELL JAMES
on
Lemmy Caution

There I am, thirteen years old, bored in class, reading a Hank Janson under my desk. It is one of those well-thumbed American paperbacks with a gorgeous dame on the cover. She wears a thin negligée, opaque as crumpled cellophane. You should see the dame inside.

You *can* see the dame inside.

Suddenly a shadow falls across the page that I am reading. When I look up, I find that I am staring into the face of my English teacher. I turn red.

'If you want to read thrillers,' he says, 'why don't you choose someone who can write?'

'Such as who?' I ask nervously.

The three names that he feeds me are Hemingway, Charteris and Peter Cheyney. Safe names in the 1950s, though bold enough from a schoolteacher. I try them. After a week I reject Charteris as being too facetious for a grown-up thirteen-year-old. I get on well with Ernest Hemingway. And I am hooked on Peter Cheyney.

This Man Is Dangerous comes first in the Lemmy Caution series. It opens with Lemmy standing in the shadows outside a nightclub somewhere in wartime England, waiting to thump a guy over the head before rifling through his pockets. This Caution character, you should understand, is a wisecracking American who has not given a damn since old Ma Caution taught him how to pin his own diapers. Lemmy carves through the first half of the book, carrying a gun beneath his shoulder, slugging men with his blackjack, and kissing every dame who looks as if she might know what a kiss is supposed to mean. Which in this book, as in the whole Caution series, includes some of the swellest sets of dangerous curves a guy could hope to clap his eyes upon.

There is a twist, of course—as always with Cheyney. Three-quarters of the way through the fast-turning pages, Lemmy Caution reveals himself as an undercover FBI agent. (This is in the days when the FBI were the good guys.) Being on the side of law and order (almost) means Lemmy is *entitled* to do the exciting things that he keeps doing.

For loyal readers, Lemmy Caution's FBI cover is now blown for the rest of the series. But in each book, Cheyney pulls further surprises. There is the beautiful heroine who at the climax of one tale turns out to be the blackest of villainesses. There is the beautiful villainess who at another climax—yeah, you guessed—but you would not in the original. Every one of Cheyney's tales contains more twists and stings than in a packet of hungry scorpions. Every story has fast dialogue, fast action, and deliciously fast women.

And each book was written in the first person, present tense. When I write *my* books this way I don't deny my debt to Peter Cheyney. Sure, the guy eventually fell from top form. When Cheyney started turning out more than two books a year it is not surprising he got slipshod. So did his editor. But most Lemmy Caution stories are clever, inventive and fun. Lemmy Caution himself was my hero for years. And as old Ma Caution used to say: 'Always repay your debts, son—especially when it don't cost you nothin'.

THE CASES OF LEMMY CAUTION, BY PETER CHEYNEY

Novels

This Man is Dangerous, 1936. *Poison Ivy*, 1937. *Dames don't Care*, 1937. *Can Ladies Kill?*, 1938. *Don't Get me Wrong*, 1939. *You'd be Surprised*, 1940. *Your Deal, my Lovely*, 1941. *Never a Dull Moment*, 1942. *You Can Always Duck*, 1943. *I'll Say She Does!*, 1945.

Story collections

Mister Caution—Mister Callaghan, 1941. *Time for Caution*, 1946.

21
ANTHONY LEJEUNE
on
Charlie Chan

C harlie Chan belongs, perhaps marginally, but unquestionably, to that small élite group of fictional characters—Sherlock Holmes, Jeeves, Tarzan who seem as familiar as old friends even to people who have never read a word of the stories in which they originated. To think of Charlie Chan principally in terms of the books about him is anyway misleading. There were only six books: but from them grew 46 feature films (not including a comic aberration with Peter Ustinov), plus stage plays, radio and television series, and a picture strip. The films were more than just a spin-off: they extended and strengthened the character.

Chan's creator, Earl Derr Biggers, was a Harvard-educated Boston journalist, who had already written several plays and novels when, in 1919, while on holiday in Hawaii, he read in a newspaper about a Chinese detective called Chang Apana. The idea intrigued him, if only because Orientals in popular fiction had chiefly been like Dr Fu Manchu, exotic villains. It bore fruit in 1925 when *The House without a Key* was published, featuring Sergeant (later to be Inspector) Chan of the Honolulu Police. Pathé bought the rights and turned it into a silent-film serial, in which Chan was reduced to a minor character, played by a veteran Japanese actor. The next four books, *The Chinese Parrot*, *Behind That Curtain*, *The Black Camel* and *Charlie Chan Carries On* all became feature films, some more than once. The last book, *Keeper of the Keys*, in which Charlie Chan solves a murder at Lake Tahoe, was published not long before Earl Derr Biggers' death in 1933, and, oddly enough, has never been filmed.

The title-role in *Charlie Chan Carries On* was given by Fox to Warner Oland, a Swedish-born actor who had previously played Oriental villains. His became the definitive screen version of Charlie Chan. When he died, seven years and 16 films later, he was replaced by Sidney Toler, who copied the details but never quite captured the spirit; the scripts too began to deteriorate.

Although the films were always cheaply made, the best were adroitly and amusingly written and involved genuine detection. Charlie Chan's own character had been clearly established in the books. He had come to Hawaii from China as a young man, lived in a Chinese-style house on Punchbowl Hill, was plump, uxorious and the affectionate father of many children, whose brash American manners and slang sometimes jarred on his own nostalgic traditionalism. He was unfailingly polite, discreet, meditative, highly regarded by his colleagues and given to quaint turns of speech and aphorisms ('A fool in a hurry drinks his tea with a fork'). Warner Oland not only looked the part and played it very warmly and humorously, but managed to make the most extravagant phrases ('Mud of obscurity begins to clear from pool of mind') and the most implausible Chinoiserie ('Always very hard winter when honourable cheese runs after mouse') appear profound. Keye Luke, as Number One son, became an important adjunct, hindering and helping his father.

In the books, Charlie Chan never travelled further than the west coast of America, but the films took him, very succesfully, much further afield—to London, Paris, Egypt and Shanghai. In 1968, after a Charlie Chan film festival at the Museum of Modern Art in New York, a slim volume of quotations from the scripts was published, containing such apophthegms as 'Hasty conclusion like toy balloon—easy to blow up, easy pop' and 'Front seldom tell truth—to know occupants of house always look in backyard.' The orientalism may have been spurious, the character was never played by a Chinese actor and the cultural implications which had intrigued

Earl Derr Biggers were not fully exploited: but the fact remains that no detective is more fondly remembered, and there could hardly be a more charming, courteous, altogether admirable stereotype, than Charlie Chan.

THE CASES OF CHARLIE CHAN, BY EARL DERR BIGGERS

The House Without a Key, 1925. *The Chinese Parrot*, 1926. *Behind That Curtain*, 1928. *The Black Camel*, 1929. *Charlie Chan Carries on*, 1930. *Keeper of the Keys*, 1932.

22
SOEUR VAN FOLLY
on
The Clewseys

I have chosen to write about not one detective but sixty-four. Have I missed the entire point of this distinguished volume? I think not.

For my choice is the single—if extended (and I do not for one moment agree with Jacques Barzun's 'distended')—*family* of detectives whose saga was presented over more than four decades by that severely under-appreciated master, Simon Smith (1911–78), in his *Clewsey Chronicles*.

It seems to me that the sixty-three *Chronicles* represent the supreme working out of two elegant concepts. The first was Smith's ('bigamous': Jakubowski) marriage of the family saga to the many formats of detective fiction. The second was the recognition of the manifold benefits of presenting as 'detective' a different family member in each book (two detectives only in the generative volume.) Offering a tree in which the family traits are so clear and repetitive that one would suspect Pharaonic inbreeding if the whole tenor of the series weren't so tasteful, Smith offers the reader both the enrichment of series fiction *and* the excitement of meeting new characters. They were two brilliant decisions. The result is that Smith's *Chronicles* offer something to everyone.

It all began with *The Skinny Woman* (1932). In this brilliantly understated work, both the matriarch and patriarch of the Clewsey clan took centre stage. Because character development has ever been 'of the essence' for Smith, for much of *Skinny* we hardly know what crime has been committed. Yet the people are flesh and blood *real*. Floozy Clewsey *is* mother of all Clewseys and Boozy Clewsey *is* the father, which no perceptive reader would gainsay.

What crime do they unravel? Not for me to give hints that might spoil the delight for an uninitiate: it does not do to be a *mal* teaser, if you will forgive the lapse into my own first, sweet tongue.

The quintessence of the *Chronicles*, however, is that they resolve the light-and-shadow issues that have ravaged and divided crime fiction since its inception. Is a character fully explored in a single novel? Or do we benefit from the continuity and familiarity provided by the same character appearing book after book? Dick Francis says the one, Agatha Christie the other. Which millionaire do you argue with?

But with *The Clewsey Chronicles* the reader gets it both ways. The *Chronicles* are the AC/DC of crime. Each book explores characters who do not then recur (often being killed on the final page.) This most versatile of Smiths has managed to join a scarcely believable range of novels on a single sexto-trilogical voyage. The cosy Clewsey exists as sibling to the hard-boiled Clewsey and the procedural Clewsey. The Cornish spy (Smiley Clewsey, one of my personal favourites) is first cousin to the anonymous wartime Clewsey featured in *Flask of Detritus* (1939).

Of course if you're going to write a lot of books and use each member only once, you need a big family. Smith denies foreplanning (as Boozy Clewsey explicitly denies foreplay—an author's in-joke, I believe.) Indeed, he is on record ('Red Herrings', April 1977) as saying 'I only writes [sic] when inspiration grabs me by the nob.' But a critical decision for the entire future of the *Chronicles* was made on the final page of that first book.

Floozy Clewsey on her deathbed, trying to tell Inspector Clewseau the location of the golden key whilst giving birth to the last of her infant octuplets. Was ever an *oeuvre* more memorably generated?

The Clewsey Octuplets: seven little girls and . . . the other one. Each later to breed like a bunny and to feature in its own book.

Another writer—most Americans, one is tempted to say—would have treated the *magnifique* seven with a less subtle pen, harping, for instance, on their slight—not to be coy—height. But nowhere in the whole canon is the word 'dwarf' or the more modern 'person of diminished stature' used in relation to even one of those gamboling, bounteous Clewsey gals as each matures and finds her place in the world—and in a book.

First, of course—and who could forget—Chanteusey Clewsey as she warbles her way out of danger in *The Milkman Always Sings Twice*. Then Zoozy Clewsey, the vet of *Murder in the Rue Moggy*. And Woozy Clewsey, as valium was used as a poison for the first time in *The Anaemic Pony*.

Oh those girls: strapping Canoesy Clewsey in her *Death on the Congo*, wispy, allergic Atissuesy Clewsey in *The Big Sneeze*, Waterloosy Clewsey, chief spotter of *Dangers on a Train*, and not least, Nosy Newsy Clewsey, the scoop-merchant in *Page Twenty-Three*, later adapted for the stage, though still, regretfully, unperformed.

And what of the eighth of the Octet, the only brother, Oo's-he Clewsey? The silent hero of *A Clewsey Vanishes*, of course, though not every reader got it.

There are too many books and favourite characters to list them all here. Settle for a few highlights, for, to be frank, there *are* less successful *Chronicles*. I do feel that the books featuring the Clewsey pets strained the concept, especially *Puss of the Baskervilles* featuring Mewsey Clewsey, and Tortoosy Clewsey whose pace was just too slow. Of this group *Odds Versus*, featuring Appaloosy Clewsey, was probably the closest to a winner.

But there were many many peaks, making, as it were, a full mountain range of achievement with snowcaps galore. A special favourite, for personal reasons, is the psychological study of Juicy Clewsey, Youhoosy Clewsey and Whoopsy Clewsey, the multiple personalities at the bottom of the tangle with *The Nine Sailors*. And of the television adaptations I think I most enjoyed *Dragbath*, with Sgt Jacuzzi Clewsey of the L.A. P.D.

But a raft, nay, a catamaran of Clewsey characters will float on forever in *la mer* of readers' spirits: Toulousy Clewsey, the artist; Bruisey Clewsey, the wrestler; Courbousy Clewsey, the architect; Carousy Clewsey, the first female tenor; and Debussey Clewsey, whose tunes so tickled. More contemporary were Masseusie Clewsey, Fusey Clewsey the ersatz terrorist, Siouxie Clewsey the Banshee, and Shoesy Clewsey who *does*—and here I agree with

Keating—have an excessive (and unexplained) attachment to red footware.

And the *coup de* Clewsey, if you will forgive another lapse: the final volume, left by Simon Smith with his publishers *as if he knew all along* about that Number 73 bus. (All my researches have been unable to establish whether the body bore clean underwear: some witnesses say uh-huh, others uh-uh. No matter.) It is a masterpiece and the final refinement: *Murder on the Intercity*, with child detective Cluesy Clewsey screaming 'Eureka' and pulling the emergency cord at, yes, Pewsey. In Wiltshire.

Who but Smith?

THE CASES OF THE CLEWSEYS, BY SIMON SMITH

The Skinny Woman, 1932. *The Milkman Always Rings Twice*, 1933. *The Nine Sailors*, 1933. *Murder One*, 1934. *Return to Murder One*, 1935. *New Worlds*, 1936. *Heart Lines*, 1937. *The Big Sneeze*, 1938. *Flask of Detritus*, 1939. *The Secret of Pearl Harbour*, 1940. *A Farewell to Legs*, 1941. *The Silence of the Sheep*, 1942. *Murder in the Rue Moggy*, 1943. *A Year to Remember*, 1944. *Trouble Ain't my Business*, 1945. *A Mysterious Affair of Style*, 1946. *Death at the Prime Minister's Lodging*, 1947. *A Mysterious Bookshop*, 1948. *Dangers on a Train*, 1949. *The Brown Thumb Mark*, 1950. *The List of Otto Messenger*, 1951. *Puss of the Baskervilles*, 1952. *One, Two, Three Buckle my Shoe*, 1954. *The Name of the Daffodil* 1955. *Dragbath*, 1956. *From Doom with Death*, 1957. *Death in the Congo*, 1958. *The Big Knock-Out*, 1959. *Page Twenty-Three*, 1960. *Sgt Lombino And the 78th Precinct*, 1961. *The Anaemic Pony*, 1962. *Odds Versus*, 1963. *G is For Grafton*, 1964. *From Frome to Welshmill*, 1965. *A Clewsey Vanishes*, 1966. *Chihuahua Springs*, 1967. *The Wench is Alive*, 1968. *Mystery Scene*, 1969. *The Armchair Detective*, 1970. *New Crimes*, 1971. *The Groom Wore Black*, 1972. *The Black Drape*, 1973. *Black Witness*, 1974. *The Black Seraphim*, 1975. *The Black Road of Fear*, 1976. *Meeting in Black*, 1977. *The Big Watch*, 1977. *The Detective Who Came in from the Cold*, 1977. *The Mark of Apocrypha*, 1977. *Murder on the Intercity*, 1979 (Posthumous).

23

RICHARD A. LUPOFF

on

The Continental Op

Ah, the Op, the Op! When Karl Shub's mind was cluttered by dreadful music he would cleanse his auditory circuits with Mozart, not a bad idea. And I have borrowed and modified it; when my linguistic circuits get clogged by reading too much bad prose I cleanse them with Hammett. With anything by Hammett, but especially with a Continental Op short story.

He started writing about the Continental Op in 1923. Hammett was 29 years old at the time. 'Arson Plus,' the first Op story, appeared under Hammett's Peter Collinson pseudonym; thereafter, as *by Dashiell Hammett*. The conventional critics like to point out that Carroll John Daly got into *Black Mask* with 'The False Burton Combs' and 'Knights of the Open Palm' a few months ahead of Hammett. They claim for Daly and his gunman Race Williams pride of priority in inventing the hardboiled detective story.

They admit that Daly was a lousy writer (he was) and that Hammett was a very good one (he was), but still Daly was *first*. That's a dubious claim. Daly's stories were blood-and-hate-drenched exercises that presaged the mindless violence and mysogyny of Mickey Spillane and the whole Destroyer/Penetrator/Executioner school of killer-porn.

Hammett was doing something altogether different. He was writing stories of a man driven by a sense of duty, of righteousness. His was a morality that no amount of professional detachment could dampen. Follow Hammett with Chandler, Macdonald, Michael Collins, Joe Gores, Bill Pronzini. There are no female Hammetts. That isn't sexism. It's simple fact. A female Dashiell Hammett would make about as much sense as a male Agatha Christie.

I reread the Op stories and I'm in San Francisco in 1923. It's a very different San Francisco from today's. There are only ferries to industrial Oakland or bucolic Marin County. No Bay Bridge, no Golden Gate Bridge, no underwater rail line. They rode in tall, square automobiles. Radio was a novelty. Prohibition was a joke. For entertainment they went to a fight or a play. The movies had yet to find their voice and lose their heart.

Steven Marcus says that Hammett's best work was his short stories. Robert B. Parker holds out for the novels. I'm with Marcus. There were two Op novels, but *Red Harvest* was too episodic and it tilted too far toward the Daly blood-and-anger school for my money, even though Jacques Barzun called it, 'in many ways Dashiell Hammett's best novel.' And while I like *The Dain Curse* better, it's really too melodramatic and silly in the long run, despite its several fine moments. No, if you want to read one Hammett novel it has to be *The Maltese Falcon*, a modern masterpiece that for once lives up to its billing in spades. But of course the Op is not in its pages.

There are plenty of terrific Op stories. Most of them take place in or near San Francisco. And what makes them work—among their many virtues—is simply Hammett's clean vision of what he was writing, and the clean way in which he wrote it. Read the first few paragraphs of 'The Big Knockover:'

> I found Paddy the Mex in Jean Larrouy's dive.
> Paddy—an amiable conman who looked like the King of Spain—showed me his big white teeth in a smile, pushed a chair out for me with one foot, and told the girl who shared his table, 'Nellie, meet the biggest-hearted dick in San Francisco. This little fat guy will do anything for anybody, if only he can send 'em over for life in the end.' He turned to me, waving his cigar at the girl: 'Nellie Wade, and you can't get anything on her. She don't have to work—her old man's a bootlegger.'
> She was a slim girl in blue—white skin, long green eyes, short chestnut hair. Her sullen face livened into beauty when she put a hand across the table to me, and we both laughed at Paddy.

That's all it takes. Good God, that man could write! I said that most of the Op stories were San Francisco stories, but 'Corkscrew' is an Arizona western. It isn't among my favorites, which include 'Fly Paper,' 'The Whosis Kid' (ah, boxing!), and 'Dead Yellow Women' (despite the unfortunate Fu Manchu-like Chang Li Ching).

'The King Business' is a piece of Hammett silliness about a missing heir who winds up in *Muravia*, a sort of Graustark/Ruritania type Mitteleuropean country and gets involved in a nutty kind of comic-opera political struggle. Totally goofy but totally fun. And 'The Tenth Clew' has a scene in it that Joe Gores points out I must have plagiarized for a mystery novel of my own—except that I wrote my book *before* I read this particular Op story.

A couple of Op novels and fewer than a score of short stories. For these I'll give up my Chandlers, even give up my *Maltese Falcon* (although with a dreadful cry of pain). The Op, that fat, middle-aged fellow. Where did he live? What was his home like? Did he have any friends outside the Continental Detective Agency? Did he have any interests outside of his work? If there is a Heaven, I will meet him there and ask him.

THE CASES OF THE CONTINENTAL OP, BY DASHIELL HAMMETT

Novels
Red Harvest, 1929. *The Dain Curse*, 1929. *The Big Knock-Over*, 1948.

Story collections
The Continental Op, 1945. *The Return of the Continental Op*, 1945.

24
ERIC WRIGHT
on
Benny Cooperman

Hello, operator. Yes, this *is* Anna Abraham speaking. Yes, I'll take the call. Hi, Mom. Where are you? Yes, I thought you might have heard. Who told you? One of the Grantham Jewish Mafia? All right, what do you want to know about him?

His name's Benny Cooperman, and he's a private detective. I met him through Dad, when Benny solved a problem for him. Okay, I'll try.

First, yes, it's all right, Mom, he's Jewish, so you can relax.

But he's actually Jew-ish. You know? I mean he doesn't own a yarmulkah and if his mother didn't light candles on Fridays, he'd never notice. She might not, either. Well, she's kosher-ish. Candles, but no menorah. No gefilte fish, either, because her idea of a special dinner is two cans of tuna fish instead one. Benny takes after her: he seems to live on chopped egg sandwiches.

You've been reading too many thrillers, Mom, this is Ontario. Benny isn't allowed to carry a gun. He's no gourmet, either. He does drink a little beer, but if you ever see him with a drink in his hand and his eyes glazed it's because someone is trying to talk to him about the virtues of different brands of scotch. Benny thinks a single malt is a weak milk shake. And he's trying to give up smoking.

What else can I tell you? His father was in ladies' ready-to-wear in a small way, like your father, Mom. He's retired now, spends his time playing gin rummy at his club. They call him The Hammer. No, it's a gin rummy term. Oh, yes, his brother is head surgeon at Toronto General. That's good, isn't it? And his cousin's a lawyer. So he's got good genes. But he dropped out after high school, himself. Not very: he reads mostly crime novels, like you. He gets a bit bewildered by literary discussions. How do you mean—failure? He's solved every case he's been on, mostly around Grantham, but one was on a movie lot in Niagara Falls, and another up in Algonquin Park. Not too many mean streets, no. Sure he drives a car. He's had a succession of second-hand Oldsmobiles. Don't ask me where he finds them.

His friends? No one you would know. Mostly night people, janitors and waiters and such. The one I know best is the guy who has an office next to him. Frank Bushmill, a drunken Irish chiropodist, always quoting Joyce. And gay. Bushmill, not Benny. How do you think I know? You could say Benny and I are walking out, but we sleep in occasionally. Well, don't ask, then.

I'm not sure about his age. Miriam said he was thirty-five when she met him ten years ago, but he doesn't look forty-five yet. He's ageing very slowly, unlike a lot of my other friends. I guess the job agrees with him.

Because I like him, Mom. He's not a nice Jewish boy: he's a sweet guy who's found a job he likes. He's a kind of tidier. He likes things tidy, and he worries away at them, trusting to a hunch (he calls it an itch behind the knee) to tell him what to do. Don't worry about it, Mom. I won't waste my education on him. I don't think he'll ever ask. Stay in touch.

THE CASES OF BENNY COOPERMAN, BY HOWARD ENGEL

Novels
The Suicide Murders, 1980. *The Ransom Game*, 1981. *Murder on Location*, 1982. *Murder Sees the Light*, 1984. *A City Called July*, 1986. *A Victim must be Found*, 1988.

Uncollected story
'The Three Wise Guys', 1989.

25
PAUL BUCK
on
Bill Crane

I don't like detectives, private or state. I don't like enforcers of laws. Full stop. I grew up in the same road as Commander Drury, the first big fish from Scotland Yard to be jailed for corruption. As a writer, editor and publisher over the last twenty years I've suffered all manner of censorships. There are other reasons I could mention.

I don't go out of my way to read detective fiction, but I do home in on fiction and non-fiction about crimes and criminals. That's the approach that captivates me. Not the solving of a mystery or the bringing of a wrongdoer to justice. However, I will read an author who has a quality in his or her writing that appeals to me. Sometimes I discover a detective in the stories. One such writer is Jonathan Latimer. One such detective is Bill Crane. Latimer wrote five books in the Thirties with Crane as his central figure, namely: *Murder in the Madhouse*, *Headed for a Hearse*, *The Lady in the Morgue*, *The Dead Don't Care* and *Red Gardenias*. I like Latimer primarily for his sparse, tough style, though I also like some of his humour. But like many of his time, and even many today, his wisecracks are regularly at the expense of women. The mouth is the focal point of Crane's body. Crane would like to think that his ability with women could involve other parts of his anatomy, and events are occasionally indicated to prove the point, though his desire for wealthy women is never fulfilled, he only succeeds with the also-rans. Like many men, Crane is mostly mouth, not trousers.

Crane's cut and thrust with his tongue is his main weapon, not his fists. His sidekicks do the physical stuff. The other use for his mouth is as an orifice into which he pours drink. Any drink. Dry martinis, Bacardis, whiskies, beers, absinthe . . . even embalming fluid (contained in a Dewar's White Label bottle). Many detectives drink, their personal lives apparently shot to pieces, an occupational hazard it seems. Crane drinks because his brain doesn't work unless it's fuelled by alcohol. He can only reason through a haze of drink. If he's not drinking then he's not working. It's interesting that he can rationalize better in a stupor, whereas from a sexual point of view his performance must be reduced by drink, whether he thinks so or not. Once again it's the male view, no thought for the female's position.

Why have I singled out Crane if I seem to despise him? Of course I don't despise him, but I do find he never lets me forget my distaste for the law and its agents. Crane reminds me that the crime business works best if those participating on both sides of the fence are unbalanced, or have the ability to bend or be above the law. Crime is big business, it provides an income for a large network of police, lawyers, court officials and prison staff, as well as for many of the felons. It is in the interest of both sides to cooperate and thus maintain their jobs. (Murderers upset the cart, and are thus despised by both camps.) Police as criminals. Law enforcement as a bent career, that's when I get interested. Much detective fiction seems to be about justice, fairness, honour and honesty. That's not the real world. I know that if I want the real world I can read of G.F. Newman's corrupt policeman, or Andrew Vachss' brutal investigator, or others, but when I do I know very specifically that these are works of social fiction. Crane lives in books written as entertainment. That's why I like him. I like the idea that I'm reading Latimer as an entertainment and yet I'm not allowed to get off the hook, I'm still made to think of the real world. Others would hate that, wanting to find escape. But then perversity is my middle name.

THE CASES OF BILL CRANE, BY JOHNATHAN LATIMER

Murder in the Madhouse, 1935. *Headed for a Hearse*, 1935. *The Lady in the Morgue*, 1936. *The Dead don't Care*, 1938. *Red Gardenias*, 1939.

26

MARK SCHORR

on

Jack Crawford

Jack Crawford? Who's he?

Crawford heads the FBI's Behavioral Sciences unit in Thomas Harris's two captivating thrillers. Crawford directs a small army of experts on blood, fingerprints, and other forensic evidence. He knows how to marshal and advance the troops, within the constraints of the criminal justice system. As Harris describes him, the 53-year-old Crawford looks like 'a fit, middle-aged engineer who might have paid his way through college playing baseball—a crafty catcher, tough when he blocked the plate.'

Tucked away in the federal bureaucracy, Crawford lacks the flash of a Nero Wolfe or the rugged individualism of Sam Spade. But he is the last person you want on your tail, determined, dedicated, and damn good at what he does. His very blending into the bureaucracy is a part of his camouflage, like a predator in the shadows waiting for his prey.

Even after the death of his wife, Crawford is immediately back at his desk. No time to grieve. There are telexes to file, special agents to be nudged, villains to be captured.

Readers of Harris's novels are far more likely to remember Harris's villain, Dr 'Hannibal the Cannibal' Lecter, the psychopsychiatrist who is as brilliant as he is brutal. In *Red Dragon*, the empathetic FBI agent Will Graham nearly loses his life in pursuit of Lecter, and the serial killer nicknamed 'The Tooth Fairy.' In *The Silence of the Lambs*, the bright and ambitious young agent Clarice Starling is teased by Lecter in her pursuit of the serial killer known as 'Buffalo Bill.' But in both novels, the agents are manipulated by Crawford.

It is Crawford who is really Lecter's adversary, in his own way as ruthless as the sociopathic doctor. As head of the Behavioral Sciences unit, Crawford has the same sort of insight into human character and weakness as Lecter. While Lecter uses his skills for his perverse sense of 'fun,' Crawford uses his abilities for law enforcement.

Crawford risks Graham's life, and perhaps sanity, by bringing him out of retirement. He sends Starling in to meet, and intrigue, the caged Lecter. Yet Crawford has a certain humanity, repressed, buried, controlled, but there nevertheless. He tries to convey his concerns to Graham and Starling, but he is better at manipulating than sharing emotions. He is like the biblical Abraham, willing to sacrifice his child as a test of faith. No doubt convinced that if there is a fair and just god in the universe, his offspring will not be taken. And there is a certain utilitarian logic to his use of his agents. The most good for the most people.

Obviously Crawford does the right thing, for in both novels the bad guy is ultimately caught and Crawford's minions live on. But Lecter escapes at the end of the second novel, and Harris reportedly got a million dollar plus advance for his next two novels. It's a safe bet that once again Hannibal the Cannibal will threaten humanity. And Crawford will again move his human chess pieces in the battle against him.

THE CASES OF JACK CRAWFORD, BY THOMAS HARRIS
Red Dragon, 1982. *The Silence of the Lambs*, 1988.

27
BARRY FANTONI
on
John Dalmas

As any bright schoolkid knows, all enduring stories, from Christmas pantos to Greek tragedies are based on myths and all myths have a hero. If they don't, then they aren't proper myths and the figure who poses as the hero is a phony and he won't get the girl and ride off into the sunset. Because that's what heroes do. They kill the dragon and marry the princess. Or they get killed and their soul lives on and marries the princess. Its great being a hero. You can't lose. Mutant Hero Turtles create a myth. So do Spaghetti westerns and Star Wars and James Bond. Private investigators, especially the kind that carry .38 caliber revolvers, wear snap brim hats and walk mean streets are definitely heroes and the stories they tell are as near as damn it to a myth as you'd get this side of Euripides. But there's something else a bright schoolkid will tell you. Before the hero, there is usually another hero, who I call a pre-hero.

The pre-hero is a feature in many classical myths. Their role is to carry the banner and proclaim that there's to be one greater than he [the one with the banner], who will come after and clean up. John the Baptist was a pre-hero and a perfect example. His job was to set the scene and do the dirty work for Jesus. The John the Baptists are usually pretty crude, direct kind of guys. But then they have to be, since their position in the unfolding myth is to create the opening for the Perfect Hero. Preparing the path is usually an uphill struggle and getting bumped off early is also part of the deal. Few heroes can take the stage unless there has been at least one John the Baptist to cry in the wilderness. Before Raymond Chandler invented Philip Marlowe, he had first to create his pre-hero, John Dalmas.

Dalmas got his first chance to crack a case in 'Mandarin's Jade', which was later to become Marlowe's in *The Big Sleep*, and he quickly established himself as the kind of hero that Chandler would eventually perfect. And Dalmas embodies to the letter the qualities of those particular heroes who rescue damsels in distress and go home empty-handed (Remember that some heroes have other tasks, like bringing home the Golden Fleece or shooting Lee Van Cleef). In common with Marlowe, John Dalmas has little time for the idle rich, abusers of authority and bullies. He is self-effacing, idealistic and above all, honourable. Heroes must be honourable. It is no good putting evil to the sword if you are going to run off and stash the recovered spoils in your Swiss deposit account. And as the precursor to Marlowe, Dalmas had the most important of all the hero private investigator's gifts—the one-liner. We only need to read three short paragraphs of 'Mandarin's Jade', to get the precise tone of this voice in the wilderness. I quote;

> 'He gave me the name address and telephone number of a man named Lyndley Paul who lived at Castellamare, was a socialite and went everywhere except to work, lived alone with a Jap servant, and drove a very large car. The sherriff's office had nothing against him except that he had too much fun.'

The life of Christ was a perfect myth, but it could not have happened without John. Same goes for Marlowe.

THE CASES OF JOHN DALMAS, BY RAYMOND CHANDLER

'*Mandarin's Jade*', 1937. '*Bay City Blues*', 1938. '*Trouble is my Business*', 1939. '*The Lady in the Lake*', 1939.

28

JOHN MALCOLM

on

Dalziel and Pascoe

It is, at first view, a straightforward ringful. On the right, the gross, aggressive, repulsive figure of the nasty senior policeman Dalziel, bully-Northern to the core, scratching his porcine back on his corner-post like a prize bull and leering suggestively. To the left Ellie Pascoe, née Soper, the feminist, social-working, committed, moral-mongering sort of woman that every red-blooded male dreads to find There Indoors. In the centre, holding the ring, the decent, hard-working, balanced Peter Pascoe, keeping his intelligent and professional end up against a cunning and experienced superior, quite apart from the criminals, and his domestic end up (if that is not a description Ellie would pounce on as sexist) against the demands of a loyal partner with high standards of social awareness and self-expression. Great, one can hear the lip-smacking publisher say; someone for most people to identify with. Lots for the gentleman readers and plenty for the ladies. Write away, Mr Hill; it's a formula that must please.

There, however, is where the ringside image begins to fade. The corners, and the middle, blur. Formula it is not. For as Reginald Hill writes, nothing comes out as a formula. The crimes, the stories, and the people are all different. They are all real, living now, in the England we know, not an invented, timbered falsity nor a raw Osbornian kitchen, but where something of both extremes and the commonplace exist together. And the three protagonists begin to overlap and fuse, to draw apart and reposition themselves, not as figures in a dance, for it is impossible to associate Dalziel with dancing, but as those who have lived their lives in close association so often do.

Take Dalziel: the aggressive enjoyment of being rude to people, the great gulps of whisky, the bad food greedily shovelled down, the pungent remarks intended not just to deflate but to hurt hard; every woman's nightmare of a man. God knows what Dalziel really looks like. His reaction to a medical examination, one where samples of everything 'extractable or removable' have been taken from him, is to have two large stiff Scotches (pure malt, of course) to replace the food banned by the doctor. Dalziel is one of the Wild Bunch, hardly constrained by belonging to a police force. Yet Dalziel's intuition and his success with older, mettlesome women can not have been garnered by a blind, aggressive bigot. Dalziel can ruminate that if a man has devoted his life to something—even, some might say, have destroyed it for that something, as he has—then the least that something can do is not bore him. And then, on the very same page, Dalziel can draw a really biting come-back from Ellie, 'the authentic liberal radical left-wing pinko Dalziel-hating note' and enjoy it thoroughly, as a bout with a worthy opponent. His course-assessment superiors, avoiding his deep-set vein-crazed eyes, make the mistake of rebuking him as 'insubordinate, disruptive, inattentive and absent'. Dalziel responds, doubtless truculently, that such adjectives are not compatible with each other.

With Ellie Pascoe, for the male reader, a feeling of nervous recognition arises. The Dalziel and Pascoe novels are not about two people; Ellie makes sure of that, intruding as every wife does on the balance, comfortable or uncomfortable, that men working together try to create. Ellie Pascoe is dreadfully real. Forthright, crisp, opposed to any idea that a woman's place is in the home, fond of a whisky, combative, stressed by the conflict of being simultaneously a policeman's wife, a mother and a class warrior, one can not help liking Ellie and sympathizing with her even though there is no doubt that she is there to put forward the Other View.

Peter Pascoe is, of course, the chap we all know ourselves to be: decent, honest, intelligent, hard-working, sympathetic, a good father, tolerant husband and steady salary-earner. The sort of fellow who responds to a challenge. Oh no he isn't; those two sentences describe a smug bore. Pascoe is never that; Pascoe is a modern policeman with a modern policeman's problems. He has not yet snapped and wrung Ellie's neck but he gives as good as he gets and can corral Dalziel like a clever cowhand rounding a prize bull. Pascoe is the hero, keeping his cool, taking the blows, understanding the system even if he doesn't like it, but working it.

Add to these three characters plots that are excellent and varied, prose that can sketch a flat and flooded Lincolnshire like a Flemish painter on an incestuous community like an Iris Murdoch, and you have a series whose virtuosity must make many other crime novelists feel as though they're practising with only one hand.

THE CASES OF DALZIEL AND PASCOE, BY REGINALD HILL

Novels

A Clubbable Woman, 1970. *An Advancement of Learning*, 1971. *Ruling Passion*, 1973. *April Shroud*, 1975. *A Pinch of Snuff*, 1978. *A Killing Kindness*, 1980. *Deadheads*, 1983. *Exit Lines*, 1984. *Child's Play*, 1987. *Under World*, 1988. *Bones and Silence*, 1990. *One Small Step*, 1990.

Story collections

Pascoe's Ghost, 1979 (seven stories, two with Dalziel and Pascoe) *There are no Ghosts in the Soviet Union*, 1987 (six stories, one with Dalziel, one with Pascoe).

29

RALPH H. PECK

on

Charlie Dark

B rian Garfield's Charlie Dark—obese and as rumpled as a slept-in bed, too old to change, beyond retirement age—dubs himself as the world's best sleuth. Charlie informs his boss, his cohorts in the CIA, and just about everybody else that he's 'the best'. He's the conceited Nemesis of international terrorists, assassins, the world's most nettling criminous caste, whom he brings to pseudo-Islamic justice.

An unabashed glutton, Charlie gnaws his way through multiplying loaves and fishes, fatted cattle, chops by the multi-kilo, slabs of ham. Charlie's co-workers are repelled by the caloric count of this most Deadly Sin: 'You are preposterously fat,' exploded

Myerson, Charlie's boss. 'You disgust me.' (*Myerson's not in a particularly savage mood, obviously ... was* Charlie's thought-response.) Somebody also wondered if Charlie buys his suits at a tent shop.

Because of his girth, Charlie—who, in contrast to his button-down CIA cohorts, doesn't pack a gun—is an elephantine target, beyond disguise. Though he probably can yodel as grandly as Pavarotti (Charlie does everything well) he'd be absurd if he tried to pass for a local in lederhosen and a Tyrolean hat.

Never mind. On a jet-lagged beat through Byzantine physical and mental landscapes, Charlie Dark is awesomely seductive.

Since 1976, when his first short story—'Joe Cutter's Game'—was published, Brian Garfield has featured Charlie Dark only in short stories. To write sequel novels about a character he's already explored thoroughly in a book has no appeal to Garfield. But short stories? OK.

Difficult puzzles are Garfield's forte in both his novels and short stories. He stacks the cards against Charlie Dark, blocking Charlie's most logical moves with diabolical *Don't Touch!—Off Limits!* restrictions. I can just imagine Garfield at his typewriter, giggling away when Charlie resolves another 'impossible' case.

After penning a shelf of international travel guide books (not quite the accidental tourist) I especially enjoy Brian Garfield's foreign backdrops. We've gumshoed (separately—we haven't met) through many of the same back alleys. While I was merely in quest of the perfect *couscous* and hand-massaged *kobe* beef, the best gypsy flamenco dancer, the little sins that give the blue-rinsed traveler a whiff of the underbelly—like peeking furtively at the whores showcasing their wares in windows along Hamburg's Reeperbahn—Garfield's delicious research included delicatessen to stoke Charlie's food fetish.

Garfield's ear for words is true. When we hear behind-the-barn homespun truths, we know a cowpoke is drawling them. Ditto for the patter of a sybarite at a formal bash in Paris. Garfield captures the lilt of language, tailors it to his characters, and his stories are all the wittier for it—as if told in an Irish brogue or in Victor Borge's rollicking Danish accent.

Garfield's urbane sense of the ridiculous also is rare among contemporary American authors. Though '*meaningful' sociology buried in baroque syntax* is the boring fiction fad on this writer's (American) side of the unpacific Atlantic, Garfield is too fine a writer to fall for it.

As Charlie Dark waddles after fiends on all the inhabited continents, he's vulnerable, likeable, fun to read about, my favorite contemporary mystery-story hero. I wish I'd created him. I'd be thrilled if I could star Charlie in a novel, an odd coupling of sorts; obesity repels me, too.

'If Charlie Dark is not on the roster with the Scarlet Pimpernel, Mr Moto, Sherlock Holmes, Travis McGee, Raffles, Miss Marple and other legendary mystery and suspense detectives, he richly deserves to be.

THE CASES OF CHARLIE DARK, BY BRIAN GARFIELD

Checkpoint Charlie, 1981 (story collection).

30

SUSAN DUNLAP

on

Chief Inspector Wilfred Dover

The mystery world is dividing into two camps: those who love Chief Inspector Wilfred Dover, and those who can't bring themselves to believe that there are readers so low-minded, so tasteless, so, well, Dover-like, to wallow in the slimy realms of 'the most idle and avaricious policeman in the United Kingdom.'

Having failed in their foremost goal of giving Dover the boot, Scotland Yard accepts second best, i.e. keeping the beady-eyed, hippo-gutted, and universally offensive Chief Inspector out of London. Woe to the far-flung constabulary that needs a small assist. For Wilfred Dover anything beyond placing his jowly, unshaven face next to a beer glass would be more effort than he planned to give. Effort, in Dover's lexicon, is a four-letter word (to others it would be a six-letter one, but that would be too much effort for our boy.)

I can't decide whether the British Tourist Board employed wry British wit when they posted notices in the Underground saying: 'Tired of cleaning, Do a Dover.' Or 'Having a wet season? Do a Dover.' (Pictured is a toddler seated on toilet, in just the position the Chief Inspector might choose from which to speak to his prissy assistant, the long-suffering Sergeant MacGregor.)

Most frequently we find the Chief Inspector set up in a pub in the unfortunate host village, accepting the largesse of the slowly-suspecting host, while he complains about the poor quality and insufficient quantity of the food he's been pigging down, and the lumpiness of the mattress on which he plans to spend his afternoon. Dover's idea of investigating is to tolerate with as little grace as possible the increasingly panicked suggestions and reports of MacGregor, while he cadges the sergeant's cigarettes and wheedles another half pint. While MacGregor rushes out to interview suspects, Dover settles down to snore. But somehow, with a perversity that never fails to astound the unfortunate sergeant, in the end it is Dover, dealing in the familiar, who recognizes the invidious nature of one of the suspects and uncovers the killer.

Perhaps Joyce Porter spent too many years with Wilfred Dover. Perhaps she was taken over by the particular Doverian rules of minimalism—never stand when you can sit, never sit when you can lie, never swallow before you speak, and never under any circumstances pick up the tab—for she has entitled three of the Dover books *Dover One*, *Dover Two* and *Dover Three*. However, in a spurt of malevolent energy akin to Dover's rising from a chair to snatch the last piece of pie from the tired and hungry MacGregor, Joyce Porter has spurted forth with the unforgettable title *Dover and the Unkindest Cut of All*. The good news is that you must read the book to understand why the title is such a classic.

THE CASES OF DOVER, BY JOYCE PORTER

Novels

Dover One, 1964. *Dover Two*, 1965. *Dover Three*, 1965. *Dover and the Unkindest Cut of All*, 1967. *Dover Goes to Pott*, 1968. *Dover Strikes Again*, 1970. *It's Murder with Dover*, 1973. *Dover and the Claret Tappers*, 1976. *Dead Easy for Dover*, 1978. *Dover Beats the Band*, 1980.

Short stories

'*Dover Pulls a Rabbit*', 1969. '*Dover Tangles with High Finance*', 1970. '*Dover and the Dark Lady*', 1972. '*Dover Does Some Spade-work*', 1976. '*Dover Goes to School*', 1978. '*Dover without Perks*', 1978. '*Dover and the Smallest Room*', 1979. '*Sweating it out with Dover*', 1980. '*Dover Weighs the Evidence*', 1982. '*Dover Sees the Trees*', 1982. '*A Souvenir for Dover*', 1985.

31

MICHAEL EATON

on

C. Auguste Dupin

Two years before the word 'detective' appeared in the English language a master of ratiocination made his first analytical outing: C. Auguste Dupin, the Armchair Detective before there were professionals. What little we know of him is contained in three tales recorded by Edgar Allan Poe: 'The Murders in the Rue Morgue' (1841)—a locked room mystery; 'The Mystery of Marie Roget' (1842–3)—the solution of an unsolved true-life crime; and 'The Purloined Letter' (1845) a piece of psychological detection.

Emanating from an illustrious family down on its luck, Dupin exhibited the refinement of sensibilities, not to say snobbery, appropriate to his class. Living in indolent seclusion he turned his back on the society of his fellows, yet he could read its ways as easily as he read the books with which he was surrounded.

Above all, he was a creature of darkness: 'enamoured of the Night for her own sake'. In daylight hours he was wont to close tight the shutters and illuminate his dusty lodgings with tapers. He had no desire for the sun to compete with the penetrating gaze of his intellect. And yet he was also a creature of the city: impossible to conceive of his like outside the Metropolis, where criminal acts can be committed without attracting attention. On his nocturnal perambulations the anonymous *flâneur* can pass through the maze that is Paris. The world is in code, and he can crack it.

This little we know of him: he exists as a character only through the methods he used. In Poe's three stories it is Pure Intellect who is the protagonist and Dupin is an Intellect with a name, a man who existed only for the demonstration of the analytical method for its own sake. The superiority of his reasoning powers are his only 'source of liveliest enjoyment.' The detective exists, in Poe's phrase, to 'play the Oedipus', to provide a full solution to the riddle, to read the identity of the assassin on the corpse of his victim, to listen to the secret discourse of dumb objects—what we would now call 'clues', to give the answers to those puzzling questions which are not beyond *all* conjecture.

The objectivity of the mathematician, working with the Calculus of Probabilities, meets the intuition and the psychological empathy of the poet who can throw himself into the spirit of his opponent. Dupin can identify with the intellect of the one who has committed an act which throws society into temporary chaos. So the detective must be always two, for he carries within his own soul the soul of the one he seeks. And, as is often remarked, the detective story is always two: the story of a crime and the story of its solution. In these pioneering accounts of Poe the earliest events are never recounted first. Though the process of deduction is linear the story always proceeds through flashbacks. The detective exists to shed light on the darkness of the past.

But if the detective is also a dilettante, and if his intellect is so far above that of the *gendarmerie*, the newspapers and public opinion, he will be far too disdainfully preoccupied to be his own autobiographer. So the creation of the detective implies the creation of another character: the recorder, the first-person intimate who can outline his friend's amazing powers for us, the gaping audience. Because this character is, by definition, obtuse to a greater or lesser degree the detective will have to spell out for him (on our behalf) the paths of his reasoning.

We can only know the detective through his self-effacing Boswell. Thus the writer can be inscribed into the texture of the tale through these two alter egos, being simultaneously the Writer as Brilliant Deducer and as Humble Recorder.

The Ultimate Object of this display of the rational is the revelation of Truth, which exists in the positivistic philosophy of the last century as an Absolute whose loss we now mourn with nostalgia (anagrammatic of 'lost again'). All the detectives who have sprung from Dupin's side return us that reassurance: that which we thought concealed has in fact been staring us in the face all the while.

THE CASES OF C. AUGUSTE DUPIN, BY EDGAR ALLAN POE

'The Murders in the Rue Morgue', 1841. 'The Mystery of Marie Roget', 1842–1843. 'The Purloined Letter', 1845 collected in *Tales of Mystery and Imagination*.

32
MICHAEL GILBERT
on
Montague Egg

Late one evening, in the confessional atmosphere of the old Detection Club in Kingsley Street, Dorothy Sayers said: 'I sometimes wish that Lord Peter was not so infernally polite and well-bred'. The company to whom she made this comment included half a dozen of the leading detective-story writers of the time. One of them said: 'You are suffering, then, from *nostalgie de la boue*. You would like him to be a bit more common.' Dorothy, who was a stickler for accuracy in the use of words, replied: 'Not just common; I'd like him, every now and then, to be exceedingly coarse.'

To those who knew her well this was not a surprising confession. One of the dons at Somerville had noted in Dorothy 'a continuing streak of coarseness'; and did she not, later, make a speech on 'The Importance of Being Vulgar'? But by that time she was stuck with Lord Peter Wimsey. He was a scholar, a gentleman and a spare-time diplomat. Vulgarity was unthinkable.

And so Montague Egg, the travelling representative of Plummet and Rose, Wines and Spirits, was born. He was the perfect foil, the complete antithesis of the aristocratic and sometimes saccharine persona of Lord Peter. He appeared to have no home, and was unmarried. 'No wedding bells for Monty Egg.' His life was spent in the Commercial Rooms of country hotels, with frequent excursions to the Saloon Bar. He did not read *The Times*, preferring *The Daily Trumpet* (specialising in the matrimonial entanglements of film stars); he called Lord Borrodale 'a tough nut', and was capable, before he learned better, of calling an undergraduate 'an Oxford gent'. He admitted to an ingenious method of swindling the Railway.

But do not let this deceive you. The blurb on the jacket of *Hangman's Holiday*, a collection in which six of the eleven stories about him occur, says, patronisingly, that 'his powers of deduction were at least equal to those of Lord Peter.' This is a considerable understatement. His deductive powers are fantastic. He spotted a butler as murderer on the grounds that he called him 'sir'. ('Last time he addressed me as 'young fellow' and told me that tradesmen must go round to the back door.'). He is an expert on grandfather clocks, scent bottles, corkscrews and watches. He knows about the deadly possibilities of the liqueur 'Noyau', and the likelihood that garages would have a clock set to warn their customers about lighting-up time.

In addition, he had one facility that attached him particularly to his creator. Few people now could quote a single line of all the poems Dorothy wrote in her youth, but there are many alive today who can recall the advertising jingles at which she excelled.

> If he can say, as you can,
> Guinness is good for you,
> How grand to be a toucan.
> Just think what toucan do.

This was Monty's forte as well:

> To call an Oxford man an undergrad
> Proclaims you an outsider and a cad.
> To call the University the Varsity
> Is out of date, if not precisely narsity.

Who can help liking such an agreeable and unpretentious soul?

THE CASES OF MONTAGUE EGG, BY DOROTHY L. SAYERS

Hangman's Holiday, 1933 (twelve stories, six with Egg). *In the Teeth of the Evidence*, 1939 (seventeen stories, five with Egg).

33

PATRICIA MOYES

on

Amelia Peabody Emerson

H aven't you always admired those intrepid Victorian English ladies, in their long khaki skirts, solar topees and stout shoes, who—armed only with their parasols—strode across the Near and even the Far East during the second half of the nineteenth century? It brings a blush to my cheeks to have to admit that their magnificent fictional counterpart has been created by an American author. What have we all been doing, we lackadaisical British, to allow Amelia Peabody Emerson to slip through our fingers and into the brilliant imagination of Elizabeth Peters of Maryland? Shame on us.

For anybody who has unaccountably missed her, Amelia Peabody is a rich, spunky, grown-up and delicately sexy English lady. With her Egyptologist husband Radcliffe Emerson (whom she first meets in *Crocodile on the Sandbank*) she solves crimes among the pyramids and rock tombs of the Pharaohs during the period of the great excavations of the late nineteenth and early twentieth centuries.

Emerson (known to his Egyptian workforce as 'Lord of Curses'), Amelia and their infuriatingly bright son, Rameses—not to mention the cat Bastet—have become absolutely real characters to millions of readers. I use the word 'characters' advisedly, because it is accurate: I do not use the word 'friends', because I don't think that Peabody, Emerson, Rameses or Bastet would welcome it applied so loosely. They choose their friends, from whatever walk of life, with exquisite care.

Peabody (as her husband always calls her, unless he is really angry, when he resorts to 'Amelia') is indomitable. In her improvised divided skirt, for easy movement, and with her chatelaine of useful small tools and her inevitable parasol, she pursues villains across the sands of the desert, the fashionable hotels of Cairo and the peasoup fogs of London. She never loses her firmness of character nor her gentility of upbringing. I would give anything to have dreamed up Peabody. Barbara, I hate you!

Did I say Barbara, rather than Elizabeth? A slip of the hat. Elizabeth Peters has three literary hats (and many more of the outrageously decorated variety). In her persona of Barbara Michaels, she writes wonderfully funny and crisp Gothic novels: but as herself, Barbara Mertz, she is a distinguished Egyptologist who has published two scholarly books on the subject. This gives an added dimension of delight to those Peabody enthusiasts who, like myself, are fervent amateurs in the discipline. Every detail accurate, and those who know will have appreciated the throw-away moment when Peabody and Emerson fail to excavate the mound of rubble which, in fact, concealed the entrance to Tutankhamen's tomb. Real-life Egyptologists such as Petrie and Howard Carter make fleeting but entirely justified appearances. The combination of scholarship, humour, period atmosphere, fine character drawing and brilliant plotting is quite irresistible.

Over the series of books (five so far) Amelia Peabody Emerson dominates effortlessly, taming the immemorial sands of Egypt with the firm footprints of her sensible boots. She is a loving and adoring wife: a loving and exasperated mother: and a loving and relentless pursuer of truth and justice. No Master Criminal nor tomb-robber is safe from her avenging parasol. No hard-done-by young woman need be afraid once she has Peabody's protection from the world of unscrupulous gentlemen—or, come to that, mummies.

Barbara, I withdraw that remark about hating you. I am just wildly jealous. Please, please, write us another Peabody.

THE CASES OF AMELIA PEABODY EMERSON, BY ELIZABETH PETERS

Crocodile on the Sandbank, 1975. *The Curse of the Pharaohs*, 1981. *The Mummy Case*, 1985. *Lion in the Valley*, 1986. *The Deeds of the Disturber*, 1988.

34

MAXIM JAKUBOWSKI
on

The Eye

He is the Eye. He has no name.

He works for Watchmen, Inc., a vast worldwide private investigation network. He is no knight of the mean streets, he is just an employee. His boss is called Baker and, every morning when he is at his desk in the office in the Carlyle Tower, at eleven thirty, he takes a photo of a group of schoolgirls out of his desk, studies it and mentally weeps. One of the fifteen anonymous faces is that of his daughter. It was taken in Washington when she was eight or nine years old. With the photograph, there had been an obscene note from his wife who had snatched the kid.

His daughter.

She would be twenty-four years old this July.

He is the protagonist of Marc Behm's *The Eye of the Beholder*, for me, the ultimate Private Eye novel. One of the most heartbreaking novels in the annals of crime and mystery fiction, one of the great love stories of our time, a novel that explores the limits of obsession like no other. The only crime novel Behm has written, a 'story of God in disguise as a Private Eye, searching for his daughter: a quest for Grace'.

In Claude Miller's movie of the novel, which transposes the action from America to Europe, the girl is portrayed by Isabelle Adjani whose combination of vulnerability, emotion and subdued but fiery eroticism is all that I did first encounter between the lines of the book.

She is the beautiful but deranged young woman the Eye comes across on a routine investigation to determine whether the new girlfriend of Paul Hugo, a shoe-store chain heir, is after the family fortune or not. The Eye makes contact, follows the long-haired skinny girl in his company Porsche and begins his long day's journey into night. Maybe she is his long-lost daughter, maybe she is not, after the first few deaths it doesn't really matter any more, does it? She has become his obsession, his nemesis, his sole reason for living. She meets men, she loves them, she kills them. Soon, he is no longer tailing her, he is protecting her from herself, from the police, cleaning up behind her, eliminating the obvious clues she leaves obliviously in her own descent through the spirals of hell. He could walk over, talk to her, tell her he knows all, threaten her, blackmail her, but he will not. He now lives through her. She is his demonic but oh so tender child.

Sometime, the Eye loses her. But he is a professional, an experienced Private Eye who always finds his prey. What else can he do but follow her through the magic of the American highways? From skyscraper to cheap motel, from desert road to roadside cafés, the Eye is the lone crusader of American cars and roads, following in the obsessive footsteps of *Lolita*'s Humbert Humbert.

He is the Eye. He sees all, absolves her transgressions, forgives her sins, her wild fornication, her thefts, her murders. He is the Eye. And this is His story, of how a broken man can also find a reason to live, chasing the past unknown in fourth gear, from bush to hotel room, from airport to highway.

The Eye is pathetic, but I identify with him fully. The Eye is crazy but I love him because of that. The Eye is invisible, a grey man others cannot see. He lurks in car parks, shelters in bus garages, watches in airport departure lounges, and I picture his shadow over the whole wonderful, terrible continent of America.

> He went into the vestry and tiptoed into the nave. He sat down wearily in the last pew.
>
> Eve and Dr Brice were standing at the altar, getting married.
>
> Her new name was Josephine Brunswick.
>
> ....
>
> Who was she?
>
> She turned slightly, glancing over her shoulder, looking at—what? God Almighty? She was unutterably lovely. Her beauty stung him. He sat there, her scorpion's caress paralyzing him with rapture, her venom warming his blood. Who on earth was this girl? She had gray-blue-green eyes.

The Eye beholds beauty and it bewitches him until death do them part. He is a man I can do business with, I can understand how one can be blinded by the sheer presence of beauty, and follow unreasonable paths all the time knowing 'this is wrong, this leads nowhere' but still venture hardily down that road of no return, particularly if it is an American highway which holds such fascination for us Europeans, in search of a love which is not only impossible, but forbidden.

Like the Eye, I know there are no imaginable limits to the depths of all-consuming love, but he sacrifices his life, or what there is of it, to pursuing the awesome dream. He is the character I might want to be, if society hadn't installed all those fail-safe systems in me. That is why I admire and fear him (and worship at the footsteps of his enigmatic, beautiful, unknown woman).

There are hundreds, nay thousands of valiant sleuths, private eyes, dicks of all sizes and shapes, feisty or sordid investigators, but there is only one Eye.

THE CASE OF 'THE EYE', BY MARC BEHM
The Eye of the Beholder, 1980.

35
DAVID LANGFORD
on
Dr Fell

A true Great Detective needs great cases to solve and a formidable personal presence. Dr Gideon Fell scores highly on both counts. Nobody in 'golden age' crime was as unfailingly ingenious in plot construction as John Dickson Carr, who boasted more than eighty variants on the classic puzzle of murder in a locked room. And few literary figures of the 1930s were as gigantic (in either sense) and recognizable as G.K. Chesterton, from whom Carr borrowed Fell's appearance, mannerisms, and fondness for beer.

In the best of these books, it's a very Chestertonian world through which Dr Fell makes his clumsy-seeming way—wheezing, supporting himself on two canes, occasionally working on his forever unfinished *The Drinking Customs of England from the*

Earliest Days. The plots are full of high melodrama, seeming impossibilities and eerie background lore, such as the European vampire legends which darken the atmosphere of *The Hollow Man* (1935) and *He Who Whispers* (1946), or the smoky pall of witchcraft in *The Crooked Hinge* (1938) . . . all highly recommended.

The mystery tradition stated clearly that supernatural hints might be introduced, but only if later dispelled by the light of reason. Carr broke this 'rule' elsewhere, but never in the 23 novels and handful of short stories about Fell. As an eccentric polymath, Fell always knows more arcana than anyone else; as an ex-schoolmaster, he's accustomed to seeing through elaborate and consistent lies. Because he is a large, comforting figure like Santa Claus or Old King Cole, we believe him when he claims to be frightened, and let him convince us that far from being a let-down, the rational solutions are even more startling than ghosts or vampires—as in the above titles they certainly are.

Sometimes, when Carr wants light relief, Fell grows too determinedly comical. More often he does a creditable version of his original's fluency with absurd examples as a route to serious points. In the tortuous *Death-Watch* (1935), Fell persuades his friend Chief Inspector Hadley against a disastrous arrest, by showing how the case would collapse in court—and can't resist addressing an imaginary jury: 'Gentlemen, it is a well-known rule in poultry-farming . . .'

The most notorious example of Fell's rhetoric forms Chapter XVII of *The Hollow Man*: 'The Locked-Room Lecture'. As he frankly begins, 'We're in a detective story, and we don't fool the reader by pretending we're not. Let's not invent elaborate excuses to drag in a discussion of detective stories. Let's candidly glory in the noblest pursuits possible to characters in a book.'

This isn't mere self-indulgence. What follows is a rumbustious defence and analysis of the locked-room tradition . . . not only an erudite and entertaining essay but a taunting challenge to the reader. Two murders have already been committed, 'in such fashion that the murderer must not only have been invisible, but lighter than air.' They remain, in this chapter, unsolved. Fell's lecture openly lists the category and subcategory of deception into which both puzzles fall, while Carr's misdirecting hand ensures that even as it's pushed under your nose, you fail to see it.

Other notable appearances of Dr Fell are in his debut novel *Hag's Nook* (1933), which buzzes with vermin, plague, and superstition, and logically explains a family curse consisting of a hereditary broken neck; in *The Black Spectacles* (1939), a *tour de force* wherein a psychological demonstration of witnesses' inability to observe is so successful that no one can tell who entered and—under the glare of a photoflood lamp—unhurriedly murdered the demonstrator; in *The Case of the Constant Suicides* (1941), whose mingling of spookiness and farce skates over one awkward scientific lapse; and in *The Seat of the Scornful* (1942), concluding with one of Fell's most magisterial games of bluff against a murderer who 'cannot be convicted'.

The doctor never regained his best form after 1946, but in the above titles he presides over some of the most dazzlingly implausible confections in the annals of mystery. Let's leave him on a characteristic note of melodrama and compassion, in the final line of *The Hollow Man*:

'I have committed another crime, Hadley,' he said. 'I have guessed the truth again.'

THE CASES OF DR. FELL, BY JOHN DICKSON CARR

Novels

Hag's Nook, 1933. *The Mad Hatter Mystery*, 1933. *The Eight of Swords*, 1934. *The Blind Barber*, 1934. *Death Watch*, 1935. *The Hollow Man* (US: *The Three Coffins*), 1935. *The Arabian Nights Murder*, 1936. *To Wake The Dead*, 1937. *The Crooked Hinge*, 1938. *The Black Spectacles* (US: *The Problem of the Green Capsule*), 1939. *The Problem of the Wire Cage*, 1939. *The Man who could not Shudder*, 1940. *The Case of the Constant Suicides*, 1941. *The Seat of the Scornful* (US: *Death Turns the Tables*), 1941. *Till Death Do us Part*, 1944. *He Who Whispers*, 1946. *The Sleeping Sphinx*, 1947. *Below Suspicion*, 1949. *The Dead Man's Knock*, 1958. *In Spite of Thunder*, 1960. *The House at Satan's Elbow*, 1965. *Panic in Box C*, 1966. *Dark of the Moon*, 1967.

Story collections

Dr Fell, Detective, 1947 (eight stories, five with Fell). *The Third Bullet and Other Stories*, 1954 (seven stories, three with Fell). *The Men Who Explained Miracles*, 1963 (seven stories, two with Fell). *The Door to Doom*, 1980 (eighteen stories, one Fell radio play). *Fell and Foul Play*, 1991 (collects all Fell short material).

36
SUSAN MOODY
on

Gervase Fen

I first bestowed my heart on an unreciprocating male when I was twelve and my extreme youth perhaps accounts for the fact that it took me two years to realise that my passion for Lord Peter Wimsey was a passing fancy, a mere infatuation. The Real Thing hit me with a wallop when I was fourteen.

Looking back, I am perhaps a little embarrassed by the fickle speed with which I exchanged Wimsey's sleek yellow hair for the dark brown stuff which broke into mutinous spikes on the crown of Gervase Fen's boyish head, and lordly grey eyes for ice-blue humorous ones. But as the daughter of an Oxford don, I immediately recognised the type; I knew Wimsey was out of my class, but Gervase was a man I could do business with, if only in my adolescent dreams.

The fact that Fen was married failed to dampen my ardour: the wife was, after all (according to Crispin), plain and bespectacled while I had youth on my side: I could afford to wait.

It was his exuberance I loved, his extrovert character, his deliciously unconventional behaviour, his literary puns, his fitful enthusiasms. He was always slightly larger than life, whether singing lustily to the hedgerows, driving erratically through Oxford traffic, standing for (and being adopted as) a prospective member of Parliament, or simply grumbling, which he did frequently and with enthusiasm.

He brought out the maternal in me: he remained essentially boyish, with a strong resemblance to Richmal Crompton's William, despite his learning (he was, after all, the Professor of English Language and Literature at the University of Oxford, had produced a definitive edition of Langland, a volume on the minor satirists of the 18th Century, was (in *Glimpses of the Moon*) in the process of starting to begin the preliminary reading for a book on modern

British novelists and might even have produced it in due course had the publisher not gone into voluntary liquidation). He had even begun (in *Love Lies Bleeding*) to write a detective novel, though from the little he vouchsafes of this, he was probably best advised to stick to scholarship. (I was particularly taken with the title of one piece of projected work, a novel to be called *A Manx Cat*).

And now? Well, love grows old and waxes cold—now, I find him perhaps a little tiring, a little facetious, the boyishness turned irritatingly to immaturity. Other more adult detectives have taken most of the place he once held in my affections. Most, but not all: there'll always be a corner of my heart which is forever Fen's.

THE CASES OF GERVASE FEN, BY EDMUND CRISPIN

Novels

The Case of the Gilded Fly, 1944. *Holy Disorders*, 1945. *The Moving Toyshop*, 1946. *Swan Song*, 1947. *Love Lies Bleeding*, 1948. *Buried For Pleasure*, 1948. *Frequent Hearses*, 1950. *The Long Divorce*, 1951. *The Glimpses of the Moon*, 1977.

Story collections

Beware of the Trains, 1953 (16 stories, 14 with Fen). *Fen Country*, 1979 (26 stories, 17 with Fen).

37

DAVID WILLIAMS

on

Reuben Frost

Reuben Frost is the quintessential, well heeled, impeccably connected New Yorker—and an utterly warm and charming man besides. A septuagenarian Wall Street lawyer now retired, he's much involved with charity and the arts. A long standing member of the Gotham Club on East 56th St, he dresses at Brooks Brothers (though with the occasional touch of Italian high fashion), drinks freshly-pressed orange juice at breakfast, martinis at other times of the day, lunches when downtown at Bouley, takes his adorable, intelligent wife Cynthia to dinner at Elaine's, Grenouille, and other in-places, but never to restaurants like Giardi's where you may run into 'the bridge and tunnel crowd' from Queens, the Bronx, and New Jersey! Establishment upper-East-siders are very protective of their territory. The Frosts live in a brownstone townhouse on East 70th St., from where Reuben Frost walks, or takes Avenue buses, or the subway to go about his business—and taxis only if he's very late or very, very tired.

Reuben and Cynthia Frost are exactly the kind of people that Harold Ross, first editor of the *New Yorker*, surely had in mind as potential readers in 1926. They were even around at the time—Frost would have been fourteen: Cynthia somewhat younger. I met Frost six years ago, at a meeting of the Foreign Affairs Forum, the organisation founded in the 1930s to combat isolationism—an endearing concept to the British. Our friendship dates from that time: I wish it had started earlier.

It was in 1945 that Frost married Cynthia Hanson, from Kansas City, at the Little Church Around the Corner (where else?). They were good for each other then, and they still are. Cynthia was a principal dancer at the American Ballet Theatre with Anton Dolin. After giving up dancing in 1955, she became ballet mistress at the new National Ballet (where her husband later became Chairman of the Board). She left Nat Ballet eventually to administer the performing arts grants programme of the private Brigham Foundation. Busy, competent Cynthia still heads that programme.

Frost is a graduate of Princeton and the Harvard Law School. He joined the respected law firm of Chase and Ward in 1935 at a salary of $2,000 a year, and stayed there all his working life. Now a retired Executive Partner, 'of counsel' to the firm, he still has his own modest office and other privileges at Chase and Ward. His faculties are in remarkably good shape, saving only for a very slight failing in his hearing, and he looks less than his age, thanks partly to a full and distinguished head of grey hair.

As one of the finest legal craftsmen and draftsmen of his or any other day, Reuben Frost is still frequently consulted by his old clients and younger colleagues. It's his legal counselling and his public service activities that by curious coincidence have so often got him caught up in those murder investigations you see reported. Of course, it's not curious at all that, once involved, he gets to the heart of such matters before everyone else, and invariably solves the cases. His sharp, analytical mind, his encyclopaedic knowledge of the law, especially corporate law, and his practised ability to cut corners by taking an unofficial enquiry route, all combine to put him sometimes several jumps ahead of the police. I'm still reassured though that his Puerto Rican friend, Detective First Class Luis Bautista, NYPD, is usually around to watch Reuben's back when he's sleuthing, because the going can get quite tough.

Reuben Frost makes few concessions to his age, and fewer still to the changes and, as some insist, the dangers of contemporary city life. Although he was once mugged outside his house, he continues to move about with the insouciance of a high-IQ Mr Magoo, and I've no doubt he'll continue that way. More strength to him, because when his chronicler Haughton Murphy sends me those enthralling, civilised, highly literate accounts of Frost's sallies into the (better class) criminal world, they not only demonstrate Frost's incredible ingenuity and his Robert Benchley wit, but they also rekindle my love for a sophisticated, old values New York society that I know is still surviving: Reuben Frost is the urbane living proof of that.

THE CASES OF REUBEN FROST, BY HAUGHTON MURPHY

Murder for Lunch, 1986. *Murder Takes a Partner*, 1987. *Murder and Acquisitions*, 1988. *Murder Keeps a Secret*, 1989. *Murder Times Two*, 1990. *Murder Saves Face*, 1991.

38

GWENDOLINE BUTLER
on

Henry Gamadge

Henry Gamadge came into my life at a time of mild depression (I think the owner of a house I wanted to buy had refused to sell to me on the grounds that academics shouldn't live in big houses), and gave me an immediate uplift in spirits. Reading an Elizabeth Daly-Henry Gamadge mystery has never failed to divert me ever since.

Deadly Nightshade was my introduction to the Gamadge world, and from the moment I met him, on the first page, sitting at his open library window, examining a yellowing piece of paper and listening to the strains of Norma on a street organ, I knew I was in good company. He was a consulting expert on old books and manuscripts, an occasional detective.

He lived in an old brownstone house and he had a marmalade cat. I knew that brownstone houses were good detective territory. Did not Nero Wolfe live in one? And surely the young Ellery Queen occasionally dropped into one?

I felt happy and secure in Henry's company and not a bit jealous when he found a wife because she brought not only a dog but some splendidly diverting murders with her, as in *Evidence of Things Seen*.

For me there has always been a pleasantly spine-chilling element to the mysteries in which Henry Gamadge was involved: a sense of the past haunting the present. Nothing supernatural, but ghosts walked all the same, creeping out of long dead mysteries to create a murder, with luck, several, in the contemporary everyday world.

Henry Gamadge was well-read and knowledgeable, he was comfortably off and the world he moved in and deciphered was rich and sociable. The women had good jewellery and elegant clothes. The men belonged to the right clubs. The few flashy characters were always redeemed by being good people, or else due for a speedy death, sometimes both, as in *The Wrong Way Down* or *The House Without a Door*.

The Gamadge style of detecting was urbane and intuitive. He usually seemed to read the answer to the mystery from the very beginning. A small, fascinating puzzle like the antique engraving of The Lady Audley, which appears to change into another Lady Audley without any human agency (*The Wrong Way Down*), or some strange messages in a paper ball dropped in the street (*Arrow Pointing Nowhere*), alerted him at once to a deeper and more dangerous set of events to come. Nothing is predictable in a Gamadge mystery and nothing is to be taken for granted.

Henry Gamadge had the same inscrutable mastery of events that Reggie Fortune displayed. Both know the answers and pull the strings; thus the end comes about, with the mystery solved and the murderer revealed, because they have contrived it so, and never a boring moment. I think of the chilling final scenes in *The Wrong Way Down* as we watch the killer slowly undress and unmask.

I enjoy Henry Gamadge's investigation enough to reread them. Over the years I have collected most, but not all of the stories in which he displays his acumen. Even knowing the answer to a puzzle I am still given pleasure. Why should this be so, when it not true of other detective stories? There are many fictional detectives whom I am glad to meet in new adventures yet I do not turn back to read the old ones. But for me Henry Gamadge, as with Reggie Fortune and Sherlock Holmes, can always be met again. Perhaps the answer must be that these are interesting characters with a nice line in conversation and a gift to surprise.

'THE CASES OF HENRY GAMADGE, BY ELIZABETH DALY

Unexpected Night, 1940. *Deadly Nightshade*, 1940. *Murders in Volume 2*, 1941. *The House Without the Door*, 1942. *Evidence of Things Seen*, 1943. *Nothing Can Rescue Me*, 1943. *Arrow Pointing Nowhere*, 1944. *The Book of the Dead*, 1944. *Any Shape or Form*, 1945. *Somewhere in the House*, 1946. *The Wrong Way Down*, 1946. *Night Walk*, 1947. *The Book of the Lion*, 1948. *And Dangerous to Know*, 1949. *Death and Letters*, 1950. *The Book of the Crime*, 1951.

39

JAMES MELVILLE
on

Inspector Ghote

Since you're reading this book, the chances are that any mention of the city of Bombay will make you—as it certainly does countless others—think of the dogged, self-effacing and frequently put-upon Inspector Ganesh Ghote. Not bad for such a modest chap. True, he has been around for a quarter of a century, but so have a good many other fictional detectives who haven't caught the imagination and engaged the affections of readers all over the world to anything like the same extent.

It's hard to account for the huge and continuing success of H.R.F. Keating's creation beyond limply asserting that Ghote is above all marvellously credible, not only to those who are acquainted with India but also to those who aren't (and who are diverted by the fact that Keating himself didn't go there until a good many years after Ghote sprang to life).

The inspector is certainly no hero in the conventional sense. Professionally, he is a not very senior officer operating within and often in spite of a creaking bureaucracy starved of resources, and therefore having to improvise, make do and wheedle people into cooperating.

At home he's a hard-up, middle-class Indian husband and father enjoying modest domestic pleasures and coping with everyday problems and occasional crises. Mrs Ghote is loyal and generally supportive, but has a mind of her own, grumbles when she feels like it and quite often needs to be placated. His young son is the apple of Ghote's eye, and in the way of children both a great joy and a hostage to fortune.

On the whole, then, it wouldn't be accurate to suggest that the odds are stacked against Ghote. He's certainly a lot better off than the overwhelming majority of the citizens of Bombay, where, as Mr Keating once shook me by pointing out, it's quite logical for the police to search for days for 'a man in a blue shirt' because he's most unlikely to have changed it. Poor men in Bombay who wear shirts at all possess just the one, you see.

On the other hand Ghote faces his fair share of problems and frustrations, particularly since in many of his cases he's up against people who play in the big league and are both capable of and accustomed to manipulating the system in which a CID inspector must work. The very rich or politically influential tend to regard Ghote as a person of little account, and if they are also corrupt and ruthless, definitely expendable.

We know they're wrong, don't we? Because Ghote has the strength of his very limitations. An honest man, he knows what it is to face a conflict of loyalties and muddle through to a resolution of them. Being neither a genius nor a superman, he simply perseveres, doing his duty as he sees it and bloody-mindedly refusing to be deflected from the point at issue.

Ghote's cases don't solve themselves. Ghote is a creature of the imagination of a British crime writer, operating within an administrative framework that is still in many respects recognisably part of the British colonial legacy; but he is also firmly rooted in his own Indian culture. He usually knows where to look and who to ask for the information he needs, and we in our alien world revel in the fascinating insights we are afforded by following him.

More than anything else, though, Ghote is Everyman with whom each of us can identify in some way. He is part champion, part underdog; part avenger, and part victim. He is as flawed, perplexed and occasionally irritable as we know ourselves to be; as amiable, determined and honourable as we would like to be. He's great.

THE CASES OF INSPECTOR GHOTE, BY H. R. F. KEATING

Novels

The Perfect Murder, 1964. *Inspector Ghote's Good Crusade*, 1966. *Inspector Ghote Caught in Meshes*, 1967. *Inspector Ghote Hunts the Peacock*, 1968. *Inspector Ghote Plays a Joker*, 1969. *Inspector Ghote Breaks an Egg*, 1970. *Inspector Ghote Goes by Train*, 1971. *Inspector Ghote Trusts the Heart*, 1972. *Bats Fly Up For Inspector Ghote*, 1974. *Filmi, Filmi, Inspector Ghote*, 1976. *Inspector Ghote Draws a Line*, 1979. *Go West, Inspector Ghote*, 1981. *The Sheriff of Bombay*, 1984. *Under a Monsoon Cloud*, 1986. *The Body in the Billiard Room*, 1987. *Dead on Time*, 1988. *The Iciest Sin*, 1990.

Story collection
Inspector Ghote, His Life and Crimes, 1990.

Uncollected stories
'*Inspector Ghote and the Loose End*', 1977. '*Inspector Ghote and the Film Star*', 1977. '*Softly, Softly Catchee Monkey*', 1990.

40
JILL McGOWN
on
Alan Grant

To the readership of the thirties, when *The Man in the Queue* first made its appearance, Alan Grant must have come as something of a shock. Well-countenanced, well-liked, a little smug, a touch patronising, the obsessive Alan Grant is like no other fictional detective of his day. True, he could have retired on the legacy left him by an aunt; true, he had been to prep school and public school, an unusual background for a Scotland Yard DI—but in all essentials Alan Grant was a living, breathing human being, with hang-ups and prejudices as well as the 'flair' which made his colleagues admire him, the professionalism which made them respect him, and the egalitarianism which made them *like* him.

The flair was both his strength and his weakness; it made him a reputation, but it amounted almost to obsession. Grant was a man driven by sheer frustration to explain the apparently inexplicable, however irrelevant it may seem, and his mind was unable to rest until it found the answer. The professionalism was complete. Grant took deep exception to crime; he did not stand back and admire it. He investigated it, painstakingly and thoroughly, using all the resources at his command, including his colleagues at the Yard. He was not a one-man-band, he was not infallible, and he was not an amateur. Indeed, he describes himself as 'just a hard-working, well-meaning, ordinarily intelligent Detective Inspector'. The egalitarianism was entirely natural; Grant was equally at home with best-selling authors, safebreakers, gay playwrights or beat bobbies; he knew how to conduct himself in a four-star restaurant or a four-ale bar.

In his punishing searches for the truth, Grant encounters not the old, reassuring *dramatis personae* of the detective novel, but men and women who inhabit a world entirely recognisable today. His Britain is one which has to contend with the IRA gunning people down on their doorsteps, and with a yellow press which hounds celebrities for the sake of circulation; his police force deals with thugs and organised crime, and is accused of brutality towards suspects; his generation pities youngsters who live without fantasy and dreams, and despairs of their education. He even observes that to travel first class on a British railway makes one practically a millionaire. This very real world has very real, complex people living in it—no-one has the decency to leave hand-made Turkish cigarette ends lying around for him to find.

All Grant has is experience of life, of crime, and of human nature, and a mind that worries at a problem until it is solved. Laid up in hospital with a broken leg in *The Daughter of Time* (1951), bored to distraction, he sets this terrier-like mind on the murder of the Princes in the Tower, and even this academic exercise becomes a personal crusade to clear Richard III's name.

This self-destructive approach leads, almost inevitably, to a break-down, and *The Singing Sands* (1952) finds him journeying to Scotland on sick leave, ashamed and afraid of his weakness, only to encounter the dead body of a young man on the train. There is no mystery about the death; only a strange little verse scribbled on a newspaper. But Grant has to know what it *means*, and thus the obsessive curiosity which is at once his downfall and his salvation drives out the very demons it admitted in the first place. We leave him, recovered, at a point in his life when he might have fallen in love, had not his quest made such a thing irrelevant, and the lady a mere intruder.

So, no cosy domestic set-up for the eminently fanciable but quite unmarriageable Grant. To sustain a marriage, he would have to resign his job, and since he has just spent his sick leave getting to the bottom of the death of that young man on the London mail train, it is small wonder that he regards this briefly-contemplated course of action as a quite extraordinary idea.

The untimely death of Josephine Tey makes that Grant's final thought; a fitting epitaph for the lady herself. A hard-working, well-meaning, ordinarily intelligent Detective Inspector as hero? A quite extraordinary idea.

THE CASES OF ALAN GRANT, BY JOSEPHINE TEY

A Shilling for Candles, 1936. *The Franchise Affair*, 1948. *To Love and Be Wise*, 1950. *The Daughter of Time*, 1951. *The Singing Sands*, 1952.

41
DEBORAH VALENTINE
on
Cordelia Grey

It was rather like seeing a woman at a party and not liking the look of her. Word of mouth brings out a few details, all equally unpromising. A young woman as detective. As *private* detective. Twenty-two. Pretty brown hair. Attractive (what else?). Intelligent (yeah, yeah). All adding up to a young woman to whom that revolting term 'spunky' could be applied. Enough to put you off your canapés. When I was twenty-two I was having a life crisis—suddenly realizing myself too old to be a child prodigy. I don't know exactly what sort of prodigy I expected to be; I thought by twenty-two something would have turned up. Imagine the thrill of meeting a woman solving cases at an age when I still couldn't solve the enigma of my chequebook.

I discovered P.D. James late, at *A Taste for Death*, and it could only have been that first flush of enthusiasm for a new (to me) author that pushed me to read *An Unsuitable Job for a Woman*. It was much like being caught at the bar with this distasteful woman; so desperate for a drink that any company would be braved. I needed my P.D. fix.

My first inkling that there might be some more appealing

aspects to Cordelia Grey was when, on the day of her partner Bernie Pryde's suicide, she goes to their usual pub only to be confronted by that Tartar of conventionality, Mavis the barmaid. Mavis suggests that Cordelia couldn't possibly keep up Pryde's Detective Agency, using this confounding logic: that Cordelia's mother certainly wouldn't approve of the job. Sensibly, Cordelia points out that since she only had a mother the first hour of her life, her opinions posed no problems; a statement that manages to shock the entire bar. She '. . . wonders again at the capacity of older people to be outraged by simple facts when they seemed capable of accepting any amount of perverse or shocking opinion.' The pleasantness of shared observation, a good sign. Cordelia defies the careless assumption that a young, pretty, well-bred woman has the world at her feet. As we find out more of her background we realize how it has left her the kind of fatalism that accepts the inevitability of strange and unpleasant happenings, and to view the good unsentimentally. Even in that notably tetchy relationship, that of mother/daughter, she recognizes her fantasies as necessary indulgence, and that consulting this imaginary woman and having her approve of Cordelia's 'unsuitable' job is a comforting convenience. We know she feels more naïve, more eager than she looks. She retains an elusiveness that is peculiarly feminine. Not a Mata Hari mystery, but Cordelia knows how to keep her secrets—as is splendidly illustrated by the conclusion of the book.

Cool, calm and collected—admirable qualities perhaps; certainly preferable to the ball-bashing techniques of many detectives, male or female. There is a steely finesse that can only become finer in the way she handles the patronizing attitudes that dog many female endeavors. All this is good. But it was her attitude to love that won me. Not romantic love, but her unfailing loyalty to her luckless now-dead partner, Bernie Pryde. Never seeing herself as powerful enough to change his luck, she nevertheless gave him something life did not. Respect. She learned his lessons in detection well, gave him what camaraderie she could, and when the time came to defend him did so with all her heart. Clear-eyed acceptance—what more can you ask of a friend?

Is private detection an unsuitable job for a woman? I suspect so. It seems to require an unhealthy curiosity and I like to think a woman has more sense. In Cordelia's defense, she seems to have arrived at the job more out of accident than inclination. And how many friends do we have whose furniture makes us cringe, whose wardrobe could use an infusion of good taste or whose mates could be classified as 'unsuitable'? So what? I can only hope by the end of the party Cordelia and I would be making an appointment for lunch.

THE CASES OF CORDELIA GREY, BY P. D. JAMES

An Unsuitable Job for a Woman, 1972. *The Skull beneath the Skin*, 1982.

42

PHILIP L. SCOWCROFT

on

Inspector Hanaud

A E. W. Mason, writing in the mid-1920s, considered that 'the most important necessity in a detective novel is the detective himself, an outstanding person, actual, picturesque, amusing, a creature of power and singularity'. Some fifteen years earlier, when he turned to write detective fiction himself, his aim was to create a French detective who should be a professional, as physically unlike Sherlock Holmes as possible, genial and friendly and, finally, ready to trust his flair or intuition and to risk acting on it (as French detectives are, and were, supposed to do). Inspector Hanaud was the result and he is said to have been based on MM. Goron and Macé, two distinguished real chiefs of the Paris Sûreté. Yet many of Hanaud's characteristics—the quick questions, the razor-sharp observation, the incredible memory for detail—he shares with his creator.

When we first meet Hanaud in *At the Villa Rose* he is described as 'stout and broad-shouldered with a full and almost heavy face . . . he looked like a prosperous comedian'. His humour is often heavy, too, and frequently his English dilettante friend and associate Julius Ricardo, is the butt of this. Ricardo shrewdly sums him up in that very case as 'a heavy, clever, middle-aged man, liable to become a little gutter-boy at a moment's notice', and years later tells the solicitor Jim Frobisher that he (Frobisher) 'must expect to be awed at one moment, leaped upon unpleasantly at the next, ridiculed at a third and treated with great courtesy and friendship at the fourth'.

Hanaud (the Christian name Gabriel is only mentioned in the early short story 'The Affair at the Semiramis Hotel', and he usually dubs himself by his surname only) is thus a man of rapidly-changing moods and therefore more than a moderately good actor. For all his heavy-handed humour he can be impressive, ruthless even, as the representative of Justice and (like so many of fiction's Great Detectives) the avenger of wrong. For all his brilliance as an investigator, about which he has no false modesty, he has a basic humility. He says: 'We are the servants of chance, the very best of us. Our skill is to seize quickly the hem of her skirt when it flashes for the fraction of a second before our eyes'.

Only twice, and then fleetingly, do we see Hanaud in his office at the Sûreté (in *The House of the Arrow* and *The House in Lordship Lane*) and we never hear of his investigating a case in the French capital. His recorded cases take him to Aix-les-Bains in the Savoy Alps (in *At the Villa Rose*), Dijon (in *The House of the Arrow*), Bordeaux and its wine region (in *The Prisoner in the Opal*) and Normandy (in *They Wouldn't Be Chessmen*). He has successes on English soil, too, while on visits to Ricardo, in 'The Affair at the Semiramis Hotel', 'The Ginger King' (another short), *The House in Lordship Lane* and in one brilliant chapter of *The Sapphire*, where he exposes a Mayfair gambling fraud with supreme ebullience.

He is apparently unmarried, but his courtesy and gentleness to the ladies—especially those (and there are several in Mason's novels) who have been hurt or ill-treated—is legendary. They in their turn love him. He enjoys his food and his holidays, whether in Aix or in England. He is a (silent) cinema buff and takes an interest in church architecture. He delights in 'collecting' English idioms and re-using them, to Ricardo's distress, slightly wrongly, a trait particularly to be found in the later books. His fictional career was a long one, spanning (in publication dates) the years 1910 to 1946, but throughout he remains middle-aged. Yet, for all his brilliance, he is never promoted above the rank of Inspector. Can it be that his face 'did not fit' with the Sûreté's top brass; or was it that his allowing, even encouraging, the killer in *The Prisoner in the Opal* to commit suicide went against him in the promotion stakes? Whatever the reason it should not obscure the undoubted fact that he is the most interesting, as well as the most acute, of all fictional police detectives in the Golden Age period. He combines in one person the flair of the classic private detective with all the advantages of the official machine.

THE CASES OF INSPECTOR HANAUD, BY A. E. W. MASON

Novels

At the Villa Rose, 1910. *The House of the Arrow*, 1928. *The Prisoner in the Opal*, 1928. *The Sapphire*, 1933. *They Wouldn't Be Chessmen*, 1935. *The House in Lordship Lane*, 1946.

Uncollected stories

'*The Affair at the Semiramis Hotel*', 1917. '*The Ginger King*', 1940.

43
JOHN CONQUEST
on
Hazell

CONQUEST INVESTIGATIONS
Discreet & Confidential Inquiries Since 1927

Dear Mr Jakubowski,

With reference to our recent conversation, I regret to have to inform you that this agency is unable to accept your commission.

However, I would like, if I may, to take the liberty of recommending to your attention a Mr James Hazell, of 147 Shepherd Market, Mayfair, W.1. While we would not consider Hazell suitable for permanent employment, we have, on occasion, contracted his services on a freelance basis and have found him resourceful, enacious, flexible in ethical and legal matters and physically competent, characteristics which render him particularly suitable for your needs.

Originally from Haggerston, in East London, Hazell was formerly a detective constable in the Metropolitan Police, attached to the Flying Squad, Fulham Division. One of our sources, Inspector Minty, is of the opinion that Hazell was corrupt: what I understand is known in the vernacular as 'a bent copper.' Be that as it may, no charges were ever brought against him and my feeling is that Minty harbours some personal prejudice towards Hazell. Hazell left the police force after the perpetrators of an armed robbery attempted to close a car door several times while his right ankle presented an obstacle. He underwent considerable surgery, but appears to have made a complete recovery.

Following his injury and the consequent termination of a promising career, Hazell experienced a personal crisis. His marriage broke up, he drifted through a number of occupations, as a barman, van-driver and bouncer, and developed what can only be called a drinking problem. However, he seems also to have made a complete recovery from this.

Three cases on which Hazell has worked have come to my attention. They have, I believe, formed the basis of a popular series of paperbacked books of the kind sold at railway station kiosks and also, I am told, of a television series transmitted on a commercial channel. His first professional engagement was with Venables, Venables, Williams & Gregory, for whom he worked very creditably on a complex child custody case, hence the title of the subsequent 'thriller' *Hazell Plays Solomon*. Unfortunately, while committing a serious professional error in becoming involved with a principal in the case, he displayed far better judgement than the partner who was instructing him by querying the credibility of the client, thus saving the firm considerable embarrassment, for which his reward was the termination of his employment.

During the same period, Hazell shot and killed one Keith O'Rourke, a convicted felon who considered that he had a grievance against Hazell and had, on his release from a seven year sentence for attempted murder, intimated that he intended to kill Hazell. While the circumstances of this fatal encounter were, to say the least, ambiguous, no charges were brought.

Deciding to become an independent private investigator, Hazell, by pure coincidence, took over the offices of a recently deceased investigator, a Mr Fitch, and his first commission was in the nature of a legacy from this gentleman. In this matter, entitled *Hazell and the Three-Card Trick*, he was able to demonstrate that an apparent suicide was in fact an accidental death, thus enabling a widow to claim a substantial insurance payment. This he did by tracking down a very elusive criminal and, regrettably but unavoidably, offering financial inducements to gain essential testimony. At the same time, he very foolishly allowed himself to be hoodwinked into offering substantially reduced rates to an affluent client.

In point of fact, Hazell's recorded career has been beset with devious clients, particularly in his third case, entitled *Hazell and the Menacing Jester*, which is also noteworthy as his most violent. Normally Hazell, the O'Rourke affair notwithstanding, prefers to defuse potential violence by assuming the manner of an amiably minatory East End 'hard case.' In this matter, however, he was twice obliged, successfully, to demonstrate the reality behind it.

Other points, worth mentioning, are that Hazell is extremely attached to, and has developed a wry philosophy about, the London metropolis, and, as manifested most clearly in his third case, in which he was involved with persons of superficial glamour and affluence, is acutely class conscious, with a tendency to exaggerate his Cockney background when offended by social situations or when patronised. He also has a wry, if sometimes wilfully obscure, sense of humour.

I hope this information will be of use to you in helping to resolve your somewhat unusual problems.

Yours etc.

THE CASES OF HAZELL, BY P. B. YUILL

Hazell Plays Solomon. 1974 *Hazell and the Three Card Trick*, 1975. *Hazell and the Menacing Jester*, 1976.

44

H.R.F. KEATING

on

Sherlock Holmes

It would take someone as simply good as Dr Watson ever to have wanted to share rooms with Sherlock Holmes. Other people's untidiness is irksome enough, but think of the perpetual arrogant teasing, the tobacco smog, the unsavoury if sometimes picturesque visitors, the stink of chemical experiments, that bloody violin, the not listening to a word you said and the expectation that every word *he* said would not only be listened to but noted down.

Yet the man, safely in the pages, is my favourite investigator. And has been ever since I first read those wonderful tales, at about the age of ten. And this is not because of the powers he is shown as possessing, though I suppose that even as a boy I was internally illuminated by the mythical figure of the Great Detective, he who shows us that no mystery is impenetrable, no problem unsolvable, no danger insurmountable. No, it is because besides all that Sherlock Holmes is human.

Nor is his humanity a carefully contrived business, that addition of a calculated measure of weakness to offset omniscience. Holmes, of course, had his little weaknesses. There is the touch of vanity. There is the waiting hypodermic. But these, however much they may have been schematic in the first place, soon became as the stories of his adventures unfolded just two among many others. They are a couple of aspects of a complex person we can recognise as someone like ourselves, however much superior his 'little brain attic'.

At one and the same time Holmes is a single stamped figure, the emblem most people think of, the Great Detective, the contrivance for solving crimes, and he is a mass of contradictions. So he is excessively rational, yet he described himself, as the adventure of the Copper Beeches began, as a 'man who loves art for its own sake'. He is the athlete who was, in Watson's words, 'undoubtedly one of the finest boxers of his weight that I have ever seen', yet he would lie for hours upon the sofa toying with that wretched violin. He handed over 'the fair sex' to poor old Watson as his department, yet he was notable for 'a remarkable courtesy and gentleness' to women and, when he wished to burgle Charles Augustus Milverton's Hampstead house, he swiftly wooed, and won, that arch-blackmailer's housemaid. He showed on occasion a 'red-Indian composure', and at other times he was as restless and excitable as a two-year-old. And we believe both.

We believe everything about him. No wonder people reading the stories in the last decade of the twentieth century, a hundred years after some of them came from Conan Doyle's pen, write to 221B Baker Street seeking help over real problems causing them real distress. They, unthinkingly, see Sherlock Holmes as a human being like themselves.

And I do, too. With my conscious mind I know that at that marvellous mythical address there is only the Abbey National Building Society grinding out its dull, everyday business. But another part of me knows and feels that Holmes is. Is somehow still to be found in that 'single large airy sitting-room, cheerfully furnished, and illuminated by two broad windows'. And ever more shall be so.

THE CASES OF SHERLOCK HOLMES, BY A. CONAN DOYLE

Novels

A Study in Scarlet, 1888. *The Sign of Four*, 1890. *The Hound of the Baskervilles*, 1902. *The Valley of Fear*, 1914.

Story collections

The Adventures of Sherlock Holmes, 1892. *The Memoirs of Sherlock Holmes*, 1894. *The Return of Sherlock Holmes*, 1905. *His Last Bow*, 1917. *The Case-Book of Sherlock Holmes*, 1927.

There are, of course, innumerable other novels and stories by other hands featuring Sherlock Holmes. The Holmes pastiche is a thriving industry, for which there is an ever-hungry reading public. To list all would fill page after page of this book unnecessarily.

45

SCOTT A. CUPP
on

Ed and Am Hunter

Beginning in 1947, Ed and Am Hunter roamed through Chicago and Illinois like quiet whirlwinds, never too loud or terrifying, but leaving damage in their wake. Their adventures were chronicled in seven novels beginning with *The Fabulous Clipjoint* followed by *The Dead Ringer* (1948), *The Bloody Moonlight* (1949), *Compliments of a Fiend* (1950), *Death Has Many Doors* (1951), *The Late Lamented* (1959), and *Mrs Murphy's Underpants* (1963).

The novels are notable as they represent the only consistent characters utilized by Fredric Brown. The Hunters are introduced in *The Fabulous Clipjoint* when Ed (then 18) finds out that his father has been murdered in a dark Chicago alley. Having no other true family, he turns to his uncle Ambrose who runs a concession with a travelling carnival. The two strike a good friendship and Ed finds out that Am had been a private detective. They convince each other that they should solve the murder. Taking a leave from the carnival, they travel to Chicago, investigate and eventually solve the murder. The novel won an Edgar for the Best First Novel of 1947.

Ed Hunter represented the impetuous youth of post-World War II America—restless, energetic and ready to tackle a world that has opened up for them. Am is the steady figure who has sown his wild oats and travelled extensively. It is through Am that Ed gradually realizes that he never really knew his father and he substitutes Am in the role. Ed demonstrates a phenomenal memory and strong rational mind. Love is not his strong suit as he frequently falls for either the wrong girl or the right girl at the wrong time. Am provides the stable father-figure, able to pick him up when he falls and aloof enough to allow him the opportunity to make his own mistakes. The two work the carnival and then return to Chicago to work as private detectives—first for the Ben Starbuck agency, then on their own.

The cases handled by the pair get pretty wild. In *The Dead Ringer* they are faced with the murders of a midget, a chimpanzee, and a nude black boy. In *Death Has Many Doors* a young woman is convinced that she will be murdered by men from Mars. She dies in a 'locked room' scenario and is soon followed by her look-alike sister. The craziness of Charles Fort's research shows up when Ed believes Am to have been kidnapped by Fort's 'Ambrose Collector' in *Compliments of a Fiend*.

The books are distinguished by crisp, clean writing and by Brown's insights into the human psyche. The settings are memorable, particularly the carnival scenes which drew on Brown's own experiences. The Chicago locales he describes in the various novels remain much as he saw them thirty and forty years ago. The corner bar may be gone, but the feel for the areas is still there. They are not the best Brown, like *Night of the Jabberwock* or *The Screaming Mimi*, but *The Fabulous Clipjoint* and *Compliments of a Fiend* do not miss that level by much. The books do show some wear—characters drink and smoke too much, there are racial comments spoken out of habit more than rancor—but they are eminently readable and enjoyable.

THE CASES OF ED AND AM HUNTER, BY FREDRIC BROWN

The Fabulous Clipjoint, 1947. *The Dead Ringer*, 1948. *The Bloody Moonlight*, 1949. *Compliments of a Fiend*, 1950. *Death Has Many Doors*, 1951. *The Late Lamented*, 1959. *Mrs Murphy's Underpants*, 1963.

46

MARGARET MARON
on

Johnson Johnson

'Men with bifocal glasses: I spit.' Tina Rossi, *Dolly and the Singing Bird*.

'Bifocal glasses are common. So Janey Lloyd used to say.' Sarah Cassells, *Dolly and the Cookie Bird*.

'I shall call it, with levity, the bifocals syndrome.' Dr Beltanno Douglas MacRannoch, *Dolly and the Doctor Bird*.

'I have nothing, even yet, against bifocal glasses.' Ruth Russell, *Dolly and the Starry Bird*.

'Everyone knows three boring facts about Eskimos. I'll tell you another. Whenever I think about Eskimos, I think about bifocal glasses.' Joanna Emerson, *Dolly and the Nanny Bird*.

Each of the first five Johnson Johnson books opens with a comment by one of the 'birds' about his glasses; but the sixth trumps all the others in delicious cunning: 'To most of my clients, bifocal glasses are asthma. All those words are spelled correctly. I looked them up.' Rita Geddes, *Dolly and the Bird of Paradise*.

These three sentences distill the essence of a Johnson Johnson mystery. They are quirky, intriguing, define the narrator's character, and conceal a brilliant fair play clue all at once.

With his landed gentry background of public school, university, and Royal Navy, Dorothy Dunnett's enigmatic hero can, at first glance, seem a modern version of the silly ass sleuth. Certainly he's not above letting others think that when it serves his purpose: 'I had a first impression only of a pair of bifocal glasses, their half moons bright in the light, and a smile of boundless vacuity.' (*Singing Bird*.) Yet he's much more original and interesting. Those shining glasses may hide the real man, yet he's reflected in bits and shards of crazily-angled Fun House mirrors by those around him. His quicksilver character isn't so much revealed by how *he* acts, as by how others react to him.

He can turn up in formal evening splendor, but usually wears baggy trousers and misshapen wool sweaters which are so awful that one believes his claims that they're hand-knitted by an elderly uncle. A world-class portrait painter, he sails the oceans in a gaff-rigged auxiliary ketch named *Dolly*, ostensibly painting portraits of the rich and famous when he isn't competing in the latest regatta. In reality, he's also a trouble-shooter for British intelligence and puts in wherever a resident agent is in trouble, be it the Scottish Hebrides, the Bahamas, Rome or Ibiza.

Each book solves a surface mystery, but there's also a deeper mystery about Johnson himself which overarches the last two or three books. One almost has to read between the lines to ferret out details because Dunnett doesn't employ flashing arrows; and many subtle nuggets of information are delivered elliptically, in understatement, or in frivolous throwaway. According to official reports, he and his beautiful young wife were in a plane crash. He barely survived; she was killed. 'Plane crash, my arse,' says the narrator of *Paradise*, who sees that his friends are worried about his drinking.

> 'Of course it was,' said Lady Emerson. 'There is no other explanation that could possibly be put about without doing a lot of harm, and most of it to Jay himself.'
> 'How?' I asked. 'By the people who did it? Are they still about?'
> 'He doesn't think so,' she said.

Knowing Johnson, they probably aren't. He may be an engaging human being, intelligent, self-deprecating, and basically decent; but he accepts danger and has shown himself quite willing to sacrifice himself and others, too, for certain matters of principle.

Despite the buried tragedy, the books are rich in comic detail, lush scenery, and vivid characters. Johnson moves in sophisticated circles among the wealthy and leisured and their hangers-on. Violence is precipitated by those greedy for more—more love, more money, more power.

Many are the trumpeted successors to Agatha Christie. Every time a female writer sets one literate word behind another and produces three competent novels in a row, someone tries to fit her with the crown. The *Dolly* books are written with such grace, wit and sheer generosity of spirit that readers will no doubt be looking around next century for Dorothy Dunnett's heirs and successors.

THE CASES OF JOHNSON JOHNSON, BY DOROTHY DUNNETT

Dolly and the Singing Bird, 1968. *Dolly and the Cookie Bird*, 1970. *Dolly and the Doctor Bird*, 1971. *Dolly and the Starry Bird*, 1973. *Dolly and the Nanny Bird*, 1976. *Dolly and the Bird of Paradise*, 1983. *Moroccan Traffic*, 1991.

47

CAY VAN ASH

on

Moris Klaw

S ax Rohmer is best known for his creation of the diabolical Dr Fu Manchu but, in a working career of nearly sixty years, he contributed his quota of fictional detectives.

There was the irascible Chief Inspector Kerry of Scotland Yard, the vivacious Frenchman, Gaston Max—who first came upon the scene five years before Hercule Poirot—and Paul Harley of Chancery Lane, a solicitor-detective who preceded Perry Mason by more than a decade. But, for sheer ingenuity, I prefer the bizarre figure of Moris Klaw, known as the Dream Detective.

Moris Klaw was as much a mystery as the cases he investigated. Neither his true name nor his nationality was known. He spoke English with 'an indescribable accent' though his mannerisms were chiefly French. Even his age was uncertain; he might have been old, or a young man prematurely aged. He came out of nowhere and went back there.

His appearance, to say nothing of his behaviour, was eccentric in the extreme. He wore a scraggy beard, gold-rimmed pince-nez, shabby clothes, a caped black cloak, and an archaic bowler hat. This latter item served as a receptacle for a small scent spray; he had the habit of spraying his high, domed forehead with verbena in times of stress—a custom, he said, borrowed from the Romans.

In the early years of this century, when he was active in London, Moris Klaw was regarded as something of a magician. Nowadays, we would call him an exponent of ESP. He believed the universe to be pervaded by a kind of force-field upon which human emotions, if sufficiently intense, might be recorded, as though upon a magnetic tape, and retrieved by those who knew how.

This, incidentally, was no figment of the author's vivid imagination but the theory of Baron von Reichenbach, a sober 19th-century scientist, who proposed the existence of such a force and named it 'the Od'.

Thus Moris Klaw often obtained the starting-point for his investigations by literally sleeping on the job. Laying his head on his 'odically sterilised pillow', he would promptly go to sleep, which he was able to do at will, and dream what had been in the mind of someone present at the time of the incident.

'Thoughts are things!' he declared. 'You would snort less if you had waked screaming, out in the desert; screaming out with fear of the dripping beaks of the vultures—the last dreadful fear which the mind had known of him who had died of thirst upon that haunted spot!'

In conjunction with this unorthodox procedure, the Dream Detective often based his enquiries on what he termed the 'Cycle of Crime'—the periodic repetition of untoward events in connection with certain objects and places. He had travelled widely and amassed an encylopaedic knowledge of artifacts which bore a sinister reputation and allegedly 'haunted' houses. By this means, he was able to identify such deadly items as the Athenean Harp of the Borgias, and to solve the mystery of the Whispering Poplars.

Crimes which possessed no aspect of the macabre did not interest him. He sought no publicity and did not offer his services to the general public. As a rule, he was consulted by such gentlemen as museum curators, or dealers in precious art objects, who knew his name as a specialist in his peculiar field. But he had also a few problems submitted to him by baffled CID officers who had seen him at work and come to appreciate him at his true value.

No doubt in order that his adversaries might think him a harmless old fool, Moris Klaw operated out of a disreputable junk shop and pet store in Wapping. Threading your way through a clutter of domestic débris stacked up outside, and finding the place unoccupied, your arrival would be announced by the raucous screech of a parrot.

'Moris Klaw! Moris Klaw! The devil's come for you!'

Then the Dream Detective would appear and, if you were lucky, go out with you on your errand, leaving the premises in the dubious care of his drunken and half-witted handyman.

'You hear me, William! You are to sell nothing—unless it is the washstand! Forget not to change the canaries' water. If there is no mouse in the trap by eight o'clock, give the owl a herring . . .'

THE CASES OF MORIS KLAW, BY SAX ROHMER
The Dream Detective, 1920 (short stories).

48

BENJAMIN M. SCHUTZ

on

Laidlaw

Two books, only two books! But Detective Inspector Jack Laidlaw is my favorite character in all of crime fiction. I'm not alone in my admiration as both books, *Laidlaw* (1977) and *The Papers of Tony Veitch* (1983), were awarded Silver Daggers by the Crime Writers Association and were short-listed for the Edgar Allan Poe Award by the Mystery Writers Association. (Laidlaw also appears briefly as a minor character in a third novel, *The Big Man* (1985). But it's a minor appearance the way a dorsal fin on the horizon is a minor event.)

Nominally of the Scottish Crime Division, he is really in the employ of the dead, the dead of Glasgow—'the city of the stare'. Laidlaw stands squarely in the tradition of the Great Detective, a man apart, by virtue of his gifts or talents. What is Laidlaw's gift? I think it's an enormous capacity for empathy, a capacity that can leave him on the verge of paralysis. When the common wisdom of the day is that it's Us vs Them, victims or villains, Laidlaw trolls the depths of Glasglow, an angry Jeremiah, reminding people that

'We share in every one else or forgo ourselves,' and that there are 'No fairies, no monsters. Just people.'

Crime for Laidlaw is a failure of brotherhood, a failure of humanist salvation, a refusal to 'Adopt each other in our care.' He investigates not just to catch the criminals but to understand the fundamental human failures that lead to each crime and to reaffirm in the 'shitty urban machine' that there is a significance to each life and its loss, even if at the end he feels 'Lumbered with information I can't ignore. And I can't understand. As if I've been reading God's mail.'

In Laidlaw's eyes, we fail each other for two main reasons. 'One's a kind of total cynicism. Using other people. Reducing them to objects because you find nothing to believe in but yourself. That's crime in all the multifarious forms, most of them legal.' The other is 'The need to be God's relative.' The way out is 'If everybody could waken up tomorrow morning and have the courage of their doubts, not their convictions, the millenium would be here. I think false certainties are what destroy us. What's murder but a willed absolute, an invented certainty? An existential failure of nerve.'

What a refreshing change from the narcissism of the 'code heroes' rampant in today's crime fiction, whose response to the complexity of life is to erect a code, sit a virtue on its head like a totem, (honor being a current favorite) and shake it in the face of other people's claims on them. Laidlaw goes a step further into the maw of uncertainty, aware that his own vision may be no better than anyone else.

To watch Laidlaw is to watch a man try to live without false certainty, a man whose nature is 'A wrack of paradox,' and who 'knew nothing to do but inhabit the paradox.' That may be the best definition of 'hardness,' the quintessential Glasgwegian virtue: the ability to inhabit paradox without resorting to false certainties to ease the task. This is what distinguishes him from men such as the gangster John Rhodes who 'Whenever the contradictions became too much for him, that terrible anger was waiting to resolve things into immediacy, confrontation.'

This doesn't make Laidlaw an easy man to befriend or live with. It's no wonder with all the conflicts he tries to contain that he gives himself migraines, or exasperates those who try to get close to him. He's not a sanitized hero with nary a wayward impulse and perfect moral pitch. Rather he's a man with great compassion for those few small weapons we have to keep sorrow at bay and an equal anger at how we misuse them.

Where is he now, and why has he been gone so long? When last seen, his lover, Jan, described him as 'Walking the edge of himself like a ledge. She remembered him once saying to her in bed in that wild dispensation sometime achieved there "You know what I believe? There is no centre as such. The sum of the edges is the centre. You have to keep walking the line. But that's how you fell off." She sensed him teetering.'

A large part of the appeal of Jack Laidlaw is the fascination of watching a good man grapple with his demons and doing so on a tightrope. Without a net.

THE CASES OF LAIDLAW, BY WILLIAM McILVANNEY

Laidlaw, 1977. *The Papers of Tony Veitch*, 1983. *The Man in the Green Coat*, 1991 (published after this piece was received).

49

JIM HUANG

on

Julia Larwood

Yoo-hoo there Larwood, I wonder if you know how it is with detectives. Even among one's favorites, there can be a certain qualification to one's affections. Certainly there are more admirable sleuths, more stylish, dashing or brilliant detectives. There are detectives whose every move commands respect, whose powers of deduction are breathtaking, whose physical prowess keeps them from harm. Some detectives are paragons of virtue, role models for us all. Then, of course, there's you, Julia.

You may protest—with some justice—that you're not exactly a detective, that you merely happen to get into trouble or know people who become involved in murder. You might also suggest that it is your friend, Professor Hilary Tamar, who deserves the acclaim. Naturally, Hilary would demur any such honor; the professor's participation in the matters of the death in Venice, the disposition of the estate of Jocasta Fiske-Purefoy and the Daffodil settlement merely demonstrates that the methods of the Scholar may be applied with success in a more worldly realm. If Hilary provides the ratiocination, you and the others at 62 and 63 New Square, Lincoln's Inn also play important roles. A fair-minded observer would recognize all of you—Hilary, Cantrip, Selena, Timothy, Ragwort and, you, Julia—as a great team, and would understand that it would be inappropriate to single out any one.

But a 'nubile tax barrister' such as yourself is impossible to overlook. Now that phrase, taken from a description of you in *The Daily Scuttle*, by itself suggests some of your allure. 'Tax barrister' and 'nubile' are two contrary concepts, rarely linked. In your case, the description is unquestionably accurate (if put in a somewhat unflattering manner). Your command of tax matters is exceptional, and your devotion to your work is impressive. I take particular note of the incident involving champagne and the 'rather special' fudge, described in *The Shortest Way to Hades*; you'll recall that the result was to leave you explaining to your hostess 'the effect of Section 478 of the Taxes Act; but I kept forgetting half way through my sentences how they were meant to end, so I fear that I may have given her an imperfect understanding of these provisions.' In such a situation, it's a rare individual whose primary concern would be how well they had explained the provisions in question.

The appropriateness of the other part of the *Scuttle*'s description, viz. the 'nubile' part, is well documented in two incidents. In *The Sirens Sang of Murder*, Patrick Ardmore adopts 'a course of conduct so precisely calculated to reduce Julia to a state of hopeless infatuation.' He pretends no interest in you beyond a request for free tax advice. He continues 'relentlessly with his strategy of paying no compliments, refraining from physical contact, and making frequent references to his devotion to his wife. Poor Julia, naturally finding this irresistible, had not known what to do.' The conversation about investments continues right to the hotel bed, where you break the impasse ('which I take to be the correct expression for a situation in which no one makes a pass at anyone,' as you say) by expressing yourself with perfect candor.

The other incident occurs in *Thus Was Adonis Murdered*, and is by now one of the classic moments in mystery. In a letter from Venice, you describe the procedure for taking advantage of Italian waiters. Your narrative of this episode has rather more to do with strawberries than with the tax code; it is nevertheless characteristic of your charm in action.

But there is more behind your appeal. The key characteristic that mitigates your legal prowess is the simple fact that—beyond the tax code—you're basically hopeless. Hilary describes your entrance in *The Sirens Sang of Murder* this way: 'Her hair was no more than usually dishevelled, her clothing no more than normally disordered, and she stumbled, in her progress towards the bar, over no more than the customary number of briefcases . . .' This expectation of disorder and disaster is widespread, as you note in *The Shortest Way to Hades*: 'It's an extraordinary thing how every solicitor who loses a piece of paper anywhere in the area of Greater London always claims that it's my fault. It seems to be an official policy of the Law Society.'

Next time I need some free tax advice, I'll be looking you up. And I'll be sure to keep copies of anything important.

THE CASES OF JULIA LARWOOD, BY SARAH CAUDWELL

Thus Was Adonis Murdered, 1981. *The Shortest Way to Hades*, 1984. *The Sirens Sang of Murder*, 1989.

50

HAROLD ADAMS

on

Lieutenant LaSala

———————————

Lieutenant LaSala is as hard to classify as the novel, *The Captain*, Seymour Shubin's finest work to date. LaSala is no genius like Holmes or Wolfe, doesn't beat up or shoot bad guys by the dozen like Hammer or Spenser. He is a fifty-one year old cop with nearly thirty years of service, who has never killed a man. He figures he's seen it all, and nowhere in the book gets laid.

What makes the character work is his basic decency, his open-

mindedness and sympathetic nature. He was smart enough to pass
tests for the police academy, and move up steadily to a lieutenancy,
but that was it. Younger men passed him by in promotions.

The first time he appears we learn, when he sights Captain Hughes
in the nursing home, that he is loyal, proud, sensitive and kind. He
looks at the man who he remembers as a giant, nattily dressed,
'brightly bald' who led the best unit in the police department with
courage, intelligence and fairness. He remembers that 'If you were
his friend, you truly had a friend. He could bend a rule or three if
you were his friend or it meant breaking a case.'

'Even when you glimpsed the long underwear he wore on those
all-night stake-outs, you'd see a perfectly white line, and somehow
the underwear never even crumpled his socks.'

Now he looks at the old wreck and thinks, 'Mother of God—is
that what happens to you?'

He approaches this shell of the man he considered the best cop
who ever walked the earth, 'a real cop', and tries to talk, but gets
no response and is deeply depressed.

Probably nothing tells us more about ourselves than the kinds of
people we admire and respect.

What makes the book so effective is the relationship between this
conscientious, unimaginative cop, and his old hero, the captain. The
captain haunts LaSala, fills him with guilt because he doesn't want
to expose himself to the sight of the dying man and thoughts of his
own near future. The reader knows from the beginning that the killer
being hunted is the Captain, and what Shubin does so skilfully, by
subtle touches, never pat or overdone, is prepare us for the climax
without ever quite fortifying us against its impact.

LaSala is far from stupid and, when events permit, makes quick
and accurate judgements, such as when he recognizes who the next
victim will be in the series of killings he is investigating which seem
unrelated but all hang together because of the common means of
murder.

There is a steady development of inevitability, which only
becomes clear with the ending.

Shubin inserts lovely touches, such as the moment when LaSala
is in the home of the recently murdered couple, and observes the
panting dog in the living-room where he'd evidently been at the
time of the assault.

'You,' he says, 'they should have shot.'

When LaSala first makes the direct connection between the old
captain and the killings, he finds it impossible to believe and works

frantically to learn who, close to the man, would do the killings because of him. In his final act in the book, he does what he has never done before and is shattered by it.

Nicolas LaSala is a fictional cop, but he lives in the mind of anyone who has read *The Captain*.

THE CASE OF LIEUTENANT LaSALA, BY SEYMOUR SHUBIN
The Captain, 1982.

51

BOB BIDERMAN

on

Joe Leaphorn and Jim Chee

———————————

Perhaps it's the very nature of the mystery that a community is beset by an alien force, threatening, but at the same time invisible to all but the detectives—those who possess a special understanding which allows them to see things other people fail to comprehend. However, Tony Hillerman's investigators, Joe Leaphorn and Jim Chee, stand this concept on its head. For, in fact, it is they who are the aliens serving a world that, relative to their own, exists in a different dimension of time and space.

Leaphorn and Chee are Navajo Tribal Police. They call themselves 'Dinee' or simply 'The People'. Both were born and raised on the great reservation, the vast and barren plateau carved out of the rocky lands where New Mexico meets Utah and Arizona. Both left the reservation for a time to be educated in the white man's ways, where they studied his culture, his history and his seemingly insatiable lust for money.

The elder of the two, Joe Leaphorn, has since detached himself from the Navajo way. He has incorporated the white man's logic. Yet, even though he is impatient with the mysticism of his brothers, his sense of order is clearly a product of his upbringing. A criminal act, for Leaphorn, is not so much an isolated event, it is something that throws the entire universe out of kilter. In his manner of thinking there is no such thing as coincidence.

Leaphorn may not believe in the supernatural Navajo wolves or the 'skinwalkers' who fly through the night spreading sickness but he has internalised the ancient Navajo philosophy that in any jumble of events there must be a pattern, a reason that the laws of natural harmony dictate. For the concept of harmony has been bred into his bones. He is sensitive to the land and the sky and to all earthly events. He enjoy storms as well as tranquillity, for storms are right and natural. Thus, nothing happens without cause and everything is intermeshed, from the mood of a man to the music of the wind.

Chee, the younger one, is different. As a child he had wanted to be a shaman, but his uncle had told him that as a first step he must study the ways of the white man. Only when he came to understand them could Chee then make a decision whether to remain a Navajo.

Even as a graduate of the FBI Academy, Chee carries with him a medicine pouch and each morning says a brief Navajo prayer of greeting to the dawn. He subscribes to magazines like *Esquire* and *Newsweek*, but memorizes a chant which he recorded on tape while driving to work. And he has a 'secret name', a Navajo name which few, if any, white men know.

Leaphorn and Chee realise that the world outside can never understand the Navajo. But it is the world outside that is the source of their livelihood—and their troubles. Unlike the reservation where violence is usually associated with the supernatural, they find that crime in the white man's world is often abstract and unemotional—an individual matter of improving one's odds in the game of life. To Chee, the motivations for white greed make little sense, like his favorite tale from the white man's culture, *Alice in Wonderland*.

So what kind of detectives are they, Leaphorn and Chee? Very good ones, I'd say. They listen more than they speak. Instead of being experts on ballistics, they are connoisseurs of sunsets. They don't clutter up their brains with details of genetic fingerprinting but memories of cloudscapes and horizons. And they recognise the flaw that big city cops have in generalising people. For on the reservation people are scarce and scattered and even the lowliest sheep molester is treated with a modicum of dignity. In fact, unlike their hardboiled counterparts outside the reservation, they place the greatest value on human life. And even for Leaphorn, the questioning one, the mindless brutality of the outside world can't hold a candle to the inner peace and beauty of the Navajo way.

THE CASES OF LEAPHORN AND CHEE, BY TONY HILLERMAN

Novels

The Blessing Way (Leaphorn), 1970. *Dance Hall of the Dead* (Leaphorn), 1973. *The Listening Woman* (Leaphorn), 1978. *People of Darkness* (Chee), 1980. *The Dark Wind* (Chee), 1982. *The Ghostway* (Chee), 1984. *Skinwalkers* (Leaphorn & Chee), 1986. *A Thief of Time* (Leaphorn & Chee), 1988. *Talking God* (Leaphorn & Chee), 1989. *Coyote Waits* (Leaphorn & Chee), 1990.

Uncollected stories

'The Witch, Yazzie, and The Nine of Clubs', 1981. 'Chee's Witch', 1986.

52

MICHAEL Z. LEWIN

on

Anna Lee

Anna Lee was one of the first professional women detectives in mystery fiction. Although the field is more crowded now, Anna Lee remains—for me—the deepest and most interesting, the funniest and the best.

From the beginning she was a crossover character in more ways than gender. Private detective she may be, but she is *not* a mean streets loner. Anna Lee is an agency underling and by instinct a team player, so in many ways she is as much a part of the police procedural tradition as the private eye. Liza Cody is able to draw strength from each format while being freed from either's limitations. A cop couldn't reasonably risk breaking and entering;

Anna can. A lone P.I. doesn't have colleagues at hand to call on when numbers are needed; Anna does. Anna Lee is a part of crime fiction, but not defined by it.

All the other female detectives I've read about—including the most famous—are substantially determined by the male characters they are not being. We may be given Lew Archer in a skirt or an air hostess with Spenser's brain, but they all suffer because they are too conscious of what they'd be doing as a private eye if they were male.

By being less categorizable Anna Lee is more a humanist character than a feminist one and, I would argue, more likely to be a feminizing influence. Anna Lee is herself and is not defined by male prototypes. She is an original.

Indeed, in many ways Anna Lee is not 'defined' at all. She is personally elusive and rarely reflective.

In a genre that courts personal extremes like a brat screaming for attention Anna Lee stands out because she is normal. Anna Lee is *not* the biggest, the strongest, the smartest. She is not replete with arcana but happily apposite knowledge, either from a Ph.D. programme or self-instruction. She does not have the most contacts or influential people who owe her favours. She's not the best shot, the fastest runner, the hardest puncher. She hasn't been to jail, she isn't on the lam. She's not an actor, H.I.V. positive, a lawyer or in any of the other infectious conditions. Nor is she blessed with intuition verging on the supernatural.

Anna Lee is a physical woman with an enquiring mind. She has one of the most human senses of humour you'll ever want to read. Anna Lee is great because she is a real person in a real world. Her job happens occasionally to lead her into extraordinary situations and the readerly pleasure comes from accompanying a perceptive human being as she copes, understands and overcomes.

THE CASES OF ANNA LEE, BY LIZA CODY

Dupe, 1980. *Bad company*, 1982. *Stalker*, 1984. *Head case*, 1985. *Under Contract*, 1986. *Backhand*, 1991.

53

REGINALD HILL
on

Mackintosh, Bunfit and Gager

L et hacks and historians plot the frozen past. I sing what might
have been, the lost detective stories of Anthony Trollope.

The novelist's art is to disguise fact as fiction. For most writers
the real fiction only begins when they start telling you how they
do it, and even Trollope, famous for the demystifying frankness
of his artistic self-analysis, cannot be trusted here. How can we
accept his claim to lack the skill of constructing plots that need to
be unravelled, or his alleged refusal to keep from the reader any
secret known to himself, when his books abound with the stuff of
classical crime plots and he clearly doles out 'secrets' at exactly the
rate that suits his present purpose? If you don't believe me, read
The Last Chronicle of Barset, *Orley Farm*, *Is he Popenjoy?*, *Cousin
Henry* and a dozen others. It is probably true, as he states, that he
did not know how most of his books were going to develop as he
started out on them, but so what? If that were a disqualification
from writing crime novels, the dole queues of England would be
even longer than they are.

Alas, even if his reasons do not persuade us, they persuade himself,
and he wrote no pure novels of detection, though he shows us clearly
in *The Eustace Diamonds* what might have been.

Here two of his detective trio make their sole appearances, and
the third, Major Mackintosh, the Head of Scotland Yard, his most
significant, though he does figure briefly in the investigation of the
Bonteen murder case in *Phineas Redux*.

Major Mackintosh is a tall, thin man of about forty with large
good-natured eyes and, fortunately for his self-preservation in his
dealings with lovely Lizzie Eustace, the strong domestic anchor of
a wife and seven children. His reputation for infallibility is such
that, despite the fact that he works for sixteen hours a day, he's
accused of idleness if a case isn't solved at once. Bunfit and Gager

are his subordinates. We are not given their ranks nor much in the way of description but from their conversation we see them very clearly. They are Londoners, working-class in origin, dedicated to their calling. Bunfit is the older and steadier, a stolid comfortable sort of man, feeling his way forward methodically. Gager we learn is a young man in a hurry, 'almost too clever and certainly a little too fast.' The essential differences between the three are sketched with typical Trollopian economy when he writes of their efforts to crack the Eustace Diamonds case, 'Bunfit would have jeopardized his right hand and Gager his life to get at the secret. Even Major Mackintosh was anxious.' Their individually favoured theories all contain aspects of the truth which finally come together to form a full picture. Bunfit keeps his right hand, but Gager in a sense does give up his life, having promised to marry Lizzie Eustace's absconding maid to get her to appear as a witness—and keeping his promise.

Add to these their foes in the opposite camp—Mr Benjamin, jeweller, fence and mastermind; little Billy Cann, most diminutive and most expert of burglars; Smiler, the great housebreaker for whom the police entertain a feeling close to veneration—and we have a cast and a plot which could have crystallised into a crime novel to outshine *The Moonstone*.

Instead, of course, we have the third of the Palliser novels, that series in which Trollope essays the far more arduous task of creating art out of politics. I wouldn't have it any other way. Yet I find my mind dwells on Mackintosh, Bunfit and Gager long after many larger political characters have faded away. I get a sense that Trollope enjoyed them very much too. Indeed he creates three detectives when for the purposes of his tale one would have sufficed; and where a great writer gives us more of anything than is strictly necessary, it is usually safe to guess that he loves his own creation too much to stint.

THE CASES OF MACKINTOSH, BUNFIT & GAGER,
BY ANTHONY TROLLOPE
The Eustace Diamonds, 1873. *Phineas Redux*, 1874.

54

PETER ROBINSON

on

Inspector Maigret

I first started reading the Maigret stories because they were my father's favourites. He said they reminded him of his time in Paris after the Liberation. I had never been to Paris then, but with the help of a street map, I soon managed to locate the Quai des Orfèvres. At the same time, the Rupert Davies TV series gave me a strong visual image of the setting.

Before long, I was hunting out my own Maigret books on market stalls in Leeds and Bradford. I was quick to spot the old green and white Penguin Crime series covers, most of which were yellowed around the edges and touched with mildew on the inside. I still seek them out, and just last year I found one I didn't have (a double, *A Crime in Holland* and *A Face for a Clue*) in a second-hand bookshop in Lincoln. Its musty smell reminded me of the children's library in Armley, where I grew up.

When I start to read the stories, though, that smell is soon replaced by the atmosphere of pipe-smoke, Calvados and zinc-topped bars. It has been said that Maigret is more interested in *people* than in places, yet Georges Simenon certainly evokes the sights, sounds and smells of Paris (which I have since visited) with great economy.

Ultimately, though, it is Maigret's fascination with people that sets him apart. This slow-moving, slightly-grumpy police inspector stands behind the modern English versions—Wexford, Dalgliesh, Thanet and the rest—far more than any other earlier fictional detective. This becomes especially obvious when one considers that Maigret's American contemporaries of the '30s were Sam Spade and Philip Marlowe, his English ones Miss Marple and Lord Peter Wimsey—hardly models for a Finch or a Quantrill!

H.R.F. Keating has noted that the Maigret stories represent the first examples of the detective as *writer*. Part of this clearly stems from Maigret's desire to understand human motivation and his need to soak up the atmosphere of a place and immerse himself in a complex mesh of relationships until the solution to the crime becomes clear. Simenon's plots are often flimsy or far-fetched, and Maigret's actual detective-work can be minimal at times. What makes the books so absorbing is his empathy with the characters he encounters (including criminals) and his interest in their lives above and beyond his need for information to solve the crime. Maigret possesses in abundance the writer's essential characteristic: curiosity.

But it goes even further than that. Not only does Maigret piece together the answer to a psychological puzzle, he is often affected, even changed, by what he discovers. Maigret *learns* through his investigations; every case extends the range of his compassion. It may be wishful thinking that we should all grow through our excursions into writing crime fiction, but, for me, reading the Maigret stories makes it clear that some of us are not quite so different from the detectives we create as we would often like people to think we are.

THE CASES OF INSPECTOR MAIGRET, BY GEORGES SIMENON

To provide a complete and accurate bibliography of the Simenon titles featuring Inspector Jules Maigret would, if done properly, occupy 30 to 40 pages of this book!

He first appeared in French in *Pietr-Le-Letton*, 1931 (translated at *The Strange Case of Peter The Lett*, 1933, also as *Maigret and the Enigmatic Lett*, 1933); the novel can also be found in the twosome *Inspector Maigret Investigates*, 1933. This gives an idea of the bibliographical complexities of the works of Simenon in translation.

Allen J. Hubin's major reference work *Crime Fiction*, 1949–1980 (plus the 1981–1985 supplement) lists 138 Maigret titles in English, many of which also appear with more than one alternative title, and many of which do not correspond with equivalent French editions, due to the multiplication of omnibus volumes with varying combinations of novels or stories.

Strictly speaking, a bibliography of French first editions would, of course, be more accurate and informative, but sadly of little use to readers in the UK and the USA.

Enjoy the Maigret books anyway!

55

LOREN D. ESTLEMAN

on

Philip Marlowe

He's six feet tall, weighs 190 pounds, has brown hair going gray and brown eyes; likes chess, smokes Camels—a lot of Camels—when he's not in the mood for his pipe, drinks Old Grand-Dad, and dresses well, if a bit exotically (I'm talking about his dark blue dress shirts, not his black wool socks with dark blue clocks, a common design feature in gentlemen's hose of the period and not, as some uninformed later critics believe, clock faces with hands and numerals). Hats—yes; trenchcoat—occasionally, but only when it's raining. His preferred weaponry is a Smith & Wesson Police Special worn in an underarm holster, but in the early days it was a Luger. He prefers not to wear either and does so only when it looks like there will be danger. There is usually danger.

Philip Marlowe—before 1939 aka Mallory and Johnny Dalmas (see separate essay on the latter)—was born in Santa Rosa, California in either 1906 or 1907, and attended college, where his nose was broken during a football scrimmage but later repaired. He served his apprenticeship as an investigator for Mr Wilde, the Los Angeles County District Attorney, who fired him for insubordination. Insubordination and its companions—cynicism, impudence, and wit—are a Marlowe trademark, but unlike his many imitators he employs all four sparingly as both his weapons and his salvation, to keep his enemies off-guard while he plans his next move and to distance himself from the harsh realities of his world. In that world, laughter is a socially acceptable substitute for suicide.

The sky in his world is neon, the earth rain-slick asphalt. Its wildlife prowls the shadows with fangs and claws of blue steel and leaded rubber or poises in mid-flight in the beam of his flash with mascaraed eyes wide and painted lips drawn back from small teeth as white as orange pith and as sharp as daggers, then leaps away into darkness, leaving only the faint echo of sirens' laughter and the acrid scent of perfume, like dangerous musk. If he dares to follow—and he will, for in the words of his creator he is '. . .

neither tarnished nor afraid . . . a complete man and a common man and yet an unusual man . . . the best man in his world and a good enough man for any world'—he may be beaten, drugged and held prisoner, arrested, shot at, seduced, insulted, and hit on the head. And he will answer in kind, but always in moderation; for in all the adventures he cares to share with us he will kill but once, to rescue a woman.

He lives for his work. Notice the offhand affection with which he describes his little office-and-a-half on the seventh floor of the Cahuenga Building in West Hollywood: the glass-topped desk, the rug that is just something on the floor, the five tired file cabinets, three of them filled with California climate, the changing scenes on the advertising calendar on the wall. Now try to find a description of his home. Home for him is just a place to sleep, eat breakfast, and work out chess problems from his little book printed in Leipzig. The office is where he lives.

A word about Marlowe and chess. Much has been made of his Galahad Complex as an explanation for why a man of his intelligence and sensitivity should have become a private detective, but his affinity for the drawing-room sport is usually dismissed as a device to separate him from the common luggish dick or to underscore his solitude. In fact it is the key to his choice of professions. In what other walk of life except the military—where his insubordination would quickly earn him a dishonorable discharge—can a man who likes to work out problems involving kings and queens and pawns and knights and the odd bishop put his interest into practice? The Byzantine tactics and strategy of life in the Mean Streets resemble nothing so much as a demented game of chess. 'It wasn't a game for knights,' he concludes in a moment of supreme disenchantment. Ah, but it is.

As it must be for all insubordinate men who place their own unspoken rules of conduct before civil law and even the law of survival, Marlowe is without friends. The closest thing he has to a confidant, Bernie Ohls in the district attorney's office and later with the sheriff's department, is referred to as a friend-enemy. As an honest component of a corrupt system of justice, he can only be trusted so far, beyond which lies natural enmity. Terry Lennox, groomed with quiet desperation for friendship by a bleak and ageing Marlowe, proves unworthy. Anne Riordan is to be trusted, but as a woman who is not a queen she has no place on the board. Aloneness, the pillar upon which Marlowe's character is constructed, is inviolate.

He is as American as post-colonial America: Born full-grown in the Caesarean throes of revolution (Prohibition); isolated, seeking after Right on a darkling plane, sure of his aims but unsure of his mettle, sometimes irritating, always exciting. He is the light in the world he has created for himself. And he is like no other. Rather, others are like him.

THE CASES OF PHILIP MARLOWE, BY RAYMOND CHANDLER

The Big Sleep, 1939. *Farewell, My Lovely*, 1940. *The High Window*, 1942. *The Lady in the Lake*, 1943. *The Little Sister*, 1949. *The Long Goodbye*, 1953. *Playback*, 1958. *Poodle Springs*, 1989 (completed by Robert B. Parker). *Perchance to Dream*, 1991 (by Robert B. Parker).

All the original short stories by Chandler were later cannibalized by him and reutilized in his novels. In these stories, the character was not named Marlowe (see the entry on John Dalmas) with the exception of:

'Marlowe Takes on the Syndicate', 1959

There is also a collection of new Marlowe stories written by other hands: *Raymond Chandler's Philip Marlowe*, edited by Byron Preiss, 1988. This includes material by Max Allan Collins, Benjamin M. Schutz, Loren D. Estleman, Joyce Harrington, Jonathan Valin, Dick Lochte, W.R. Philbrick, Sara Paretsky, Julie Smith, Paco Ignacio Taibo II, Francis M. Nevins, Jr., Roger L. Simon, John Lutz, Simon Brett, Robert J. Randisi, Stuart M. Kaminsky, Robert Crais, Edward D. Hoch, Jeremiah Healy, Ed Gorman, James Grady, Eric Van Lustbader, Robert Campbell.

56

WENDY M. GROSSMAN
on

Miss Marple

No one would describe Miss Marple—or even Agatha Christie —as a feminist. And yet, Christie's creation follows a surprisingly modern line: Jane Marple, old female, single, somewhat poor (and dependent on her well-off nephew for handouts), and physically frail is empowered by her intuition and experience. Men in high places listen to her and make her heard, and through them she can pass the ultimate sentence: death. Only to the wicked, of course. To the merely frightened, unhappy, and foolish she is all kindness and compassion.

It is well known that Miss Marple was based on Christie's own grandmothers. They knew things—and the child watching didn't know quite how, just as we, the readers, don't quite know how Miss Marple knows things. We're given hints, of course, small ones: one character is wearing her hat the wrong way round; another wears a large choker of pearls with unsuitable clothes; a third babbles about fish. And Miss Marple can draw unexpected conclusions from these things.

It's all a matter of looking at things the right way round, like magic (which comparison Christie often invokes, especially in the Miss Marple story, *They Do It With Mirrors*). In real life, as in fiction, I find rational explanations more interesting, more fascinating, more joyous than the non-rational ones. If, for example, a man walks across hot coals, it's awfully easy to say that he must have some special mental force, and when you've said that you haven't learned anything new about how the world works. It's much harder to find out—and much more satisfying when you do—that actually anyone can walk across hot coals without getting burned (although please don't take your cue from me and try it!) because of the specific physical properties of wood ash. Christie, too, was always intrigued by the truth behind the appearances. The sound of a door closing may mean someone coming in—or going out. The landlady who swears her tenant was safely home with her the night of the crime may be protecting him—or herself.

Often what gets Miss Marple looking at things the right way round are patterns. She is, of course, famous for these: one of the suspects reminds her of the chemist in St Mary Mead who, unknown to his wife and family had two other wives and families; another suspect in another case reminds her of a woman who was single, went for a cruise, and came back married. Miss Marple is not unusual in this: the human mind is particularly rich in pattern-making abilities, and we all use familiar patterns and our experiences to evaluate new situations. What's extraordinary about Miss Marple is that hers work, and put her in touch with the truth.

Truth and justice, after all, are her passions. She might, if she were asked, say she had other things to live for, but we know better. She pursues truth with all the ruthlessness of a journalist going after a lead on a story about a government scandal. It may not be a pleasant characteristic, but it has its place in the world.

Part of Miss Marple's appeal lies in her contradictory nature. She's led a sheltered life, but she's seen every side of human nature and nothing shocks her. Her physical strength is limited, especially in the later books, but she can defeat a strong, young man. She sounds dithery and confused—but once she starts thinking along the right track she goes straight for the truth. Her village, St Mary Mead, is small and idyllic—and full of seething emotions and shocking crimes.

Contradictions like these are commonplace now, but can't have been when Christie started writing. Against the background of the fantastical exploits of Sherlock Holmes, detective story readers must have marvelled at the confusion Christie was able to weave out of homely, everyday ingredients.

Those everyday ingredients make Christie's version of evil far more sinister, as she herself knew. She said in more than one of her novels that were she directing *Macbeth* she would make the witches ordinary old women and let the contrast between their words and their ordinariness create the eerie atmosphere. She even took this advice herself, in *The Pale Horse*. Evil looks far more frightening against a background of normality, and Christie varied the theme brilliantly, especially in the Miss Marple stories, which took place in the sort of village that was the heart of Christie's England.

Miss Marple is, of course, not Christie's only old lady. Miss Marple's precursor was Caroline Sheppard, the doctor's sister in *The Murder of Roger Ackroyd*; Christie said part of her inspiration for Miss Marple was the enjoyment she had in writing about Caroline and her love of gossip. But Miss Marple stands out—like the others she loves gossip, but unlike the others she does something constructive with it.

What I continue to love about Christie's stories is the humour with which she wrote, her passion for truth, justice, and the exoneration of the innocent, the deft way she could sketch in a character with only a few strokes, and the sheer genius with which she could create a plot. Those things overcome the barriers of nationality, experience, age, and milieu. The fact that when I met Miss Marple I was (probably) a twelve-year-old living just outside New York City, with no experience of England or English people, without a grandmother Miss Marple could make me feel nostalgic about, and completely unaware of what life could be like mattered not at all. My English teacher (when I was thirteen) called it 'escapist' fiction and begged me to read something more worthy of my intelligence. Well, Mrs Taylor, wherever you are, just so you know: I'm glad I didn't listen.

THE CASES OF MISS MARPLE, BY AGATHA CHRISTIE

Novels

The Murder at the Vicarage, 1930. *The Body in the Library*, 1942. *The Moving Finger*, 1942. *A Murder is Announced*, 1950. *They do it with Mirrors*, 1952. *A Pocket Full of Rye*, 1953. *4:50 from Paddington*, 1957. *The Mirror Crack'd from Side to Side*, 1962. *A Caribbean Mystery*, 1964. *At Bertram's Hotel*, 1965. *Nemesis*, 1971. *Sleeping Murder*, 1976.

Story collections

The Thirteen Problems, 1932. *The Regatta Mystery*, 1939. (nine stories, one with Miss Marple). *Three Blind Mice* 1950 (nine stories, four with Miss Marple). *The Adventure of the Christmas Pudding*, 1960 (six stories, one with Marple). *Double Sin*, 1961 (eight stories, two with Marple). *13 Clues for Miss Marple*, 1966. *Miss Marple's Final Cases*, 1979 (eight stories, six with Marple).

(There are twenty short stories featuring Miss Marple extant; contents of British and American editions are different and duplicate stories).

57

CELIA DALE
on

The Marshal

O ver the years I've grown very fond of many of the brain-sleuths of my colleagues. Never the hard-drinking, slobbish ones: I suspect Lovejoy's sheets might be rather grubby and that Morse might smell of beer. The gentlemanly fellows don't appeal much, either, from Lord Peter and Roderick Alleyn down to Dalgliesh—too sensitive and finestrung, I feel, to protect me against the horrors of reality. Maybe Steve Carella . . .? But no, the 87th Precinct is too far away from London to be practical.

Frankly, I prefer more ordinary chaps, like Charles Paris—although I do worry about him and wish he could land a really good part in a forever-running TV series. I'm fond of irritable Inspector Evariste Clovis Desiré Pel, with his hopeless efforts to give up smoking. I feel secure with Wexford, even when he's a bit too testy with poor Burden. And I still mourn the loss of handsome but ingenuous Achille Peroni, whose creator Timothy Holme died most untimely in 1987.

Which brings me to Italy. I've always doted on Italy, from its myriad beauties down to its pasta and pizza, the cheerful unselfconsciousness of its people. Its rascals are masters of their craft: I was conned with supreme inventive skill once, when a beautiful barefoot teenage girl sold me two sheets of toilet paper outside the ladies' loo at Pompeii—a humane commercial transaction, I thought, until I found that inside the cabin was a goodly supply of the necessary, free of charge. As a scam, pure genius!

So, after much thought, I settle on Florence, and choose as my favourite, most reassuring detective the solid, almost humdrum figure of Marshal Salvatore Guarnaccia.

The Marshal is only a medium grade officer in the *Carabiniere*, the domestic rather than the criminal police. His work is as much concerned with social problems as with crime itself. He is a mild and moral fellow, who cares about the small affairs of ordinary people, lives with his wife and young sons in a flat above the *Carabiniere* barracks, his office cosy with kettle and kitchen. He has a fatherly eye on his young staff, some of them far from their homes; and he knows his city, with its beauties and brutishness, its many small communities as tightly united as any village, as a farmer knows his fields.

The Marshal isn't clever; he has no sudden shafts of brilliant intuition; he's not particularly brave; and he wishes his hours were more regular. But he has sound common sense, honesty, a dogged respect for humanity in all its forms. He cares about people, and in the end his care is their salvation.

With the Marshal we have not only a modest family man who would do his best for you in trouble but the marvellous background of the city of Florence itself. In *The Marshal's Own Case* he peers into the sleazy world of transvestites and their sad lives, in *The Marshal and the Madwoman* he enters the claustrophobic world of the half mad, explores the anxieties of the housing shortage, and listens, grieving, to recollections of the terrible floods of 1966. To whatever the setting, to however unsavoury a crime, the Marshal (and his creator Magdalen Nabb) brings a pervasive compassion and common sense.

Yes, I would trust myself to the Marshal.

THE CASES OF 'THE MARSHAL', BY MAGDALEN NABB

Death of an Englishman, 1981. *Death of a Dutchman*, 1982. *Death in Springtime*, 1983. *Death in Autumn*, 1985. *The Marshal and the Madwoman*, 1986. *The Marshal and the Murderer*, 1987. *The Marshal's Own Case*, 1990.

58

BILL PRONZINI
on

Sharon McCone

It should come as no surprise to most readers that Sharon McCone is my favorite fictional sleuth. The fact that her creator, Marcia Muller, and I are household as well as literary collaborators is well known, and I admit to a bias on that basis. But I like to think I have a fair amount of objective critical acumen where mystery fiction is concerned, and on *that* basis, for reasons of complexity of plot, depth of characterization, and emotional content, I consider McCone one of the half-dozen most important series detectives being written by anyone of either gender.

There is a third reason that Sharon is my favorite sleuth. It's that I know so much about her, so many things that nobody else except her creator knows.

What sort of things? For starters, I know that contrary to popular belief, *Edwin of the Iron Shoes* is not her first recorded case. Her first case was actually recorded two years before *Edwin*. I can't give you the title; Marcia won't tell me what it is. She won't let me read the manuscript either. Nor will she reveal much about it. 'It's unread and unpublished and it's going to stay that way,' she says darkly.

This tantalizing manuscript is packed away in one of several boxes stored in the garage. (She hasn't destroyed it because, like me, she's something of a packrat. I suspect that she has also been cannibalistically gnawing off pieces of it over the years, but she won't admit to it.) Every now and then, when I'm home and she's out, I have a devilish urge to disinter and read it on the sly. I haven't given in to the urge so far, and I expect I never will; I have too much respect for Marcia and her feelings. The fact that she has threatened to hit me over the head with an iron pot-rack if she catches me has nothing to do with it.

I know the real reason McCone broke off her personal involvement with Police Lieutenant (now Captain) Greg Marcus. (Would *you* want to have an intimate, long-term relationship with a jerk who publicly as well as privately refers to you as 'Papoose'?) I know her most amazing physical feat, performed in the rough draft of *There's Something in a Sunday*. ('My mouth went slack-jawed.') I know what happened to the baby kangaroo that lived in the pouch of Roo-Roo, the red-plush mama kangaroo Sharon had when she was little. (Poachers.) I know every nook and cranny of the old Victorian that houses All Souls Legal Cooperative, and exactly what is in each room. (A complete miniature reproduction of All Souls occupies a place of honor in our library, having been designed, built, even electrically wired by Sharon's multi-talented materfamilias.)

I know about McCone's Shocking Act.

A few years ago Marcia and I wrote a collaborative novel, *Double*, in which Sharon and my 'Nameless Detective' team up on a case that begins at a convention of private investigators in San Diego. We had a good time writing the book—and only one small argument. The argument stemmed from this Shocking Act (*I* found it shocking, anyway) perpetrated by McCone in the first draft manuscript. I can't reveal the exact nature of the Act; suffice it to say that it took place late in the novel at an isolated house in California's Anza-Borrego Desert.

Marcia wanted to leave the Act in, in all its graphic detail; I wanted it taken out. So we argued, and for a change I prevailed. McCone's Shocking Act does not appear in the published novel. Marcia still has the first-draft page on which the Act is described and periodically she threatens to take it to a Bouchercon or other mystery convention and auction it off to the highest bidder. 'I'll bet there'd be a *lot* of interest in it,' she says. She's probably right.

But I doubt if she'll ever do it. The mystery community is not ready—may never be ready—for such fictional indiscretions to be made public. Marcia, in her heart of hearts, knows this as well as I do. It's a matter of privacy, not to mention simple decency.

I know a lot of other secret things about McCone, too, but I think I'd better not divulge any more. In fact, I may have revealed too many already. I don't dare take any more liberties, lest Marcia chastise me even more roundly when she reads this little essay.

I have to live with Papoose, after all . . .

THE CASES OF SHARON McCONE, BY MARCIA MULLER

Novels

Edwin of the Iron Shoes, 1977. *Ask the Cards a Question*, 1982. *The*

Cheshire Cat's Eye, 1983. *Games to Keep the Dark Away*, 1984. *Leave a Message for Willie*, 1984. *Double*, 1984 (with Bill Pronzini). *There's Nothing to be Afraid of*, 1985. *The Eye of the Storm*, 1988. *There's Something in a Sunday*, 1989. *The Shape of Dread*, 1989. *Trophies and Dead Things*, 1990. *Where Echoes Live*, 1991.

Uncollected stories

'Merrill-Go-Round', 1981. 'Wild Mustard', 1984. 'The Broken Men', 1985. 'Deceptions', 1987. 'Cache and Carry', 1988 (with Bill Pronzini). 'Deadly Fantasies', 1989. 'All the Lonely People', 1989. 'Silent Night', 1989. 'Somewhere in the City', 1990. 'The Place That Time Forgot', 1990. 'Final Resting Place', 1990. 'Benny's Place', 1991.

59

SHARYN McCRUMB

on

Sir Henry Merrivale

John Dickson Carr, writing as Carter Dickson, created one of the best-loved sleuths in mystery fiction: Sir Henry Merrivale—doctor, lawyer, and baronet—a master of the locked-room puzzle, and a delightful character who owes less to Sherlock Holmes than he does to Mr Toad of *The Wind in the Willows*. The Old Man, as other characters are fond of calling him, appeared in twenty-three novels, beginning with *The Plague Court Murders*, in 1934.

The best description of Merrivale is in the second book, *The White Priory Murders*: '. . . He has frequently got into trouble at political meetings by making speeches in which he absent-mindedly refers to the Home Secretary as Boko and the Premier as Horseface. You will probably find him asleep, although he will pretend he is very busy

. . . His Baronetcy is two or three hundred years old, and he is also a fighting Socialist. He is a qualified barrister and physician, and he speaks the world's most slovenly grammar. His mind is scurrilous; he shocks lady typists, wears white socks, and appears in public without his necktie . . . I may add that at criminal investigation he is a good deal of a genius.'

I have long suspected that the bald, cigar-chomping aristocrat in the white suit was originally intended to be a parody of Sir Winston Churchill, but, to quote Merrivale again, 'I got a low mind.' Suffice it to note that both of them have wives named Clementine.

I identify with Merrivale, because I, too, have a childlike love of learning sensational but unprofitable things: the history of conjuring; biographies of murderers; pirate lore; and a host of other arcane subjects mostly unsuitable for serious academic pursuit. I share his tendency toward intellectual binges: to go gung-ho into a project, let it consume me completely, and then abandon it for the next attraction. HM has enlivened his detecting adventures with wheelchair stunts (*She Died a Lady*, 1943); suitcase racing (*The Night at the Mocking Widow*, 1950); the dictation of his libelous memoirs (*Seeing is Believing*, 1941); and the assembly of a scrapbook of his notorious career (*The Curse of the Bronze Lamp*, 1945).

His cases reflect this interest in the sensational. In *The Skeleton in the Clock* (1948) two men agree to spend the night in the execution cell of an abandoned prison; in *The Plague Court Murders* (1934) a house associated with the 1664 epidemic of the Black Death is the scene of the crime; and in *The Curse of the Bronze Lamp* (1945) an ancient Egyptian curse seems to have caused the heroine's disappearance. Despite these supernatural touches, there are no occult occurrences in the Merrivale books; the malefactor in each case is quite human, and the explanation for the fantastic events is always plausible.

People occasionally criticize the Merrivale series for its 'slapstick' humor, but I think that to say this is to overlook the fact that HM is the *only* humorous character in the novels. John Dickson Carr has actually created a most endearing portrait of a brilliant, but socially indifferent eccentric, and as an American Southerner, I do not even find him to be much of an exaggeration. Like the English, we have our oddballs, and we adore them. It is refreshing to find a character who is intelligent and serious about crime without being intense and somber all the time. Whether or not the game was afoot, I think that Henry Merrivale would be better company than most fictional detectives.

I am willing to overlook the paucity of the books' characterization (always the same earnest young man in love with the same spunky young woman), and the contrivance of the impossible situations, just for the pleasure of HM's company, and for the bits of history and folklore he imparts along the way.

Every outing with Sir Henry Merrivale is a daredevil ride in Toad's motorcar, and HM is one of the reasons that people say of forties mystery fiction: 'This was their finest hour.'

THE CASES OF SIR HENRY MERRIVALE, BY CARTER DICKSON

Novels

The Plague Court Murders, 1934. *The White Priory Murders*, 1934. *The Red Widow Murders*, 1935. *The Unicorn Murders*, 1935. *The Magic Lantern Murders*, 1936. *The Peacock Feather Murders*, 1937. *The Judas Window*, 1938. *Death in Five Boxes*, 1938. *The Reader is Warned*, 1939. *And So To Murder*, 1940. *Nine—And Death Makes Ten*, 1940. *Seeing is Believing*, 1941. *The Gilded Man*, 1942. *She Died A Lady*, 1943. *He Wouldn't Kill Patience*, 1944. *The Curse of the Bronze Lamp*, 1945. *My Late Wives*, 1946. *The Skeleton in the Clock*, 1948. *A Graveyard to Let*, 1949. *Night at the Mocking Widow*, 1950. *Behind the Crimson Blind*, 1952. *The Cavalier's Cup*, 1953.

Story collections

The Third Bullet and other Stories, 1954 (Seven stories, one with Merrivale). *The Men who Explained Miracles*, 1963 (Seven Stories, one with Merrivale).

60
ADRIAN WOOTTON
on
Milo Milodragovitch

Milo Milodragovitch is a large, rumpled, bear of a man; the dog-end of a long line of illustrious Milodragovitchs, pioneers who built much of the Pacific Northwest town of Meriwether, where Milo still lives. Unfortunately, while the monuments remain the family doesn't and Milo, while waiting on an inheritance (that he can't claim until he's fifty-three) ekes out a living as a, cheapish, detective.

You gather early on that while Milo has a sneaking admiration for some of his frontiersmen-type ancestors, like his great-grandfather, by and large he didn't fit the family bill and his reluctance to tolerate authority has made him an ageing ex-cop who gets by on booze, dope, the odd casual affair and, once in a while, a divorce case. The enjoyably messy state of Milo's life is further complicated by several ex-wives (one of whom still lives in Meriwether with his son, and is re-married to a local policeman who just happens to be Milo's old army buddy!). To avoid the neccessity of walking too far to get a drink Milo also has a part ownership in a bar, Mahoney's, with an adjoining room for sleep and quiet; 'All the comforts of home and a secure as a prison cell'. These things in themselves would get you interested in, if not enthralled by Milo but in fact they are simply part of the background to the two major cases/adventures of his career, described in *The Wrong Case* and *Dancing Bear*. In both, Milo is dragged out of his comfortable rut to take on something which involves him in lies, betrayal, corruption and eventually murder.

In *The Wrong Case* Milo's routine, apparently hopeless, search to find a girl's missing brother triggers off a sequence of actions including multiple murders, the exposure of a heroin dealer and a gunfight that culminates in the forced removal of several mafia hoods from the sphere of earthly influence. Milo's methods aren't subtle and James Crumley's laconic, good-humoured narrative typically shows Milo drinking, asking some questions, fighting, being beaten up and, more or less through accident (plus the assistance of various illegal stimulants), stumbling on the bad guys who he usually has to shoot. In other words unsubtle but effective.

Nevertheless in the process of Milo's work there is simultaneously the unfolding of an intense, personal odyssey about drunkenness, his father's suicide, doomed love affairs and the mythology of the Wild West, which seems inextricably linked to Milo's life. The result, as with all the best detectives, is case solved and solitary self-knowledge, yet without the women or the wherewithal. Indeed whilst Milo is constantly, self-defeatingly describing himself in the most negative physical and mental terms he remains a romantic, fascinating, contradictory character who really is a frontiersman out of his time.

Dancing Bear continues the tales of Milo and picks up on him five or so years later. At the beginning of the novel Milo is a drunk security guard terminally reluctant to ever consider playing detective again. However, all bad things come to those who wait and Milo is sucked back in by a sentimental wish to honour a plea for help by his dead father's mistress. The result is a cocaine-fueled, high-speed journey that encompasses drug-running, multinational corruption, environmental pollution and feminist conspiracies. This is Milo's great, tragic story with him as a middle-aged tough guy, driving (in his modern 'horse', a massive Trailer car) hiding and fighting (fist and gun) all over the still-Wild West, until he discovers the truth. Once again Milo manages to engage the affection of numerous women, all of whom love and then leave him because of his wildness. In *Dancing Bear* Milo tries to cast off his Cowboy mantle; 'Trigger's stuffed, love, and Gene Autry owns a football team' but it doesn't work, he can't escape his destiny, a destiny moulded by the ancestors whose ghosts surround Meriwether. Throughout the novel, while Milo chases various Indians who can help him in his search, he ponders on the land Camas Meadows bequeathed to him by his father, land which has a magical significance for the Indian people and known by them as; 'the land of the Dancing Bear'. Finally, after everything else is over, Milo gives the land up to the Indians, in a gesture of atonement that would not be out of place in a John Ford western movie (*The Searchers* or perhaps *Cheyenne Autumn*) and this above all places him in the unique position of being the only real frontier 'tec in contemporary fiction or maybe just the last real cowboy.

THE CASES OF MILO MILODRAGOVITCH, BY JAMES CRUMLEY
The Wrong Case, 1975. *Dancing Bear*, 1983.

61

SIMON BRETT

on

Kinsey Millhone

One of the great things about literature is that it offers the safest sex around. It is possible to fall in love with—and indeed have quite long complicated affairs with—fictional characters, at no personal risk whatsoever.

Fictional characters are also commendably unaffected by jealousy. No one—either inside or outside of books—frowns on the amorous reader who two-times, three-times or times in any multiple he or she chooses. It is therefore no problem for me to be in love with a great number of fictional ladies, including Shakespeare's Beatrice and Cleopatra, Sophy Western, Anne Eliot, Gwendolen Fairfax, Charles Paris' Frances, my own Mrs Pargeter and—all right, it's confession time—Kinsey Millhone.

The wonderful thing about my relationship with Kinsey is that she is totally unaware of it and that, if she were aware, she would do everything in her power to discourage it. I represent more or less everything of which she would disapprove—I am English, married, middle-aged, thickening round the waist, conformist, materialistic and not particularly brave.

By the same token, she represents everything that appeals to me enormously, but that I know I couldn't cope with in real life. She is ferociously independent ('not famous for letting guys tell me what to do'), scruffy (no make-up, jeans all the time, one dress which demonstrates the same sartorial priorities as Charles Paris' sports jacket), tenacious and courageous. She can't cook and pigs out frequently on junk food. She jogs assiduously and is aggressively unmaternal.

About the only point of contact between us is that we both hate smoking.

But all this increases rather than diminishes her appeal for me; and the real clincher is the fact that her carapace of toughness is so fragile. It's the vulnerability, the moments when she regresses to childhood comforts, that make me want to take her in my arms, give her a big hug and make it all better—knowing all the while how very profoundly she would loathe such treatment.

Kinsey Millhone has stated that her Rule Number One is: No snivelling. What is endearing about her is the frequency with which she breaks that rule. She is vulnerable in a very literal sense; one has only to count up the number of beatings, bombings, car smashes and shootings that have left their scars on her; but what makes her so appealing is the fact that they really hurt. Her confidence as well as her body is dented. She reacts to adversity in a way that is totally plausible. Kinsey Millhone is brave, but bravery needs psyching up, and she certainly knows the meaning of the word fear.

She is also very fortunate in her minder. Sue Grafton cares immaculately for her creation. She writes beautifully. She also knows the great truth—that a bit of humour never hurt anyone; and the even greater truth—that humour skilfully used can actually tighten tension rather than defusing it. As a result, Kinsey Millhone demonstrates a credibility and appeal much greater than any of the other recent rash of female private eyes. She has a proper respect for her identity as a woman, a proper contempt for men when contempt is appropriate, but her feminism is never allowed to become po-faced.

I said earlier that the great thing about our relationship is that she doesn't know about it. The other great thing is that it's ongoing. This is guaranteed by the alphabetical straitjacket into which Sue Grafton has happily strapped herself. As I write this, she is working on 'H', the follow-up to 'G is for Gumshoe'. At her current production rate, that still leaves eighteen years to the end of the alphabet. I know Kinsey Millhone'd never care about me if she knew of my passion, but that still doesn't deny me the enormously comforting prospect of a long-term relationship.

THE CASES OF KINSEY MILLHONE, BY SUE GRAFTON

Novels

A is for Alibi, 1982. *B is for Burglar*, 1985. *C is for Corpse*, 1986. *D is for Deadbeat*; 1987. *E is for Evidence*, 1988. *F is for Fugitive*, 1989. *G is for Gumshoe*, 1990. *H is for Homicide*; 1991.

Uncollected stories

'*The Parker Shotgun*', 1986. '*Non Sung Smoke*', 1988. '*Falling Off the Roof*', 1989. '*A Poison That Leaves No Trace*', 1990.

62

JOHN WILLIAMS

on

Toussaint Marcus Moore

E d Lacy provides the missing link between the fifties hardboiled style and the beat scene. He was a Jewish New Yorker who wrote a whole slew of novels during the fifties and early sixties and disappeared from view, like so many others, when crime writing went severely out of fashion in the late sixties.

His novels are mostly set in New York but would relocate on occasion to the primo hepcat holiday spots of the time—Tahiti and the south of France being particular favourites. But what really marked Lacy out from the crowd was his regular use of black protagonists, a decision perhaps influenced by the fact that Lacy was himself married to a black woman. Crime fiction has too often disappointed in its treatment of race. The genre has much potential in this area yet it has too often allowed its tone to be set by Chandler's incidental racism, so that just as in the movies black characters have mostly been maids or hookers, chauffeurs or pimps.

So for Ed Lacy, in 1957, to come out with a novel called *Room*

To Swing, which featured a black private eye with the fine black nationalist name of Toussaint Marcus Moore was a considerable flouting of convention. What is more surprising still is that Toussaint Moore isn't simply a whiter-than-white caricature of a black man, a Sidney Poitier role, but rather a regular guy (albeit with Anglophile hepcat affectations like modernist furniture and a Jaguar car) who spends much of the novel having trouble with his girlfriend, fending off white liberal advances, and wondering whether or not to take a job in the Post Office. This last is a neatly-judged theme; for the conventional white PI the very idea of such employment would seem like an admission of failure, but Lacy is well aware that for a black man in the 1950s there could be no such sniffiness about a regular job with a non-discriminatory pay structure. In fact it seems a lot more appealing than most of Moore's regular P.I. work: chasing up bad debts across Harlem, extorting money out of poor black people on behalf of rip-off credit companies.

At the start of *Room To Swing*, though, Moore is on the run in the one-horse Southern town of Bingston, North Carolina. And he's in trouble; a slick black Yankee with a set of foreign wheels stands out a mile here. A black family takes him in and after a while he gets round to telling the daughter of the family what he's doing there. It's a convoluted story involving Moore being framed for the murder in New York of a white man originally from Bingston, and as a plot it's no more than routine, but the real pleasures of the book are in its quiet passages and its detailing. Lacy is skilful enough to move Moore through settings as disparate as this small-town South and also Greenwich Village bohemia, and to allow him to deal with both middle-aged black postmen and New York media lesbians, while still maintaining a consistent and credible perspective. In short *Room To Swing* is a fine, taut piece of crime writing that never condescends to its subject, it possesses a throughgoing liberalism that also makes it one of the few period novels to invoke homosexuality without comment or censure, and it deservedly won an Edgar for its author . . .

Toussaint Moore was revived five years later in a novel called *Moment Of Untruth*, which starts off with Moore working at the Post Office but looking to earn some extra money from a little P.I. moonlighting in order to finance his impending fatherhood. It's an amiably far-fetched tale of intrigue set in the world of Mexican bullfighting, and Moore is as engaging as ever, but it bears all the signs of having been written for money just that bit too quickly (and its publisher's interest in it may be guessed from the fact that

Toussaint's name is misspelt throughout). Much better was another Lacy novel with a black protagonist, *Harlem Underground*, whose hero is a young black cop sent into Harlem to investigate Black radical movements. It's a strong, angry and even mildly prescient account of the militant phase of the civil rights movement, a time that was scarcely envisioned by Toussaint Moore in the swinging fifties. And maybe there lies the enduring charm of *Room To Swing*: its evocation of the last time in America that black and white still entertained an illusion that integration must be around the corner, to be peacefully obtained as an inevitable part of progress.

THE CASES OF TOUSSAINT MARCUS MOORE, BY ED LACY

Room to Swing, 1957. *Moment of Untruth*, 1964

63

RALPH SPURRIER

on

Inspector Morse

I f you were to go into any one of the forty pubs that can be found within a square mile of the centre of Oxford, the Black Dog in St Aldates or the Bulldog opposite Christ Church or any that serve a decent pint and were unlikely to have a blaring juke-box, the chances are you could find yourself sitting at a table next to Chief Inspector Morse.

Morse (his first name remains an enigma) is certainly not striking on first glance, and the casual observer would be surprised to know that the man with a gabardine mackintosh which has seen better days and has to be retrieved from behind the oil-can in the boot of his car when it rains, is a Chief Inspector.

He's not a big man (such as Wexford, for example), and some of the women in his past have been known to look *down* into his eyes, but he has a bulk which only becomes apparent and intimidating when he is faced with a particularly awkward witness or suspect. His ability to upset people is a double-edged sword which in turn can force an unwanted lie out of a suspect but equally exasperate his colleagues, who regard him as something of a nonconformist when it comes to playing by the rules. Even Sergeant Lewis, who is his right-hand man in the hard graft of a murder case, can find Morse's tactics a little arcane at times. It's not that he's really difficult to work with; it's just that he sees a complicated motivation for an effect which more often than not has a much simpler solution.

Still, it's the kind of cryptic by-way that an inveterate crossword-solver would love to search, and the chances are that Morse will have a copy of that day's *Times* in front of him, together with his pint of Morrell's or Hook Norton. He will glance at his watch from time to time. This doesn't mean that he has an appointment; he is checking to see if he can beat his personal limit on solving the crossword.

> Clue: Classic sinister opposition reveals author (6)

If he is not alone, Sergeant Lewis will be his companion. Morse rarely brings his female acquaintances into the pubs, much preferring the more intimate atmosphere of a restaurant. He is inordinately defensive of his private life, and little can be guessed of his success with the opposite sex except to say that he has a ready perception of what makes lovers kill each other and how the physical nature of a relationship has an all-too-powerful control over the psychological barriers to civilized behaviour. Perhaps it has been Morse's tragedy to be too observant of the violent outcome of 'domestics' that has made him somewhat cynical of the married state, and which keeps him a confirmed bachelor well into his fifties. Despite this perception, he has been known to lose a certain amount of judgement where females are concerned, and painful rebuffs have not jaded his appetite for the occasional dignified chase.

Any woman that has stayed with him for the natural progression to bed will have found herself in her own home rather than his. Morse regards his home as a retreat from the wicked world, and would gladly trade an evening of more public entertainment for three hours alone with Siegfried, Wotan and Mime after his daily fix of his favourite soap (although he would vehemently refute the term), *The Archers*. He is also very fond of a particular poet.

> Clue: Young Salopian's creator finds pride of place on bookshelf (1,1,7)

THE CASES OF INSPECTOR MORSE, BY COLIN DEXTER

Novels

Last Bus to Woodstock, 1975. *Last Seen Wearing*, 1976. *The Silent World of Nicholas Quinn*, 1977. *Service of all the Dead*, 1979. *The Dead of Jericho*, 1981. *The Riddle of the Third Mile*, 1983. *The Secret of Annexe Three*, 1986. *The Wench is Dead*, 1989. *The Jewel that was ours*, 1991.

Uncollected stories

'*Morse's Greatest Mystery*', 1987. '*Dead as a Dodo*', 1990.

64
MIKE RIPLEY
on
Hoke Moseley

If anybody reads this it means one of two things, I'm either dead before my father (and a whole lot poorer than I would've been) or I'm dead still short of retirement.

I picked up this copy of 'How To Avoid Probate' at a garage sale a coupla years ago and now I've found somebody has used the sample Will form at the back. It says you can write a will that's legal as long as you write it out. It's called a holograph will, so that's what I'm doing.

Sue Ellen should read this as the oldest, but maybe Aileen's got more sense. You'll have to figure that out between you because you'll be on your own for a while. Don't be afraid to contact my father Frank or your mother out in California. Patsy won't be shocked to hear something bad has happened to me, but tell her that on the whole I think she was better off marrying Curly Peterson.

Take my gun if it's at home, and make sure Major Willie Brownley gets it down at headquarters. I'm not worried about you girls and guns as such, because I know you're more sensible than most at your age. But use it to get in to see Willie and don't leave until he's explained all my pension rights to you.

Get what you can for the Green Lakes house and all my stuff. Split it how you want without fighting. I don't intend leaving anything specific to Ellita Sanchez, not if she's still married to that guy Donald Hutton. I know he killed his brother Virgil all those years back and Ellita was a fool to go off with him. Still, if justice was always handed out fair and square, we wouldn't need so many cops following things up.

I don't mind if you cut out a few hundred dollars for Ellita's kid. You will anyway, and you could take a shot at telling her old man Sanchez that I never was Pepe's real father.

And you could take my false teeth when you go see Major Willie. Tell him to chew on a few cold cases with them, from me. Ha, ha, ha.

Hoke Moseley, Lieutenant,
Miami PD (Internal Affairs).

THE CASES OF HOKE MOSELEY, BY CHARLES WILLEFORD
Miami Blues, 1984. *Sideswipe*, 1987. *New Hope for the Dead*, 1986. *The Way We Die Now*, 1989.

65

ED GORMAN

on

The Nameless Detective

M y favorite *noir* movies are the RKOs. The Warners stuff, to take the opposite example, rarely had anything to do with the real streets. Their men tended to be operatic rather than realistic renditions of the criminal class—long on grand gestures, short on bologna sandwiches.

If he wasn't constantly dieting, Bill Pronzini's private eye Nameless would probably eat bologna sandwiches at every opportunity. And swill down a couple of beers while he was at it.

Nameless is one of the last working-class men left in contemporary detective fiction and for that reason alone I find him admirable. Who but Pronzini would start a book: 'The bumper sticker said: JOGGING IS FOR JERKS.' In this age of Reeboks and yuppie private-eyes, that is nothing less than a call to war.

Another thing I like about Nameless is how hard he tries to make his relationships good. But he doesn't always succeed. He argues quite frequently with his lady friend Kerry and his relationship with partner Eberhardt you can forget about. Remember the scene in *Bones* where the hapless Eberhardt brings Wanda, his 'broad' of the moment, and puts the foursome through an intolerable evening? You don't know who to hate more—Eberhardt for being blind to a conniving woman, or Nameless for being so sanctimonious about Eberhardt's sad pride in Wanda. And that's exactly why the scene is so memorable—because you're both of them, Eberhardt wearing too much Old Spice and copping too many cheap feels, and Nameless knowing that he'd have a lot better sense than Eberhardt. It's so damned human, that scene, and ultimately forlorn.

As introspective as he is, Nameless is given to action. The scene in *Bindlestiff* where he's trapped down a well with two decomposing corpses that he keeps bumping against still stays with me. As does the quiet horror of *Blowback* where the radiologist tells him he's got a lesion on his lung and will have to wait the weekend before he'll know if it's malignant or not.

The San Francisco color is particularly interesting. *Quicksilver* gave me my first real sense of Japanese-Americans as a community. And *Dragonfire* told us lots about Chinese-Americans.

The middle-period Nameless novels demonstrate Pronzini's love for the classical mystery. He's the only P.I. writer I know who regularly reads John Dickson Carr, for example, and Carr's influence is apparent in such Nameless novels as *Deadfall* and *Nightshades*. Who says P.I. novels can't include classical traditional elements?

Finally, I like Nameless' prejudices. He's got good ones. In *Blowback* he meets a guy he hates immediately because the guy refers to the free beer in the room as 'rat piss' and then says 'I like imported beer.' Who the hell could could like a guy like that?

THE CASES OF THE NAMELESS DETECTIVE, BY BILL PRONZINI

Novels

The Snatch, 1971. *The Vanished*, 1973. *Undercurrent*, 1973. *Blowback*, 1977. *Twospot*, 1978 (with Colin Wilcox). *Labyrinth*, 1980. *Hoodwink*, 1981. *Scattershot*, 1982. *Dragonfire*, 1982. *Bindlestiff*, 1983. *Quicksilver*, 1984. *Nightshades*, 1984. *Double*, 1984 (with Marcia Muller). *Bones*, 1985. *Deadfall*, 1986. *Shackles*, 1988. *Jackpot*, 1990. *Breakdown*, 1991.

Story collections

Casefile, 1983 *Graveyard Plots*, 1985 (includes three Nameless stories).

Uncollected stories

'The Snatch', 1969 (expanded into the novel *The Snatch*). 'A Cold Day in November', 1969 (expanded into the novel *The Labyrinth*). 'The Crank', 1970. 'The Way the World Spins', 1970. 'Blowback', 1972 (expanded into the novel *Blowback*). 'The Scales of Justice', 1973 (expanded into the novel *Labyrinth*). 'Thin Air', 1979 (included in *Scattershot*). 'A Killing in Xanadu', 1980 (included in *Scattershot*). 'Cat's Paw', 1983. 'Skeleton Rattle Your Mouldy Leg', 1984. 'Sanctuary', 1985. 'Ace in the Hole', 1986. 'Incident in a Neighborhood Tavern', 1988. 'Something Wrong', 1988. 'Cache and Carry', 1988 (with Marcia Muller). 'Here Comes Santa Claus', 1989. 'Stakeout', 1990. 'La Bellezza delle Belleze', forthcoming 1991. 'Bedeviled', forthcoming 1991. 'Souls Burning', forthcoming 1991.

66
PETER LOVESEY
on

Detective Chief Inspector Henry Peckover

> Our 'Enry, a lamb for the slaughter,
> Got lumbered with Micks 'cross the water,
>   And not only Micks
>   But a squadron of pricks
> From Calif., New York, and etcetera.

Here, in the Bard of the Yard's virile verse—penned, aptly, at Limerick Station—are the first clues to the character of Henry Peckover: his dropping of the occasional 'h', plus anything else that helps a line to scan; his problems fitting rhymes; his suspicion of foreigners; and his unparliamentary language.

Yet there's a romantic side, manifest in these lines to his wife Miriam, when she stands in as cook in an Irish hotel:

> Fear no more the heat o' the stove,
> Nor the maître d's neuroses;
> Thou hast stirred in bay and clove,
> Basted well and prayed to Moses:
> Gourmets, gourmands, piggies, must
> At some point leave the trough, or bust.

Many a fictional detective aspires to poetry and emulating Shakespeare, but how many put their verse on record in book after book, as 'Enry does? He even put it on the lavatory walls at Scotland Yard and got demoted from Sergeant to Constable for his efforts.

Now for a quick Peckover-portrait. Born in London's Stepney ('cradle of genius'), and 45 or so, he's a straight knees-up-Muvver-Brown cockney with memories stretching back to the Hammersmith Palais and the Bethnal Green Labour Party. Happily married with two kids, Sam and Mary. Has a taste for brown hats, burgundy slacks, suede shoes and unsuitable jackets. Lives at 32 Collins Cross, somewhere near Camden Market. Pastimes, apart from poetry, are Watney's, Whitbread, Bass and Worthington; is inclined to silly horseplay, rather than violence, when drunk. His 'rhymed contributions', tapped out on a 1959 Imperial Good Companion, have appeared in *Homes and Gardens, Good Housekeeping, Punch, The Listener, Poetry Quarterly, Motor, Country Life, Taste, Slimming* and *Woman's Realm*. The poetic bent is not appreciated at Scotland Yard.

Our 'Enry is a survivor, thanks be to God and the Chief Commissioner. He was demoted from Inspector to Sergeant for breaking a suspect's arm (he's not averse to violence when sober) and his conduct as Chief Inspector suggests he may slip another rung any time. His creative skills aren't confined to poetry, for nobody can dream up an expenses claim like Peckover; in France, 'to hospitality for Gendarmerie, taxis, telephones, portable filing cabinet, subscriptions to essential French magazines, oil for handcuffs, repair to truncheon, disguise kit no. 27 comprising beret, goatee, easel and palette . . . £213.35.'

Someone at the Factory—and it must be Superintendent Veal—understands the special skills of Peckover. Someone had the vision to assign him to the Flying Squad, the Anti-Terrorist Branch and the Vice Squad. Someone is aware that Our 'Enry is the only possible man to tangle with bombers, porn merchants, born-again evangelists, fitness freaks, cocaine kings and a baby called George. In recent cases, he has been triumphantly supported by a snappy dresser, the black, towering old-Harrovian—Detective Constable Jason Twitty.

As a champion of law and order, Peckover is obliged to suffer more than most. In *A Healthy Way to Die*, he undergoes aerobics in a health farm; *The God Squad Bod* has him tambourine-bashing at revivalist meetings; he's held prisoner by a blue-movie queen in *Zigzag*; compelled to change nappies under fire in *Peckover Holds the Baby*; and, in *A Free-Range Wife*, he rides a stuffed stag and stuffs a . . . No, I won't spoil it for you.

A Peckover plot defies analysis. Line for line, Michael Kenyon's is the wittiest and freshest of all crime fiction. That's a tall claim, I know. The writing never flags. It's sharp, sparky, intelligent and warm. Seek out the Bard of the Yard; you'll be glad you read this.

Finally, a sample from *Good Housekeeping*:

> *Kitchen Catastrophe*
>
> O action-painted kitchen!
> O decorated me!
> O living, panchromatic art!
> O flying potpourri!

O hot and fishy particles
Of aubergine and squid!
The day I took my finger
Off our blender's airborne lid.

Henry Peckover

THE CASES OF HENRY PECKOVER, BY MICHAEL KENYON

Zigzag, 1981. *The Elgar Variations*, 1981. *The God Squad Bod*, 1982. *A Free-Range Wife*, 1983. *A Healthy Way to Die*, 1986. *Peckover Holds the Baby*, 1988.

67

MARTIN EDWARDS

on

Francis Pettigrew

' I suppose that it is the first time on record,' says Francis Pettigrew at the end of *Tragedy At Law*, 'that anyone has ever been driven to commit suicide by a quotation from the Law Reports.'

The tone is far removed from the self-satisfaction of the conventional amateur sleuth who has just revealed why and by whom murder came to be done. And a special bitterness deepens the irony of Pettigrew's words, for he was responsible for the quotation and he is talking about someone he once loved.

Frank Pettigrew first came onto the scene fifty years ago, at the tail end of the era of Wimsey and whimsy, of murder purely for pleasure, yet he was from the outset a reluctant detective. In this, for me, lies much of his appeal. Even though he appears in books written by Cyril Hare, who said in a characteristically entertaining essay, 'The Classic Form', that a whodunnit 'is not a serious type of book', Pettigrew is unable to treat 'murder in the raw' as a game. He is sensitive to the pain that crime leaves in its wake.

When first encountered in *Tragedy At Law*, Pettigrew has already reached 'an age, and a stage in his profession, where he did not much care to be reminded of the passage of time.' As a young barrister he had shown much promise, but the glittering prizes never materialised and now he is 'eking out a precarious practice by the drudgery of legal authorship'. That last phrase struck a chord when, as a student, I became absorbed in the book at the expense of an essay on the doctrine of privity of contract.

For all that Pettigrew made his bow during the Second World War, there is something very modern about his self-awareness. He realises that his lack of success is due to a subtle deficiency within his own make-up—'some quality that was neither character nor intellect nor luck, but without which none of these gifts would avail to carry their possessor to the front.' He is passionately opposed to capital punishment, but when Judge Barber advocates extending the death penalty, he responds by characterising this as 'stretching the stretching'—an example of gallows humour, shall we say? And typical of Pettigrew's instinct for levity which, coupled with his mistaken belief that other people would be as reasonable as himself, has cost him professional advancement.

Despite becoming involved in a number of mysteries after that chronicled in *Tragedy At Law*, Pettigrew never develops a taste for 'this business of detection', as he makes clear to MacWilliam, the Chief Constable, in *That Yew Tree's Shade*. Unlike most amateurs, he maintains a credible relationship with the police. He does not seek to supplant the official investigators and Inspector Mallett, for instance, treats him with respect but never kow-tows to him. Yet he is able to contribute scraps of legal knowledge now and then which help to pinpoint hidden motivations—insight into probate practice on one occasion, a piece of information about divorce law in another. When Crippen provides Pettigrew with a clue, it is nothing to do with a body in a coal cellar but related to a court case brought by Ethel Le Neve in connection with her claim to the doctor's estate.

The later books see Pettigrew's life taking a turn for the better. During war-time service in that bureaucratic haven Pin Control, his secretary is a young and attractive woman, Eleanor Brown, whom he later marries. As the years pass, he enjoys a tranquil retirement disturbed only by the occasional untimely death.

Yet it is that initial portrait of a lawyer steeped in disillusion that has stuck in my mind. Even Pettigrew's seemingly idle scepticism about the machinery of justice—as when he 'found time to wonder . . . whether his client would be hanged merely because the Judge had a down on his counsel'—has over the years acquired a degree of plausibility which might have disconcerted Hare himself. I do not claim Pettigrew as a giant of the genre, but in his small failings, as well as in his insights into the way that people behave, I find an enduring charm. From an author who belonged in spirit to the Golden Age came that rarity in traditional detective fiction, a character of flesh and blood.

THE CASES OF FRANCIS PETTIGREW, BY CYRIL HARE

Novels

Tragedy at Law, 1942. *With a Bare Bodkin*, 1946. *When the Wind Blows*, 1949. *That Yew Tree's Shade*, 1954. *He Should Have Died Hereafter*, 1958.

Short story collection

Best Detective Stories of Cyril Hare, 1959 (contains one Pettigrew story).

68
ANNE HART
on
Hercule Poirot

Agatha Christie's most famous detective was born in Belgium in the mid-nineteenth century (year and day unknown) into a large family of modest circumstances. As a young man he joined the Belgian police where he enjoyed a distinguished career and rose to become head of the force. His plans to retire in 1914 were overtaken by the Great War. It is likely that an association with the resistance to the German invasion of Belgium led to his arrival in England as a wounded refugee in 1916. Befriended by Mrs Emily Inglethorp of Styles Court in Essex, Poirot was given a temporary home on her estate from which he renewed earlier acquaintances with Arthur Hastings and Inspector Jimmy Japp, and subsequently solved his first English murder case, *The Mysterious Affair at Styles* (1921). Following this, Poirot and Hastings became residents of London, most notably in rooms at 14 Farraway Street, and Poirot embarked on a remarkable and lucrative career as a private detective. His earlier cases were narrated by Hastings in a lengthy series of short stories (in one of which, 'The Double Clue', Poirot first met the love of his life, the outrageous and unattainable Countess Vera Rossakoff), and the novel *Murder on the Links* (1923). Shortly thereafter, Hastings emigrated to Argentina with his bride, Cinderella Duveen, though over the next thirteen years he returned for lengthy visits and collaborations with Poirot. By the end of the 1920s, having solved *The Murder of Roger Ackroyd* (1926), the adventure of *The Big Four* (1927), and *The Mystery of the Blue Train* (1928), Poirot's reputation as the most celebrated private detective in London was secure. The 1930s saw him at the height of his powers in such cases as *Peril at End House* (1932), *Murder on the Orient Express* (1934), *The ABC Murders*, (1936), and *Death on the Nile* (1937). Occasional collaborators during this period were Superintendent Battle, Colonel Johnny Race, and Mr Satterthwaite. In about 1935 Poirot took up permanent residence at 203 Whitehaven Mansions, a meticulously ordered Mayfair flat, where his impeccable manservant, George, ministered to his household needs and his secretary, the formidable Felicity Lemon, to his business affairs. From the 1940s to his death in *Curtain* (1975), at what must have been a phenomenally old age, Poirot steadily pursued his illustrious career in such cases as *One, Two, Buckle My Shoe* (1940), *Five Little Pigs* (1942), *The Hollow* (1946), *Mrs McGinty's Dead* (1952), *Dead Man's Folly* (1956), *Cat Among the Pigeons* (1959), *Third Girl* (1966), and *Elephants Can Remember* (1972). Notable friends during these years were Superintendent Albert Spence and the memorable Ariadne Oliver, a crime writer with dozens of best sellers to her credit, who bore a distinct resemblance to Agatha Christie.

Hercule Poirot's enduring hallmarks were his magnificent black moustaches, his egg-shaped head, his foreign and eccentric mannerisms, and his enthralling ability—aided by his famous 'grey cells'—to solve crimes. In all, Agatha Christie devoted 33 books, 55 short stories (many published under more than one title), and a play, *Black Coffee* (1934), to his achievements, though not without occasional rebellions: 'I point out that by a few strokes of the pen . . . I could destroy him utterly. He replies, grandiloquently: 'Impossible to get rid of Poirot like that! He is much too clever.' Many of his cases have been adapted to the stage, film and television.

THE CASES OF HERCULE POIROT

Novels

The Mysterious Affair at Styles, 1920. *The Murder on the Links*, 1923. *The Murder of Roger Ackroyd*, 1926. *The Big Four*, 1927. *The Mystery of the Blue Train*, 1928. *Peril at End House*, 1932. *Lord Edgware Dies*, 1933. *Murder on the Orient Express*, 1934. *Murder in Three Acts*, 1934. *Death in the Clouds*, 1935. *The ABC Murders*, 1936. *Murder in Mesopotamia*, 1936. *Cards on the Table*, 1936. *Dumb Witness*, 1937. *Death on the Nile*, 1937. *Appointment with Death*, 1938. *Hercule Poirot's Christmas*, 1939. *Sad Cypress*, 1940. *One, Two, Buckle my Shoe*, 1940. *Evil Under the Sun*, 1941. *Five Little Pigs*, 1942. *The Hollow*, 1946. *Taken at the Flood*, 1948. *Mrs McGinty's Dead*, 1952. *After the Funeral*, 1953. *Hickory, Dickory, Dock*, 1955. *Dead Man's Folly*, 1956. *Cat Among the Pigeons*, 1959. *The Clocks*, 1963. *Third Girl*, 1966. *Hallowe'en Porty*, 1969. *Elephants can Remember*, 1972. *Curtain*, 1975.

Story collections

Poirot Investigates, 1928 (eleven stories). *Two New Crime Stories*, 1929 (one Poirot story). *Murder in the Mews*, 1937 (four Poirot stories). *Dead Man's Mirror*, 1937 (three Poirot stories). *The Regatta Mystery*, 1939 (nine stories, 5 with Poirot). *Poirot and the Regatta Mystery*, 1943. *Poirot on Holiday*, 1943. *Poirot knows the Murderer*, 1946. *Poirot lends a Hand*, 1946. *The Labours of Hercules*, 1947 (twelve Poirot stories). *The Witness for the Prosecution*, 1948 (nine stories, one with Poirot). *Three Blind Mice*, 1950 (nine stories, three with Poirot). *The Under Dog*, 1951 (nine Poirot stories). *The Adventures of the Christmas Pudding*, 1960 (six stories, five with Poirot). *Double Sin*, 1961 (eight stories, four with Poirot). *Poirot's Early Cases*, 1974 (eighteen Poirot stories).

(There are fifty-five short stories featuring Poirot extant; contents of British and American editions are different and duplicate stories).

69
BARBARA WILSON
on
Mrs Pollifax

At first glance Mrs Emily Pollifax seems to be a direct descendant of the Miss Marple/Miss Silver school of amateur women sleuths. She wears a flowered hat, she grows geraniums and, most important, she blends in perfectly with her surroundings—a harmless old lady who nevertheless has a sharp ear for gossip and an even sharper eye for detail. But look again: Mrs Pollifax also has a brown belt in karate, and is one of the CIA's favorite agents when it comes to smuggling, secreting and spying.

I have to admit that the CIA is not exactly my favorite organization, but I found it almost irresistible in Dorothy Gilman's first thriller (*The Unexpected Mrs Pollifax*) when the recent widow complained to her doctor of feeling 'so unused, so purposeless,' and then set off to Langley, Virginia to present herself as a potential spy. Telling a bewildered young man there that, 'It's true that my only qualifications are those of character, but when you reach my age character is what you have the most of,' Mrs Pollifax offers her life to her country. And is promptly rejected ('It's not a matter of *presenting* oneself, it's a matter of your country looking for *you*.').

Mrs Pollifax is recruited by mistake as it turns out, because she looks, in her flowered hat, so little like a spy, and so very much like a tourist, but she proves her mettle in countless ways in the first novel. Sent to Mexico, she is soon kidnapped and taken to Albania, where she finds herself in a fortress prison high in the mountains. Perhaps it's just that I've always been fascinated by Albania myself, but I found her adventures there quite impressive. Not only does she lead an escape from the jail, but she retains her energy and her dignity ('indifferent at last to how many goats stepped on her') through a series of hilarious and hair-raising adventures on the way back to the West.

Mrs Pollifax is no suave James Bond, but her sense of humor and her equilibrium rarely desert her, even in the most precarious and dire circumstances. She is a meticulous secret agent and a dependable comrade-in-arms to her fellows, most of whom are men and few of whom, interestingly enough, seem to consider her either too old or too feminine to be of use. Quite often, in fact, Mrs Pollifax's loyalty and resourcefulness are important factors in getting out of a sticky situation. Her command of karate moves is quite helpful as well.

One of the delights of the Mrs Pollifax books is their far-flung locations. Albania may have been my favorite, but I've also enjoyed Mrs Pollifax safari-ing through Africa and hurtling across Turkey, by van and by gypsy caravan. For those of us who dream of foreign places Mrs Pollifax offers the perfect escape; she's barely settled down to her gardening and humdrum life back in New Brunswick, New Jersey, when Carstairs of the CIA calls and asks if she'll be ready to leave for parts unknown in twenty minutes. Often cast in the circumspect role of tourist, Mrs Pollifax makes friends of her traveling companions in order to spy on them, and unflappably follows them everywhere they go, whether that means African savannahs, Thai jungles or even the Xinjiang Uygur Autonomous Region (that's one I had to look up in my atlas).

The cold-war atmosphere of the books can occasionally be irritating, but it's rarely taken all that seriously. Mrs Pollifax is best, in fact, when she is least serious and when the usual elements of the spy thriller turn to farce. In *The Amazing Mrs Pollifax*, she and young Colin attempt half a dozen times to rid themselves of an inconvenient corpse in and out of Istanbul in scenes reminiscent of Hitchcock's comedy, *The Trouble with Harry*.

Midway through the series Mrs Pollifax acquires a husband, the understanding but firm Cyrus Reed. I worried that he might develop a tendency to want to turn up and save the situation, and on one occasion he does just that. But on another Mrs Pollifax saves *him* after he's kidnapped—in extremely frightening and foot-blistering circumstances. I must confess I like Mrs Pollifax better on her own, especially in her earlier escapades when she's discovering unknown aspects of her character ('"I am going to shoot the first person who walks through this door after I leave," she called out, only a little embarrassed by her cliches.')

Unexpectedly, Mrs Pollifax is a delightful spy who challenges notions of femininity and old age, and as such, is a welcome change from women sleuths who don't get out of the garden. Or as Mrs P.

would put it: 'The situation is extremely fluid and unconventional, but we *are* moving in the direction of Yozgat.'

THE CASES OF MRS POLLIFAX, BY DOROTHY GILMAN

The Unexpected Mrs Pollifax, 1966. *The Amazing Mrs Pollifax*, 1970. *The Elusive Mrs Pollifax*, 1971. *A Palm for Mrs Pollifax*, 1973. *Mrs Pollifax on Safari*, 1977. *Mrs Pollifax on The China Station*, 1983. *Mrs Pollifax and the Hong Kong Buddha*, 1985. *Mrs Pollifax and the Golden Triangle*, 1988.

70

NIGEL ALGAR

on

Ralph Poteet

L ong ago, a few things could be relied on, like a female voice on the speaking clock and a male private eye on the streets. You could also put money on him being white, in possession of all his faculties and enjoying a full complement of limbs. His sense of honour was highly developed, he probably knew his way around the subjunctive and he definitely slept alone. Those guys are still around, with their battered integrity, but there is a new bunch in town, decked out with all kinds of disability, so that you get to thinking that Mungo (George C. Chesbro's Ph.D.-toting dwarf) should book a tour to Lourdes for him and all the other fictional private eyes stumbling and tapping their way down the dark alleys.

Ralph Poteet, star of Loren D. Estleman's *Peeper* (1989) is at least white and male, but there his resemblance to the classic private eye ends, unless you count his exuberantly obscene wisecracks offered to those who cross his path. *Peeper* has been described as a ribald spoof of the genre and as a brilliant satire, but it is more an extravagantly rude private-eye story that hustles the genre conventions up to the edge of the cliff and delightedly tips them over.

Poteet lives in a crummy Detroit neighbourhood, sandwiched between a dirty bookstore on the ground floor and Lyla Dane, a hooker, on the floor above. Forty-three years old and as many pounds overweight, neatly attired in a Tyrolean hat with an orange feather and a suit that has seen better decades, Poteet is summoned by Lyla in the small hours to help solve the problem posed by a dead priest in her bed. On this occasion, as on so many others, Poteet sinks to the most tasteless remark possible: 'At least he wasn't a fag'. His bristling cynicism towards religion was perhaps encouraged by the loss of sight in his right eye, inflicted upon him by his Ohio Baptist father when beating him with the family bible. Justice was nonetheless exacted upon Poteet senior by Ralph's sister Ethel, who made his Thanksgiving Day by killing him with a Black and Decker Floating Wonder cordless electric knife. Honest on a large scale, but a little shaky further down, Poteet has sticky fingers which ensure that a heterogeneous collection of objects fall into his pockets in the course of the investigation. The path from the hooker's apartment leads through murky Catholic Church politics to a corrupt US Attorney General, but the twists and turns of the plot do not deflect Poteet from his dogged venality. The lovely April Dane, apparently the sister of the hooker, does however manage to provide a whole rainbow of dazzling sexual attractions which leave Poteet feeling as if he had been 'carrying anvils up and down stairs all night'.

If ever this wild novel makes it to the screen, Burt Young would be the ideal Ralph Poteet—scuzzy, but somehow deep down irresistible. *Peeper* also offers a gallery of other entertaining characters, such as O'Leary, the arson investigator who carelessly drops lighted cigarettes wherever he goes, and Carpenter, the Bishop's cadaverous troubleshooter. Other writers have tried to give a new twist to the private eye novel, but quite often their imagination quits on them just after they have thought up the one-legged Aborigine lesbian. Estleman, however, just keeps going and his flair for incisive description and comic dialogue puts him mean streets ahead of the pack. As Poteet himself would say, dollars to dogshit you will love this book.

THE CASES OF RALPH POTEET, BY LOREN D. ESTLEMAN
Peeper, 1989. '*State of Grace*' (uncollected story, 1988).

71

DANIEL P. KING

on

Mrs Pym

Founder of the Crime Writers' Association and one-time secretary to Edgar Wallace, Nigel Morland's best-known character is Mrs Palmyra Pym.

Born before the turn of the century, she was widowed after a short marriage. She began her crime-fighting career as a policewoman in Shanghai in 1935 and, 16 years later, long after her return to England, she was an Assistant Commissioner, Criminal Investigation Department—the highest-ranking woman in the history of Scotland Yard.

She remained an employee of the British War Department, but had been assigned to Scotland Yard for 'special investigations.'

Her first 'special investigation' seemed to readers inadequate and incoherent, but the lady emerged unmistakably out for blood in adventures to come. Straight from the hard-bitten school of detectives, Mrs Pym appeared determined and resourceful and once she began investigating, there was no stopping her. Although physically tough and badly dressed, she retained her femininity throughout her escapades.

She was a terror to evil-doers and unconventional in the eyes of her superiors. Unconventional, she often packed a gun, but usually relied on her fists in tight situations. She was aggravatingly oblivious to regulations and traditions of the Yard but was permitted a freer hand than were her male colleagues.

When Mrs Pym made her appearance in 1935, she was considered too rough and unconventional for a British detective; her clothes were jaunty and eccentric and her language perhaps a bit too blunt. She was brave, skilful, outrageous—an awesome sight when she went into battle.

As the years wore on, she became something of a bore, but her clothes changed for the better and her manners became more agreeable. She continued, however, to use her third degree methods and interpreted Scotland Yard regulations to suit herself. Given Morland's background, it is not surprising that the stories themselves are often fantastic and unashamedly in imitation of Edgar Wallace. Wallace, in fact, purportedly gave Morland the idea of his heroine, the hard-bitten, glitter-eyed Mrs Pym.

Mrs Pym involved herself in a variety of strange and mysterious investigations:

The Clue of the Bricklayer's Aunt opens with the strange behavior of a bedridden paralytic—the bricklayer's aunt—whose wild dancing and throwing of furniture about attract the attention of neighbors. Mrs Pym finds the connection between this curious behavior and the robberies and murders that follow.

The next Pym book, *The Clue in the Mirror*, finds her uncovering a long and involved trail of crime which leads her from a warehouse in Wapping to respectable financial circles.

The Case Without a Clue deals with Mrs Pym's efforts to discover why the galley proof of a suppressed book was stolen from a publisher's safe and why a murder followed. The plot is well-conceived, but Mrs Pym is now engagingly proper—and boring.

A Rope for the Hanging concerns a street brawl in which a drunken laborer is killed—at first a seemingly common case in which a deputy assistant commissioner of Scotland Yard would be scarcely be interested. But once Mrs Pym begins investigation, the mystery is penetratingly illuminated.

Mrs Pym uses her unconventional third degree methods in *A Knife for the Killer* to solve the mystery of a parachutist who alights on the 'Rockefeller Building' and is found by police to be dying of a gunshot wound.

The Corpse on the Flying Trapeze had her investigating how and why an acrobat was beheaded while swinging from a trapeze in full view of a crowded theatre. The bloody beginning is only a prelude to more murders later on—all seemingly without motive until Mrs Pym comes on the scene.

The Mrs Pym stories continued through the 1940s and the plots grew better as the lady's eccentricities became less pronounced. She finally retired, or was retired by a bored Nigel Morland who confided in later years that detective stories 'bored him to tears.'

THE CASES OF MRS PYM, BY NIGEL MORLAND

Novels

The Phantom Gunman, 1935. *The Moon Murders*, 1935. *The Street of The Leopard*, 1936. *The Clue of the Bricklayer's Aunt*, 1936. *The Clue in the Mirror*, 1937. *The Case Without a Clue*, 1938. *A Rope for the Hanging*, 1938. *A Knife for the Killer*, 1939. *A Gun for a God*, 1940. *The Clue of the Careless Hangman*, 1940. *The Corpse on the Flying Trapeze*, 1941. *A Coffin for the Body*, 1943. *Dressed to Kill*, 1947. *The Lady had a Gun*, 1951. *Call Him Early for Murder*, 1952. *Sing a Song for Cyanide*, 1953. *Look in any Doorway*, 1957. *A Bullet for Midas*, 1958. *Death and the Golden Boy*, 1958. *The Concrete Maze*, 1960. *So Quiet a Death*, 1960. *The Dear, Dead Girls*, 1961.

Story collections

Mrs Pym Of Scotland Yard, 1946. *Mrs Pym and Other Stories*, 1976.

72

EDWARD D. HOCH

on

Ellery Queen

I t may not be fashionable just now to write about Ellery Queen as one of my favorite fictional sleuths. Less than twenty years after the last Ellery Queen novel appeared, there is an unfortunate tendency—especially among younger readers and critics—to view his early cases as unreadable and the later ones as mere reworkings of what has gone before.

Acceptance of this view shows a failure to appreciate what the detective story is all about. It is not an action-adventure tale, nor a thriller, nor a shocker. It is not even a novel of suspense, though certainly suspense is a key element in all good fiction. It is first and foremost a puzzle, a game between author and reader with the detective acting as the author's spokesperson.

When we first meet Ellery Queen, he is a bookish young man more interested in first editions than in murder. He owes a great deal to the mannerisms of Philo Vance. But he changes over the years, perhaps more than any other character in a long series of novels. He changes with the times, and although his age seems to remain about the same, he becomes a much more modern, contemporary man, abandoning his walking stick and pince-nez. In an early novel Ellery remarks that he is 'practically sexless,' but in later books he seems to be more aware of women's physical attributes. Julian Symons has speculated that the later Ellery seems almost like a different person, perhaps a younger brother of the original.

But if the true character of Ellery Queen is open to question, there can be no doubt about the puzzles he investigates and solves. The solutions are often brilliant, dazzling displays of the least-suspected-person technique at its most ambitious. The carefully reasoned deductions, consuming up to ten percent of the book in the early novels, sometimes focus on the level of liquid in a pitcher, or the dating of old love letters, or the indentations on a rug. A torn playing card can become a clue, as can the angle at which a horseman rides.

So vivid are the endings to the Queen novels that I can still remember the identity of the killer in each of them—a feat I find impossible to duplicate with any other lengthy series. Most of the first ten Queen novels contained a 'Challenge to the Reader' just prior to the final chapters, but even after the authors ceased using this device the books always carried an implicit challenge. We might dig through the clues and weigh the evidence, but it was rare indeed when the reader could anticipate an ending where the killer might be anyone—a seemingly minor character, a person believed to be dead, or even a member of the investigating team itself.

Some of the best Ellery Queen novels can be found in his middle period, during the 1940s, when he was equally adept at solving a small-town poisoning (*Calamity Town*) and tracking a big-city serial killer (*Cat of Many Tails*). It was during this period that he suffered uncharacteristic doubts about his ability, and twice arrived at a wrong solution before reaching the correct one. Multiple solutions are fairly common in the Queen canon, with at least one case presenting four of them before the real murderer is at least revealed.

For those who enjoy a good puzzle, there is no better companion than Ellery Queen. In his thirty-two book-length adventures the reader will discover one novel in which Ellery never meets the killer until the final scene, one in which the reader knows the killer's identity from page one but is still surprised, and even one in which the killer's name appears only twice in the entire novel—as its opening and closing words.

If the detective story is indeed the grandest game in the world, then Ellery Queen is its grandest player.

THE CASES OF ELLERY QUEEN, BY ELLERY QUEEN

Novels

The Roman Hat Mystery, 1929. *The French Powder Mystery*, 1930. *The Dutch Shoe Mystery*, 1931. *The Greek Coffin Mystery*, 1932. *The Egyptian Cross Mystery*, 1932. *The American Gun Mystery*, 1933. *The Siamese Twin Mystery*, 1933. *The Chinese Orange Mystery*, 1934. *The Spanish Cape Mystery*, 1935. *Halfway House*, 1936. *The Door Between*, 1937. *The Devil to Pay*, 1938. *The Four of Hearts*, 1938. *The Dragon's Teeth*, 1939. *Calamity Town*, 1942. *There Was An Old Woman*, 1943. *The Murderer is a Fox*, 1945. *Ten Days' Wonder*, 1948. *Cat of Many Tails*, 1949. *Double, Double*, 1950. *The Origin of Evil*, 1951. *The King is Dead*, 1952. *The Scarlet Letters*, 1953. *Inspector Queen's Own Case*, 1956. *The Finishing Stroke*, 1958. *And on the Eighth Day*, 1964. *The Fourth Side of the Triangle*, 1965. *A Study in Terror*, 1966. *Face to Face*, 1967. *The House of Brass* 1968. *The Last Woman in his Life*, 1970. *A Fine and Private Place*, 1971.

Short story collections

The Adventures of Ellery Queen, 1934. *The New Adventures of Ellery Queen*, 1940. *The Case Book of Ellery Queen*, 1945. *Calendar of Crime*, 1952. *QBI: Queen's Bureau of Investigation*, 1954. *Queen's Full*, 1965. *QED: Queen's Experiments in Detection*, 1968.

73
JERRY RAINE
on

Dave Robicheaux

I was sitting at the bar when the big man came in. He had black hair with a white patch above one ear. He walked over to the jukebox and put in some money. A song I faintly recognised came into the room.

'What's that song?' I asked, as he sat down one stool away from me.

'"La Jolie Blonde" by Iry Lejeune,' he said. 'My favourite.' Then he turned to the barman and ordered a 7-Up.

I sat there with my Jim Beam and listened to the music. I kept looking at the white patch in the big man's hair. He smiled at me and said, 'My friends call me Streak. They reckon I've got skunk blood in me.'

Then he told me his real name was Dave Robicheaux. He was an ex-homicide detective from the New Orleans police department. He had left the department some years ago because he was getting in too much trouble. Trouble had a habit of finding him he said, and too often the only way to end it would be with a sawed-off or a .45 automatic. Nowadays he owned a bait and boat rental business south of New Iberia, and although the life was a lot quieter, he still had to dust off his detective instincts now and then to get people out of trouble.

'I guess you could call me a part-time private eye,' he said.

We talked a little about his life before he became a cop, about his year in Vietnam when he was a hotshot lieutenant with a degree in English. He told me a few stories about his times there, and how they always came back to haunt him. Then he told me about his drinking problems and insomnia, about AA meetings and the alcoholic world where dragons and monsters frolicked. As we talked about this the Jim Beam in front of me looked less and less inviting, but I still knocked them back.

'Are you a married man Dave?' I asked. We were now on first name terms.

His eyes dropped to his 7-Up and a look of sadness fell over his face. 'Twice,' he said. I waited for him to elaborate, but a heavy silence fell between us. I cleared my throat uncomfortably.

'Any kids?' I asked.

Then he opened up, and talked about an adopted little girl called Alafair, a refugee from Central America who he'd rescued from a crashing aeroplane in the Gulf of Mexico.

'A crashing aeroplane in the Gulf of Mexico?' I said with disbelief. This man had some stories to tell and I listened as he unfolded that one too.

By the end of the evening the room was spinning and Dave said it was time to pick up Alafair from the babysitter. He shook my hand and I said it was a pleasure to have met him. He slipped a piece of paper in my top pocket and said, 'Read it when you get home.' Then he left.

I took the piece of paper from my pocket and read it there at the bar. It was an address for the local AA, with the time of the next meeting.

'Will you take a look at this?' I laughed at the barman.

He obviously knew what was on the paper already. 'Dave's always doing that,' he said. 'He's a good man.'

I'm only passing through this area,' I said, 'but maybe I'll go to this meeting first.'

'If Dave thinks you're in trouble,' the barman said, 'you usually are. He's a bit of a legend around these parts.'

I paid for my drinks and stood up to leave.

'You like to read?' the barman asked.

'Sure,' I said. 'Why?'

He reached under the bar and brought out a battered paperback. It was called "The Neon Rain." 'There have been four books written about Dave,' he said. 'They're all great. That's the first one. A good place to start.'

'You mean I've just been talking to a fictional character?' I said. How much had I been drinking?

The barman shook his head. 'I wouldn't say that exactly. Dave's real enough, that's for sure. He's just a great guy. A *great* guy.'

I went out into the night and headed for my pick-up. I put "The Neon Rain" on the dashboard and curled up on the seat to sleep. Outside it began to rain. I thought of Dave Robicheaux as the bourbon knocked me out. I'd try and make that AA meeting tomorrow. It should be interesting. If I didn't, I could always read the books.

THE CASES OF DAVE ROBICHEAUX, BY JAMES LEE BURKE
The Neon Rain, 1987. *Heaven's Prisoners*, 1988. *Black Cherry Blues*, 1989. *A Morning for Flamingoes*, 1990.

74
JERRY KENNEALY

on

Dan Roman

Fans of the hardboiled genre suffered a great loss with the untimely and unexpected death of Ed Mathis.

Mathis' Dan Roman books were described by one impressed reviewer as 'authentic western thrillers'. They were much more than that. Though Dan Roman worked the big oil towns and dusty back roads of Texas, the streets he prowled were every bit as mean as Chandler's Los Angeles, Spencer's Boston or Estleman's Detroit.

Six Dan Roman novels made it into print, and through the efforts of his wife, Bonnie, and agent, Dominick Abel, two additional manuscripts, *September Song* and *The Fifth Level*, are due out in 1991–1992.

Roman had much in common with a lot of his contemporaries: an ex-policeman, a bit of a drinking problem and difficulty in hanging onto his women.

Even when married, Roman remains a loner, a bit lost, a bit unsure of himself, but with that yard-wide streak of decency running down his back and the fire of justice burning in his belly, a belly that starts to sag a bit under the weight of bourbon, beer and Hungry Man TV dinners.

As with all well-written characters, the reader cares for Roman, worries about him. By the end of a book I felt like I had a smoker's cough and was pleading, please Dan, cut down on the Carltons, will you?

In a Dan Roman book, the bad guys were more likely to wear sweat-stained Stetsons and drive around in battered pickup trucks with rifle racks riveted to the back cab window, than in dark sedans with snub-nosed revolvers hidden in the car's head rest.

Being an ex-policeman myself, and a working private investigator, I was always impressed with Mathis' handling of the daily working of a private eye and his contacts with his police buddies. It had the certain ring of authenticity to it, much like a Joe Wambaugh police procedural does. Of course Wambaugh has all kinds of police credentials, and Lawrence Sanders, whose *Deadly Sins* series are every bit as authentic as Wambaugh's when it comes to police jargon and work habits, does not. What Sanders does have is a great writing talent and a 'rabbi' or two, some cops that are giving him the real story.

Mathis had no official police background, but somehow he got that 'taste' of how real cops talk and act. A pure case of talent rather than experience.

Mathis loved to sprinkle some local folklore in his books and his vivid descriptions of the Texas characters, animals and the landscape is fascinating. You could feel the dirt under his boots when Roman walked those trails. His description of how old buck squirrels raid nests and perform surgery on the young males to eliminate future competition in *The Burned Woman*, has changed my feelings about those cute furry creatures for all time.

What gives one writer that certain edge over other writers? The quality that makes him just that much better? I think the final test is that with the great ones: Chandler, Stout, the MacDonalds, you read the book, put it away, but not too far away, because in a year or two you'll want to read it again. Ed Mathis was that kind of writer.

THE CASES OF DAN ROMAN, BY EDWARD MATHIS

From a High Place, 1985. *Dark Streaks and Empty Places*, 1986. *Natural Prey*, 1987. *Another Path, Another Dragon*, 1988. *The Burned Woman*, 1989. *Out of the Shadow*, 1990. *September Song*, 1991. *The Fifth Level* (scheduled for 1992).

75

STEPHEN GALLAGHER

on

The Saint

P icture it.

Barmouth, West Wales, September 1965. It's cold and it's blowy and there's bugger-all to do. You're eleven years old and you're standing in the town's modest bookshop and you're holding a title that, if you buy it, is destined to become one of the landmark volumes of your life. But you don't know this for sure right now. All you know is that it costs twenty-five shillings and that's almost half of your total holiday money, and you've still got most of the fortnight to go.

The book is *The First Saint Omnibus*. If you take it, two things will happen. The first is that you'll be back before the end of the week to blow the rest of your holiday savings on its companion volume, the unsurprisingly-titled *Second Saint Omnibus*.

The other is that, roughly twenty-five years later, you'll get the chance to recall the day when asked to rate your all-time favourite detective.

There are some, of course, who would say that the Saint is a mystery hero and shouldn't really be classed as a detective at all—at least not in the classical, puzzle-solving sense. Which isn't strictly true; Charteris could write a tale of straight detection as well as anyone, as 'The Appalling Politician' and several others show . . . it's just that, for the Saint's creator as well as for the Saint's readers, the dogged pursuit of a detailed solution is only of incidental importance to the storytelling process. 'As a general rule,' Simon Templar says revealingly, 'problems in detection bore me stiff—it's so much more entertaining to commit the crime yourself . . .' A thesis which is pursued to the ultimate in 'The Impossible Crime', a locked-room murder mystery to which Templar provides his long-time adversary and occasional ally Chief Inspector Teal with a completely satisfying wrap-up, only to reveal in an aside half a page later that the entire solution is bogus. Templar himself is the culprit, and the absence from the room of a bronze Chinese dragon—a key element in the first and more elaborate explanation—is due to the fact that he was so offended by its ugliness that he slung it out of the window.

But that's typical of the character, and in the context of the story it's exactly what you'd expect of him. I think that what drew me to the Saint, and what draws me to him still, is that through him Charteris uses crime fiction to express a worldview that is both subversive and life-enhancing. Although his roots were in the Twenties and his major development took place in the Thirties, the Saint stands well apart from all those Hannayesque heroes who were firmly for the status quo; in Templar's eyes, the status quo is nothing more than fair game for a challenge. Consider Charteris' quintessential Public School Man, Junior Inspector Desmond Pryke, a character so daringly named that we can only assume the joke to have passed over everyone's heads back in 1934. It was in the Saint stories that I first saw a non-judgmental portrayal of a drug addict (in 'The Death Penalty'), and in 'The Affair of Hogsbotham' found an attack on ostentatious morality so well-worked that its liberal message is undimmed today.

But don't misunderstand me. For all his apparent lack of scruples Templar is actually one of the most moral characters in popular fiction, applying a rigorous personal code of fairness and justice that owes nothing to the conventional standards of the day; all of this conveyed in the kind of effortless prose that is the sure mark of a writer who works twice as hard as the one who draws praise for his or her style, which is usually only apparent because instead of being integral it sits on top of the story like an unsuitable hat.

Independent of his time, the early Saint has barely dated at all. The old George Sanders movies captured nothing of the character's spirit and recent attempts to revive his TV success have failed badly by turning him into a lightweight and conventional thriller hero; even worse, there are now Saint stories by other hands—adaptations of scripts, and with none of the wit or magic of the originals.

But go to the source. You're there, in the seaside bookshop.

So, what do you do?

THE CASES OF THE SAINT, BY LESLIE CHARTERIS

Novels

Meet the Tiger, 1928. *The Last Hero*, 1930. *Enter The Saint*, 1930. *Knight Templar*, 1930. *Featuring The Saint*, 1931. *Alias The Saint*,

1931. *She was a Lady*, 1931. *The Holy Terror*, 1932. *Getaway*, 1932. *Once More The Saint*, 1933. *The Misfortunes of Mr Teal*, 1934. *The Saint Goes On*, 1934. *The Saint in New York*, 1935. *The Saint Overboard*, 1936. *The Ace of Knaves*, 1937. *Thieves' Picnic*, 1937. *Prelude for War*, 1938. *Follow The Saint*, 1938. *The Saint in Miami*, 1940. *The Saint Goes West*, 1942. *The Saint Steps In*, 1943. *The Saint on Guard*, 1944. *The Saint Sees It Through*, 1946. *Call for The Saint*; 1948. *Vendetta for The Saint*, 1964. *The Saint in Pursuit*, 1970.

There are several other novels featuring the Saint, by other hands, adapting TV episodes, although in many cases the novels were overseen by Leslie Charteris.

Story collections

The Brighter Buccaneer, 1933. *Boodle*, 1934. *The Happy Highwayman*, 1939. *The Saint at Large*, 1943. *Saint Errant*, 1948. *The Saint in Europe*, 1953. *The Saint on the Spanish Main*, 1955. *The Saint around the World*, 1956. *Thanks to the Saint*, 1957. *Senior Saint*, 1958. *Concerning The Saint*, 1958. *The Saint to the Rescue*, 1959. *Trust The Saint*, 1962. *The Saint in the Sun*, 1963. *The Fantastic Saint*, 1982.

76

LESLEY GRANT-ADAMSON

on

Rebecca Schwartz

Favourites come and favourites go, outpaced, outsmarted, out of date. My new pet is Rebecca Schwartz, budding lawyer from Marin county, nice Jewish girl with an office across the bridge and the whole of San Francisco to play with. She's intelligent, loving, courageous, female. No grim 'exercise in role reversal', no masculine hero in drag.

Julie Smith—a slight, bright red-head with a trace of South Carolina in her accent, in other words distinctly not Rebecca Schwartz—spills out the stories with that fizzing energy American writers have on tap. But in her case it's allied to keen plotting and good writing. Try her in *Tourist Trap*, thrill for yourself.

Julie likes to talk about sending Rebecca into mean rooms, a way of saying that women writers deal with the serious pain in life, the kind you can't leave behind when you go home after adventures on the streets because the pain is too deep, too personal.

Detective fiction suffers from the glance over the shoulder, the fallacious notion that the best is long past. I saw Julie Smith once on a public platform, shouldered aside by (male) panellists who wanted to tell the world about Hammett and Chandler. Julie got in that the important thing in US crime fiction *right now* is the rise of the female writer and the female detective. Emulating their heroes, those guys zapped the lady, shut her mouth. So I'll say it for her. The major development in US crime fiction is the success of the female crime writer and the female sleuth. It's taken time for them to catch up with British crime writing (and when hasn't it?) but now women detectives feature in nationwide best seller lists and blossom in all their variety, from man-apers to man-haters, to credible creatures like Rebecca.

Julie Smith's art is in dodging the stereotype, ducking the cliché, springing the surprise that even in San Francisco is surprising. Her Rebecca stories have it all: courtroom drama that makes the *San Francisco Chronicle* cry: 'Worthy of Perry Mason'; a journalist man in Rebecca's life that allows Julie (a former reporter) to send her sleuthing on that level as well as the lawyerly one; a setting in the most amusing, frightening, anything-is-possible city in the world.

In *Tourist Trap* she's pitched against a crazy man who means to destroy the city's economy by fear. A man is crucified, her client is framed, a cable car plunges, diners are poisoned, tourists flee and locals stay indoors. Down those anxious streets goes Rebecca Schwartz who's as scared as the next woman. Too easy, given the drama that is San Francisco, to go for the big scale 'city held to ransom by madman' ending. Julie Smith shapes it otherwise, leads Rebecca to one of those mean rooms where she confronts a basic truth, a fundamental human frailty. Which is what good novelists of every genre and none have always done.

The next time Rebecca's creator wants to say a word for modern women's crimewriting, I hope they let her. But even if they don't, the Rebecca Schwartz stories speak . . . er . . . volumes.

THE CASES OF REBECCA SCHWARTZ, BY JULIE SMITH

Death Turns a Trick, 1982. *The Sourdough Wars*, 1984. *Tourist Trap*, 1986.

77

BARBARA MERTZ, BARBARA MICHAELS & ELIZABETH PETERS

on

Peter Shandy

Few fictional sleuths have had such an insanely brilliant début as Peter Shandy. To avenge himself on neighbors complaining of his lack of Yuletide spirit he sets up: eight life-sized reindeer, sixteen Santa Claus faces, sixteen sets of red and purple artifical candles, several dozen strings of orange, green and blue lights, and a couple of amplifiers endlessly blaring out such Christmas classics as 'I Don't Care Who You Are, Fatty, Get Those Reindeer Off my Roof.' Then he puts the whole thing on automatic timer and leaves town.

Peter's criminous career begins when he skulks back home to find the body of a neighbor who has presumably fallen to her death while trying to remove some of the obnoxious decorations. That's what the town cop presumes; thanks to his incurable habit of counting things, Peter knows better. At the end of *Rest You Merry*, the first book in the series featuring him and his entourage, he has not only caught a pair of murderers but found time to acquire a wife.

Peter is fifty-six years old when he woos and wins his Helen, a petite 'forty-ish' librarian; and what a joy it is to encounter a hero whose intelligence, amiability, energy and good humour render his age as irrelevant to the reader as it is to Peter himself. He is the best kind of sleuth—i.e., amateur. By profession he is an agronomist, codeveloper of the most famous rutabaga in fiction, and a professor at Balaclava Agricultural College, one of the most remarkable institutions of higher learning in or out of fiction.

The college and the county in which it is located are inhabited by a collection of characters Dickensian in the vivacity of their eccentricities, against whom Peter's affable, low-keyed normality stands out in delightful contrast. After coping with people like college president Thorkjeld Svenson, who only rips doors off their hinges when he is seriously annoyed, Cronkite Swope, star reporter of the local paper (whose brothers are of course named Brinkley and Huntley), and various relatives of Balaclava Buggins, founder of the college, Peter is unfazed by the giants and wizards of Welsh mythology whom he encounters in his most unusual adventure, *The Case of the Giant Hogweed*.

Peter needs all his agricultural expertise to solve the mysteries that plague the college and its environs, for Balaclava County killers employ decidedly unusual murder weapons—quicklime substituted for the harmless variety, a lethal manure pile, a soap factory purportedly set ablaze by a shot fired from an antique cannon. Sometimes it is Peter's wife Helen who supplies a vital clue through her knowledge of county genealogy or rare books. In a sense Peter and Helen are a detective team, though they don't conform to the old-fashioned model of a brilliant husband and a nitwitted wife who is constantly in need of rescue from villains and her own stupidity. Helen is no nit-wit and despite her diminutive size she is quite capable of leaping onto a mammoth draft horse and riding it to the rescue of others.

Why is Peter so dear to me and countless other readers? For one thing, he's a darned good detective. The suspects may be fantastic, but the clues are not, and Peter's solutions to his cases demonstrate both logic and good old Yankee common sense. For another, Peter is—simply—a very nice guy. He cares about people. He's the sort of person you'd love to have for a neighbor. So far the Shandy saga consists of eight books. One can only hope that the cat continues to drag in new cases, the luck never runs out, and Peter Shandy stays fifty-six (but who's counting?) forever.

THE CASES OF PETER SHANDY, BY CHARLOTTE MACLEOD

Rest you Merry, 1978. *The Luck Runs Out*, 1979. *Wrack and Rune*, 1982. *Something the Cat Dragged In*, 1983. *The Curse of the Giant*

Hogweed, 1985. *The Corpse in Oozak's Pond*, 1987. *Vane Pursuit*, 1989. *An Owl Too Many*, 1991.

78, 79
DUNCAN TORRENS
on
Roger Sheringham & Anthony Gethryn

Tape 1
Note to D. Torrens:
Hope this is OK; lots of background noise of eating and drinking. All spellings phonetic. Usual fee for transcribing.

Diane

DUNCAN TORRENS: Good afternoon, Colonel Gethryn, it was good of you to spare the time to talk to me.
ANTHONY GETHRYN: Glad to be needed, my boy. Not much call for old buffers like me these days.
DT: I wanted to talk about one of your contemporaries, Roger Sheringham, if you don't mind.
AG: Certainly, I remember him, the young whippersnapper. He appeared the year after I did, that'd be 1925, in connection with the Layton Court affair. Bit of a prig at the time, I thought, and damned disorganised. No military training, you see.
DT: Whereas you, Colonel, were, what—thirty-eight? before your first case?
AG: First one that chappie MacDonald wrote about, that is, yes. He called it *The Rasp*—a bit limp, I thought, but it did well enough. That would be '28 and Sheringham appeared the next year. But I outlived him in the end, going on until 1959 with that curious affair of Adrian Messenger. Sheringham seemed to pack it in in the Forties. May be he got some war work, like I did in the first show.

DT: You were an undercover agent in Germany in 1915 I believe . . .

AG: Yes, but even now I'm not supposed to talk about it.

DT: So that would make you . . . 73? . . . by the time of your last case?

AG: Well? What of it?

DT: No offence meant, Colonel. Now, Sheringham and yourself were contemporaries during, let's say, the late Twenties and early Thirties. Didn't you feel somewhat in the shadow of the others from the so-called Golden Age?

AG: You mean the little Belgian chappie, I suppose? He was older than I was! And then there was Lord Whatsit—at least he had the sense to retire; get out while the going was good. Never could stand that policeman who dabbled in poetry and theatricals either. Funny chap, spoke with a New Zealand accent, sort of a cultured Australian if you can imagine such a thing.

DT: And there was Albert Campion . . .

AG: Now I had a soft spot for him, because of the Royal connection, though we don't talk about that either. He was closer to Sheringham, though, always putting himself down and making light of things. I was much more thick-eared, that was my trouble. What you'd call hardboiled these days I suppose. Makes one sound like an egg, doesn't it?

DT: But with all this competition, don't you feel cheated that you never got the recognition you deserved? Both of you?

AG: Well, I can't speak for Sheringham, but yes, it's true, we were handicapped by having men do our writing for us. My chappie, MacDonald, went off to Hollywood and did very nicely thank you. Sheringham's bloke—Berkeley was it?—did a bit of journalism and went on to write some psychological stuff. I was always one for the direct approach—a bit of action.

DT: Both you and Sheringham dabbled, as you put it, in journalism yourself.

AG: True enough. I helped start up a little paper called The Owl and Sheringham worked for that rag The Daily Courier. That got him one of his cases, you know, the one with the silk stockings tied like this. . . .

DT: I think it best not to exert yourself, sir. Now you both solved a string of cases . . .

AG: I did more than he did!

DT: Well, I have notes on ten successful Sheringham. . . .

AG: May be, but the man kept getting things wrong, dammit. Look at the Stratton case. *Jumping Jenny* they called it. Messing about with the evidence, lying to the police . . .

DT: Some would say he had a streak of humanity and preferred justice to the letter of the law . . .

AG: Stuff and nonsense. The boy was inept!

DT: The boy was actually only five years your junior, sir, and he won the DSO during the First World War.

AG: So did I!

DT: Of course, sir, please calm down. All I meant was . . .

AG: The trouble with Sheringham was that he thought everything looked better after five or six pints of beer! Sort it all out down the pub was his method. Sometimes you had to crack heads, especially if you were dealing with the sort of mass murderer I had to face. Sheringham had it easy in comparison, you know.

DT: I'm sure, Colonel, please sit down.

AG: If you don't believe me, look at the case which everyone remembers, that affair with the poisoned chocolates. He called in all those old fuddy-duddies in the Crime Circle and they still couldn't sort it out. God knows why he wanted to form the blasted Crime Circle anyway. Not as if there weren't decent clubs about at the time. They probably wouldn't have him and his cronies, though.

DT: But surely *The Poisoned Chocolates Case* is a classic?

AG: Only from the way that fellow Berkeley—or was it Cox?— wrote it up.

DT: Sixty years on, it is still remembered . . .

AG: Because they couldn't fathom it out! That's why!

DT: But surely. . . . Please, Colonel, do not over-excite yourself.

AG: Don't patronise me, Mr Torrens, whoever you are. I'm old enough to be your grandfather.

DT: Great-grandfather, actually. But please . . .

AG: Good God, man, the chocolates case is dead simple.

DT: You mean. . . .?

AG: Of course. A half-wit could have guessed it!

DT: Colonel, please sit down . . . Don't try to do that . . .

AG: If you . . . just look at . . . (-?-) . . . the evidence . . . (Sound of breaking glass.)

DT: Colonel Gethryn. . .!

AG: . . . it could only have been . . . aaaaghh (?- spelling? Diane)

DT: Help! Get an ambulance! Is there a doctor in the club?

Unidentified Voice: What have you done to Colonel Gethryn? My God! Get the police!

DT: No, wait, you don't understand. . . .

(More breaking glass. Siren. Tape ends.)

P.S. Any chance of cash payment for this one?—Diane.

THE CASES OF ROGER SHERINGHAM, BY ANTHONY BERKELEY

The Layton Court Mystery, 1925. *The Wychford Poisoning Case*, 1926. *Roger Sheringham and the Vane Mystery*, 1927. *The Silk Stocking Murders*, 1928. *The Poisoned Chocolates Case*, 1929. *The Second Short*, 1930. *Top Storey Murder*, 1931. *Murder in the Basement*, 1932. *Jumping Jenny*, 1933. *Panic Party*, 1934.

Uncollected stories

'The Avenging Chance', 1930. 'Perfect Alibi', 1930. 'Mr Simpson Goes to the Dogs', 1934. 'White Butterfly', 1936. 'The Wrong Jar', 1940. 'Mr Bearstowe Says . . ', 1943.

THE CASES OF ANTHONY GETHRYN, BY PHILIP MACDONALD

The Rasp, 1928. *The White Crow*, 1928. *The Noose*, 1930. *The Link*, 1930. *Persons Unknown*, 1931. *The Wraith*, 1931. *The Choice*, 1931. *The Crime Conductor*, 1931. *Rope to Spare*, 1932. *Death on My Left*, 1933. *The Nursemaid Who Disappeared*, 1938. *The List of Adrian Messenger*, 1959.

short story

The-Wood-for-the-Trees, 1952.

80

ADAM BARNETT-FOSTER

on

Isaac Sidel

A h, Isaac. You still have that worm in your gut, don't you? It's your stigmata, the mirror image of your secret sins.

It's been there, gnawing away at your insides since you betrayed your surrogate son Manfred Coen, he of the blue eyes for sleeping with your mad, uncontrollable daughter Marilyn the Wild. The Peruvians put it there in you while you were working undercover to bust their gang and it has remained ever since, the image of your guilt, even though you ascended the throne of Police Commissioner in the sprawling, Balzac-like New York of Jerome Charyn.

Charyn's quartet featuring your often sad adventures is now a quintet, with at least one more volume to come, and you stand alone in the pantheon of crime investigators, lonely, without friends, without family, sometimes too close for comfort with those tenuous forces of evil you are paid to keep in check.

Your New York is a bit like the old Brooklyn where Jews, Irish and mulattos of every colour combination mingled on either side of an ill-defined sense of justice where the law would bend amiably in all the necessary directions.

You gradually took over the books, didn't you? The first one, *Blue Eyes*, wasn't really about you but concentrated on Manfred Coen, the blue-eyed detective, who was an amalgam of two brown-eyed kids, Jerome and his older brother Harvey Charyn, a Brooklyn policeman. Coen was a ping pong freak, a 'wanderer in Manhattan and the Bronx who dreamt of corpses'. You, Isaac Sidel, were only his mentor, a honcho in the First Deputy Police Commissioner's office who would later get Coen killed. He was your blue-eyed angel, poor Manfred, he dished the dirt so you could keep clean in your eternal war against the Guzmanns, the Marrano pickpockets, the renegades of your own Jewish tribe.

In *Marilyn the Wild*, which preceded Coen's death, we found out more about you and that daughter you couldn't control, who keeps on getting married and unmarried and loves Coen. You hate what you did to them although you did gain a painful victory against the Guzmanns. Or did you? You now have that tapeworm in your guts and in *The Education of Patrick Silver*, you wander through the city trying to assuage your all-consuming guilt, dreaming that Coen is still alive, the son you had always wanted, so you adopted another lost soul to wield your vengeful sword, a giant Irishman, thrown out of the police force, who never wears shoes, even in winter. He's just another pawn in the war between you and the Peruvian pimps.

In *Secret Isaac* you have finally triumphed, but the scars on a whore's cheeks send you on a desperate trip to the Dublin of James Joyce as the worm in your stomach tightens its grip on your tortured soul ever stronger. This was after the fall from grace, but ironically you are now Police Commissioner of New York, king of the hill, without a kingdom.

And we thought that was it. Charyn had left you in limbo, almost forgiven you, granted you some redemption, some piece of mind.

Then, twelve years later, you're back with *The Good Policeman* adopting criminal orphans and getting horribly mixed up with the political battles of New York, that other secret war between the Jews and the Irish police mafia. You're even sent to jail, but as usual it's all a pretence, another passage through purgatory on your way towards the inevitable, hollow triumph that police procedurals demand.

Isaac, your city of New York is an urban jungle that bears little resemblance to the New York I know, it's a soul country that is baroque, teeming with all sorts of bizarre characters and emotions given free rein, a magic, unruly country, a distorted, wonderful vision of, say, an 87th Precinct on acid or a Hill Street populated by survivors of the concentration camps.

But who cares about reality, Isaac? The artifice of your wonderful world is a sobering tonic which injects an energetic brew into the often arid landscape of contemporary crime and mystery fiction.

Give me your nightmares any time.

THE CASES OF ISAAC SIDEL, BY JEROME CHARYN

Blue Eyes, 1974. *Marilyn the Wild*, 1976. *The Education of Patrick Silver*, 1976. *Secret Isaac*, 1978. *The Good Policeman*, 1990.

81

MARCEL BERLINS

on

Professor Hilary Tamar

I finished *Thus was Adonis Murdered* with the satisfaction and pleasure of having discovered a lustrous and original talent; little did I know, as the formula obliges me to say, that I was on the verge on entering a puzzle so wickedly complex, so delicately provocative, that it has not been resolved to this day. My first inkling of the coming torment came when I was idly discussing the merits of *Adonis* with a friend who had just finished it. What I particularly liked about the book's narrator, I remarked, was the way he . . . I was never to finish that sentence. 'What do you mean, he?', my companion interrupted. 'You mean she.' I pointed out that I was referring to Professor Hilary Tamar, the Oxford don who tells the tale and solved the mystery. 'So am I' said my friend. 'She's a woman.' That evening, ten pounds wagered, I re-read *Adonis* for what I thought would be the easy task of finding a reference to Tamar's maleness.

Seven years, two further books (*The Shortest Way to Hades*; *The Sirens Sang of Murder*), and countless conversations later, I have yet to discover that elusive clue that will settle, once and for all, Hilary Tamar's sex. I have, of course, asked Sarah Caudwell, the professor's creator; she smiles enigmatically. Bribes, threats and attempted blackmail have not worked either. Caudwell laughs and claims that she doesn't know the answer either.

Perhaps, I thought at the beginning of my quest, Tamar followed the sex of the reader, men regarding him as male, women believing her to be female. But no. I have encountered every sexual per-mutation, and none is more prominent than any other. What other indications are there? The name Hilary is, statistically, more common among women than men; but on the other hand, a law professor is realistically more likely to be male than female. The surface facts cancel each other out.

We are left with one avenue of exploration—an analysis of the psychology and personality of the individual. Tamar, when at Oxford, is perpetually engaged in preparing a great work on a matter of exceptionally obscure legal history; in London, the professor is accustomed to meeting four young friends—two men, two women—all at the Chancery Bar, who have a habit of finding themselves in compromising circumstances, usually involving several unexplained deaths.

Surely, I thought, the narrator will, over a total of some 750-odd pages, leave some sexual signposts in the descriptions of, and attitudes to, the mixed foursome at the centre of the books' adventures. Not a bit of it. Just as I was persuading myself that the warmth and affection of Hilary's description of Julia's physical virtues had to denote a writer of the opposite sex to the objects of praise, there would, a few pages later, be an equally passionate assessment of the beauty of Ragwort. I am not oblivious, either, to the possibility that the professor's tastes may be devoted more to members of the same sex than to the other; but which is Hilary?

Tamar provides few personal details; those that are occasionally scattered offer little help. The liking of claret, grilled dover sole and cats (even to the extent of happily looking after other people's), a slight knowledge of tennis players—these are attributes of utmost sexual neutrality. We are reduced to sterotypical generalisations: 'No woman would speak in such a mannered, pedantic and old-fashioned way'. Ah, but 'no man would notice so many physical and emotional details'.

Sarah Caudwell's fellow crime writers, accustomed as they are to detection, have been of no assistance. A 1990 survey of their own favourite fictional detectives was divided into male and female. Hilary Tamar appeared on neither list. There was, however, a third option, the crime writers' 'favourite androgynous detective'. There was only one name, the winner and sole candidate.

THE CASES OF HILARY TAMAR, BY SARAH CAUDWELL
Thus Was Adonis Murdered, 1981. *The Shortest Way to Hades*, 1984. *The Sirens Sang of Murder*, 1989.

82

B.J. RAHN

on

Miss Silver

Knitting and gossiping in country houses while elucidating baffling murders, Patricia Wentworth's Miss Maud Hepzibah Silver is the epitome of the armchair detective. She was one of a group of redoubtable old lady sleuths to appear during the Golden Age. She made her debut in *Grey Mask* and was featured in over thirty novels between 1928 and 1961. She is a private enquiry agent rather than a gifted amateur detective but is nonetheless eccentric.

Miss Silver is described in *Latter End* as a composite portrait of a Victorian governess, and in *Poison in the Pen* the narrator states:

> . . . she was the perfect survival of a type now almost extinct. She might have stepped out of any family album to be immediately recognized as a spinster relative of slender means but indomitable character, or at a second view as the invaluable governess whose pupils, doing her credit in after life, would never forget what they owed to her ministrations.

Miss Silver really was engaged for twenty years in 'the scholastic profession' and fully expected to spend her life living in other people's houses until forced to retire on her necessarily meager savings. But a fortunate turn of events enabled her to enter her present profession and to acquire a home of her own and a devoted housekeeper, Hannah Meadows. Miss Silver is proud of her flat and grateful for its comforts.

Miss Silver takes her second career very seriously and sees herself as a servant of Justice and the Law. But despite her devotion to her profession, Miss Silver would never refer to herself as a private detective. 'She remained a gentlewoman, and she found the word repugnant to a gentlewoman's feelings'. On her card appear only her name and address and the words, 'Private Enquiries.' However, her personal code alters according to her role. As a private gentlewoman she would never listen to other people's conversations or trespass on private property, but as a private enquiry agent she does both.

Although she operates in the private sector, Miss Silver frequently works with the police. And indeed owing to her physical limitations and lack of official status, Miss Silver must often rely on the police to arrest the villain at the end of a case. Scotland Yard's Chief Inspector Lamb and Inspector Frank Abbott sometimes request her services or refer people to her, but usually her clients hear of her from grateful friends whom she has helped. Miss Silver accepts cases on the understanding that she cannot undertake to prove anyone either innocent or guilty but merely endeavor to find the truth.

Miss Silver's invincible investigative method combines keen observation of details with painstaking garnering of facts, intuitive insight into character, and analysis of human behavior to arrive at the solution to the mystery. Her sensitivity to innocence and delicate feelings as well as her awareness of human depravity lead her to an accurate assessment of people's motives. '. . . as far as she is concerned the human race is glass-fronted. She looks right through the shop-window into the back premises and detects the skeleton in the cupboard'. Having identified the culprit, she pieces together the minutiae of daily life to establish means and opportunity. Murder in Wentworth's novels is usually a personal, if not always domestic, crime.

Miss Silver works under cover. Her ability to elicit information while trading knitting patterns or helping with some domestic chore often leads her to the solution of the crime far ahead of Scotland Yard. Chief Inspector Lamb and Inspector Abbott always claim she has an unfair advantage because she can ingratiate herself where the police never could and because she can use methods they durst not. Winning confidences by a calm, kind, patient attitude augmented by perceptive remarks, incisive questions, and the occasional hortatory cough, Miss Silver establishes an aura of order and security which reminds people of the comfort of the nursery and encourages them to relax and trust her.

Never without her brightly flowered chintz knitting bag—one with a pattern of honeysuckle and humming-birds was a particular favorite—Miss Silver knits an unending series of garments for her niece Ethel's children. Because she holds her knitting in the continental style, low in her lap, Miss Silver is able to observe unobtrusively a great deal of what goes on around her. Her knitting is used deliberately to create a homely, non-threatening image which will encourage both the innocent and guilty to lose their reticence and to say a great deal more than they intended.

Miss Silver's dowdy appearance is part of her professional technique. She is quaint. By definition, that which is quaint is not intimidating. Quaintness inspires confidence and a patronizing attitude in the beholder.

> If Miss Silver's own garments were quite incredibly out of date, it was because she liked them that way and had discovered that an old-fashioned and governessy appearance was a decided asset in the profession which she had adopted. To be considered negligible may be the means of acquiring the kind of information which only becomes available when people are off their guard.

Physically, Miss Silver is a rather diminutive woman with small competent hands, trim ankles, and little feet. Her countenance seems to be rather nondescript and colourless. '. . . the small neat features, the rather pale smooth skin, washed twice a day with soap and water, belonged to a period when a lady did not use make-up and even powder was considered "fast"'. Her eyes, described as small and greyish hazel in colour, are perhaps her most remarkable feature, for she is capable of darting gimlet glances of electrifying intelligence. Her smile is reported as charming and able to inspire confidence. Her voice is ladylike and refined.

Miss Silver's distinctive mannerisms, such as her habit of pursing her lips and her genteel, prim cough—which she uses to punctuate remarks, to express disapproval, and to encourage people to speak—reveal a polite but assertive character. She uses old-fashioned expressions such as, 'Pray be seated.'

Miss Silver also has a habit of quoting passages from the Bible and from the poetry of Alfred, Lord Tennyson. Frank Abbott refers to these apothegms as 'Maudie's moralities'. Among her favorite maxims is: 'Trust me all in all, or not at all.' Another explains a great deal of human perfidy: 'The lust of gain in the heart of Cain.' According to Abbott, Miss Silver lives by a simple code: 'Love God, honour the Queen; keep the law; be kind, be good; think of others before you think of yourself; serve Justice; speak the truth'.

He speaks for all of her devoted admirers when he sums up her character: 'Maudie, so practical, so resolute, so intelligent, so inflexible in her morality, so kindly, and so prim—in all these aspects she delighted him'.

THE CASES OF MISS SILVER, BY PATRICIA WENTWORTH

Grey Mask, 1928. *The Case is Closed*, 1937. *Lonesome Road*, 1939. *In the Balance*, 1941. *The Chinese Shawl*, 1943. *Miss Silver Deals with Death*, 1943. *The Clock Strikes Twelve*, 1944. *The Key*, 1944. *She Came Back*, 1955. *Pilgrim's Rest*, 1946. *Latter End*, 1947. *Wicked End*, 1947. *Eternity Ring*, 1947. *The Case of William Smith*, 1948. *Miss Silver Comes to Stay*, 1949. *The Catherine Wheel*, 1949. *The Brading Collection*, 1950. *Through the Wall*, 1950. *The Ivory Dagger*, 1951. *Anna, Where are You?*, 1951. *The Watersplash*, 1951. *Ladies' Bane*, 1952. *Out of the Past*, 1953. *Vanishing Point*, 1953. *The Silent Pool*, 1954. *The Benevent Treasure*, 1954. *Poison in the Pen*, 1955. *The Listening Eye*, 1955. *The Gazebo*, 1956. *The Fingerprint*, 1956. *The Alington Inheritance*, 1958. *The Girl in the Cellar*, 1961.

83

ROBERT WALLACE

on

George Smiley

When I first came across George the striking thing wasn't so much the incongruity of his match with Lady Ann Sercombe but rather that he should have taken a wife at all. What on earth could he have been thinking about? I mean, he wasn't the type. A man who'd return to an empty flat, listen to Mahler! Stravinsky perhaps, or even any of the swag of classical composers, but not Mahler, surely. Hopelessly romantic. No woman should marry a man and then make him pretend to enjoy, was it the Fourth Symphony with that soprano yodelling? For Anne to listen to Mahler was another thing altogether; she liked racing drivers, young ballet dancers (the Welsh Apollo!).

You see, the thing about George—it was years before I came to think of him as Smiley, Mr Smiley never—the thing was he didn't have the faintest idea about himself, of what made him tick. Decency, as a quality, he had some vague claim to decency, but just like the rest of us, with George it only went so deep, and beneath there was the familiar abyss of human consciousness. Contrast James Bond, one layer to his mind and often as not I'll bet a body in desperate need of a course of penicillin. A happy man, James, an Aston Martin with which to share memories in old age. But George, can anybody recall a moment when it might truly be said that George was happy? Once, at a dinner in Canberra, I sat next to a man from the British High Commission. Conventional type, pissy way of spooning his soup. Well, he said he thought George's world was too Tudor. His expression. I suppose when one thinks of all that red brickwork there might be something in the Tudor remark. But I gather the chap was referring to back stabbing, nasty games, long shadows. George inhabited such a world, yes, but was it really his own? Surely nobody could accuse George of participating at that level. Or could they?

I mean, if he wasn't reading Grimmelshausen, he seemed to be regretting . . . life. That's it, living in a past which never was. And half of him dreaming of a cultural existence on the other side of the East/West divide because, I expect, of this fix on seventeenth-century German poets.

Consider when it was put to George in the late Twenties that he entertain the idea of being a spook, how readily he acquiesced. Why! What kind of a man does that make him? Trading a chance to pursue his interest in German literature for treachery; a fatal decision, with something dreadful in it. That's a George quality, bad judgement, which makes him all too human.

The absurdity of buying Anne presents like Grimmelshausen's *Simplicissimus*. Grimmelshausen, man of action, the antithesis of George. Nothing diffident about the German writer, and show him a woman, he'd go for her. The way other men went for Anne.

The point being that George did all these things to himself. Case in point: his career with the Circus. He'd either be in forced retirement, on the outer, or more or less running the joint during a rundown phase. But always a problem with his status. You'd have to describe his as an unrewarding life, particularly ideologically; his way out was to be loyal to the networks, the joes, those people taking risks, but not so loyal to the ideologies. Because beyond 'decency' all ideologies may be illusory? George Smiley, the just man struggling to render himself sufficiently partisan for action? George Smiley, peering at the world, attempting to make some sense of what he sees. Not that you could call him slow, hardly, but so much of his mind seemed to want not to know, not to participate either. Thus talking to Connie, say, and her leading him through the past, connecting things, so that he might comprehend, accept, what part of him already knew to be the case.

But George didn't want to know, did he? Yet had to in the end.

Perhaps it's all to do with Grimmelshausen. I mean, a man of action, a boastful swashbuckling old fart, Grimmelshausen. George's mind full of silly stuff like that.

And so terribly innocent, a boy, George, no more than a boy, bumping into things in this adult world. Heavens above, the model of any one of us: a dangerous creature capable of killing his friend (in George's case, Dieter Frey), then indulging in the luxury of regret.

THE CASES OF GEORGE SMILEY, BY JOHN LE CARRÉ

Call for the Dead, 1961. *A Murder of Quality*, 1962. *The Spy Who Came in from the Cold*, 1963. *Tinker, Tailor, Soldier, Spy*, 1974. *The Honourable Schoolboy*, 1977. *Smiley's People*, 1980. *The Secret Pilgrim*, 1991.

84

KIM NEWMAN

on

Dudley Smith

On page 100 of *Clandestine*, an *à clef* account of the 1958 murder of author James Ellroy's own mother, we are first introduced to Lieutenant Dudley Smith, the *éminence grise* who will come to haunt all Ellroy's subsequent works: 'A fearsome personage and legendary cop who had killed five men in the line of duty. Irish-born and Los Angeles-raised, he still clung tenaciously to his high-pitched, musical brogue, which was as finely tuned as a Stradivarius . . . He was over six feet tall and broad as a ceiling beam. He was an immense brownness—brown hair cut close, small brown eyes, and always dressed in a baggy brown vested suit . . . a huge ego who was adept at changing roles at the drop of a hat, yet who always managed to impart purity of personality to the part he was currently playing.'

A minor player in the tangle of *Clandestine*—a tangled skein of cases that, in true Chandler fashion, turn out to be one case—Smith, with his folksy stories about daughters and his habit of 'adopting' promising young cops, still made an impact, and the ripples of that impact have been felt ever since. Ellroy followed *Clandestine* with *The Black Dahlia*, the first of his major series of period-set L.A. crime novels, extrapolating from a real case and a lot of real people into a nightmare vision of American crime and society. A typical passage, giving some of the unique Ellroy sleaze flavour, reads: 'DeWitt hit the floor, then crawled over to the commode and vomited into it. When he tried to get himself upright, Fritzie pushed his head back into the bowl and held it there with a big spit-shined wing-tip brogue. The ex-bank robber-pimp drank piss water and puke.' Dudley Smith fails to appear in *The Black Dahlia*. Ellroy explains, 'You'll recall that in *Clandestine* I have Dudley Smith talk about the Black Dahlia case, and hanging up the suspects in the meat locker, but in *The Black Dahlia* I have Fritz Vogel do that. The reason for that is the novel *True Confessions*, by John Gregory Dunne, also about the Black Dahlia case. There's so much Irishness in *True Confessions* that I didn't want a character so outrageously Irish as Dudley Smith to be in *The Black Dahlia*, which was wrong. I made a mistake. The whole quartet would have been more homogeneous if Dudley Smith had been in *The Black Dahlia*.'

However, Smith did return, more potent and sinisterly amiable than ever, in *The Big Nowhere* and *L.A. Confidential*, the thematic successors to *The Black Dahlia*, and Ellroy's forthcoming-as-this-piece-is-written *White Jazz* is also due to feature him. It is in his latest appearances that Smith, 'the Dudster' as he is sometimes tagged by scandal magazines, expands to become a fully nightmarish figure. Involved in the investigations of several major homicides, pulling the strings of his apprentices and skilfully playing department politics, it gradually becomes obvious that Smith is also implicated in several major homicides. Indeed, the shocking first chapter of *L.A. Confidential* finds Smith assassinating, on behalf of historical mobster Mickey Cohen, Buzz Meeks, the sole survivor of the trio of investigators who appear in *The Big Nowhere*. Mixed up in organised crime and possessed of all manner of prejudices, Smith goes beyond the now stock figure of the corrupt top cop simply because—like all Ellroy's most potent heroes and villains—he is a genius. If he has a precedent, it is Hank Quinlan, the similarly gross, similarly Irish, similarly beyond-the-pale cop played by Orson Welles in *Touch of Evil*, but Dudley Smith is under control in a way that Quinlan is not, and the scary thing about him is that, despite everything, he is the only happy person in Ellroy's tormented universe of golf, sleaze, neon, horror, corruption and death.

So far beyond matters of law and order or good and evil that he sometimes seems like an alien, Dudley Smith strides through Ellroy's Los Angeles as its secret king, doing favours for gangsters and politicians and sometimes even deigning to shove an investigation towards a legitimate (although always advantageous to Dudley) solution. A monster and a tyrant, Smith is still worthy of inclusion in this pantheon of Great Detectives, and his motives are as pure and mysterious as the most altruistic of Holmesian busybodies. By the end of *L.A. Confidential*, Smith is a Captain of Detectives, but he seems to have forged the instrument of his own destruction in Ed Exley, newly promoted to Chief of Detectives and another sole survivor, an ambitious and complex cop who, through a painful process of deduction and the absorbing of the more direct skills of his partial döppelganger Bud White, has seen the true face of Dudley Smith and is sworn to bring him down. I asked Ellroy if this meant that *White Jazz* would see the end of the Dudster? His creator replied 'I think he's always there. I love him. Never underestimate Dudley Smith. He's smarter than everybody else.'

THE CASES OF DUDLEY SMITH, BY JAMES ELLROY

Clandestine, 1982. *The Big Nowhere*, 1988. *L.A. Confidential*, 1990. *White Jazz*, 1991.

85

JACK ADRIAN

on

The Sooper

B ut why the Sooper? Why Superintendent Patrick J. Minter (who only ever featured in a single novel, one novella and eight short stories) and not the far more celebrated, and *Queen's-Quorum*ised, J.G. Reeder, say, or the Four Just Men, or even Sanders of the River (for Sanders too is a detective, more or less)?

His offensiveness to his superiors, I think. His laconic sarcasm. His engaging detestation of Sherlock Holmes (arising, to an extent, from Wallace's on-off tiff with Conan Doyle, principally over the matter of Spiritualism, which Wallace regarded as an absurd belief in a grown man). His fondness for unspeakable cigars. His down-to-earth appreciation of precisely how the world wags.

The Sooper made his debut at a time (the early-1920s) when Wallace was truly firing on all cylinders; when he was penning (or, rather, dictating) his most enduring thrillers—*Jack O' Judgement*, *The Valley of Ghosts*, *The Crimson Circle*, *The Green Archer*, *The Fellowship of the Frog*, *The Dark Eyes of London*, and a score or more other books—a good many of them as serials for a talented and tough-minded editor called Willie Blackwood.

Blackwood was so close a friend that he had no compunction in rejecting stories he didn't think were up to snuff, despite Wallace's tiresome though understandable habit of puffing every new story as 'the best I've ever written'. His flagship was the weekly *Answers*, but he also oversaw a number of lesser papers including *Pictorial Magazine*, for which, in 1928, Wallace wrote the emphatically un-rejectable *Big Foot*.

It's archetypal Wallace: an old house, a crazed tramp who sings Spanish songs in the moonlight, a lawyer who fancies himself as an amateur sleuth, a dodgy (or seemingly dodgy) detective-sergeant, the public hangman (with which office Wallace had had an obsession since covering an execution years before for the *Daily Mail*), an Impossible Crime—and the Sooper: harassed by his superiors, imaginatively insulted by petty crooks, ambushed, shot at, but in the end triumphant over a steaming bowl of poisoned soup.

Although *Big Foot* is written in the third person the emphasis throughout is on the Sooper, whose pungent soliloquies sometimes extend over two or three pages. He is akin to Inspector (on occasion, due to Wallace's notorious forgetfulness, sergeant) Elk, for Elk too has a caustic wit when roused. But Elk is invariably subordinate to the hero, often off-stage for whole chapters.

It has been said that many of Dickens's supporting characters are a good deal more sharply defined than some of his main leads. This is an acute judgement, and much the same can be said of Wallace. His sardonic sneak-thieves, canny charwomen, pragmatic desk-sergeants, fly shopgirls, and above-stairs servants who weren't born yesterday, though their activities are often tangential to the main plot, invariably spring to life in a far more vigorous manner than his heroes or heroines. The Sooper is cut from this same cloth: a choric role, but translated to centre-spot.

Yet while *Big Foot* is hugely diverting, to get the full flavour of the Sooper you must turn to the short stories (the novella *The Lone House Mystery*, though entertaining enough, suffers from hasty construction). The first, and best, 'The Little Dragon of Jade', 'The House of the Candles' and 'The Get-Back', were commissioned by the *Saturday Evening Post*, which paid highly for 'character' stories. Wallace shrewdly turned the Sooper into a first-person narrator so that he could utilise a story-telling technique at which he was pretty nearly peerless: the domestic back-parlour or saloon-bar (not public-bar) yarn spun over a mug of tea or a jar of something dark and smelling of hops by a skilled and worldly-wise raconteur educated in the University of Life rather than Oxbridge.

It was a technique he'd stumbled into while writing his 'Smithy' soldier sketches twenty-odd years before, then sharpened and refined once he discovered he had the rare gift of perfect dictation. Significantly it's also the technique he used on the only commercial recording he ever made, in 1929: a two-sided 78 lasting well over six minutes, on which he read 'The Man in the Ditch' (Columbia 5026, for those who haunt old-record marts). Two years later he read a couple of Sooper tales on the wireless, but (alas!) these don't appeared to have survived.

Still, the stories survived, and the 'voice'—of both Wallace and the Sooper—is there, to be heard in one's head: an urbane, self-educated (he had difficulties with certain words: 'tornado' and 'naïveté', for instance, which came out as 'torr-nahdo' and 'nay-veet'), Cockney-toff drawl.

As a taster (of tone, style and humour) here's the Sooper on a certain amateur sleuth: 'He . . . had an apartment in Baker Street and played the fiddle. An' when he was short of clues, he took a shot of 'coke' an' naturally he saw more clues in a minute than a flat-footed policeman would see in a year.'

How could one not but be entranced by such an approach?

THE CASES OF THE SOOPER, BY EDGAR WALLACE

Novel
Big Foot, 1927.

Story collections
The Lone House Mystery, 1929 (contains the title story plus 'The Sooper Speaking', 'Clues' and 'Romance In It'). *The Sooper-And Others*, 1984 (contains, with other stories, 'The Little Dragon of

Jade', 'The House of Candles', 'The More-or-Less Crime', 'The Get-Back' and 'Warm and Dry').

86

JULIAN SYMONS

on

Sam Spade

In his encyclopaedic study of the P.I., *Trouble is their Business*, John Conquest says I'm not over enthusiastic about the genre or sub-genre and its practitioners. Quite right: most of them seem to me just fantasy figures, fairy-tale heroes and heroines, utterly removed from reality. Of course in a few cases—Marlowe and Archer the most notable—the idealisation is redeemed by excellent writing. But still, why Sam Spade?

In part, no doubt, because Hammett's view of him is firmly unromantic. A dream man, Hammett called him, 'what most of the private detectives I worked with would like to have been and what quite a few of them in their cockier moments thought they approached.' Spade was, Hammett added, a hard and shifty fellow. He had a code of loyalty which included his partner Archer, even though he knew Archer might not be equally loyal to him, but he was a long way off Chandler's noble character walking down mean streets and turning wrongs to rights. Spade's eye was always on the main chance. When Brigid O'Shaughnessy asks if Spade would have sent her up if the Maltese Falcon had been real and he'd been paid what he was promised, he doesn't say yes or no, but that a lot of money would have been 'one more item on the other side of the scales.' Spade may be a dream man, but his thoughts and actions are rooted in reality.

Sam Spade appeared only in *The Maltese Falcon* and three so-so short stories, although he had a separate career on the radio and as a strip-cartoon character. But early in the Thirties Hammett wrote a screenplay in which Spade was shown not just as hard and shifty, but as crooked. The story was turned down by Darryl Zanuck, resold with Spade renamed Richmond, and ended up as a crime comedy called *Mister Dynamite* with the hero's name (and he was a hero) now T.N. Thompson, long for TNT. That was the end of Sam Spade, the most truthfully seen of all P.Is.

THE CASES OF SAM SPADE, BY DASHIELL HAMMETT

Novel
The Maltese Falcon, 1930.

Short story collection
The Adventures of Sam Spade, and other stories, 1944 (seven stories, three with Spade).

87

FREDERICK NOLAN

on

Spenser

The first line of the first book read: 'The office of the university president looked like the front parlor of a successful Victorian whorehouse.' I couldn't believe my luck. I thought. Someone's writing private-eye stories this good and nobody told me?

The book was *The Godwulf Manuscript*, and the writer was Robert B. Parker (the B stands for Brown, if you care). And the private eye's name was Spenser. You didn't need a degree in English literature to spot the lineage. By Sam Spade out of Philip Marlowe as played, perhaps, by the young Robert Mitchum, but written in a style mint-fresh, compulsive, addictive.

There were only two more, then (this was 1975): *God Save The Child* and *Mortal Stakes*. I devoured them, completely hooked on

Parker's irresistible mix of Code of the West meets Down These Mean Streets. I wasn't alone. When *Promised Land* appeared in 1976, the Mystery Writers of America confirmed my feelings by naming it best mystery novel of the year.

By now I'd discovered that Parker was as unusual as his hero. It was no surprise to learn he'd grown up a Chandler fan, but it certainly was to discover he was a one-time failed management trainee and copywriter turned university professor who'd written a doctoral dissertation entitled *The Violent Hero, Wilderness Heritage and Urban Reality: a study of the private eye in the novels of Dashiell Hammett, Raymond Chandler and Ross MacDonald.*

Like Spenser, he served in Korea, he cooks, he drinks a lot of beer, he has blue eyes, likes jazz, runs, works out with weights; Spenser was too much of a maverick to remain a cop, Parker couldn't take being an Organization Man. Perhaps both of them have a romantic's belief in the possibility of a better world, but that's as far as Parker's prepared to let it go: he isn't into researching or soul-searching, and neither is Spenser.

'Explaining myself is not one of the things I do really well, like drinking beer or taking a nap,' he says in *Promised Land.* 'Explaining myself is clumsy stuff. You really ought to watch what I do, and, pretty much, I think, you'll know what I am.'

Spenser's turf is a carefully-observed Boston and the clutter of small towns surrounding it. Specialities of the house are beautifully judged and often erudite putdowns, a vitriolic line in insults, teasing references to popular song, and of course, the cooking. A Spenser novel devotes an unusually large amount of words to the acts of eating and drinking. 'I do it to break up the slow march of exposition,' says Parker. 'Spenser's a careful man who tries to impose order on the universe, and consequently, whatever he does, which includes eating and drinking, he doesn't do sloppily.'

One shudders to think what percentage Spenser's put on the sale of certain brand name beers (he's choosy, but not fussy: 'the worst beer I ever had was wonderful') or how many people he's attracted to certain Boston restaurants. He appears to have only three stable relationships: a Boston police lieutenant named Martin Quirk, his dangerous buddy Hawk and the dark and lovely Susan Silverman, who came on the scene in *God Save The Child.* You could roast chestnuts on the intensity of their commitment:

'Yeah,' I said. 'Yeah. We're lovers.'

'For how long?' Susan said.

'For as long as we live,' I said. 'Or until you can't bear me anymore. Whichever comes first.'

'For as long as we live will come first,' Susan said.

By 1980, when *Looking For Rachel Wallace* came along, Spenser was already a cult. Now, sixteen novels down and . . .? to go, he is probably the bestselling private eye of the decade. There have been—let's face it—one or two stories that were just about good enough to pass muster, but as far as I can tell, nobody cares, the way nobody cares that Spenser was thirty-seven back in 1974, which would have him pushing sixty now. Nobody cares that he doesn't have a first name (did I dream that it was—once—David?). Nobody cares that he never seems to get paid. What matters is that he's a class act. That he lives by a set of ethics we all wish we could emulate. And that he has the best line of repartee in the business. You don't read a Spenser novel for the storyline or to find out whodunnit.

Spenser *is*. Take it or leave it.

THE CASES OF SPENSER, BY ROBERT B. PARKER

Novels

The Godwulf Manuscript, 1973. *God Save the Child*, 1974. *Mortal Stakes*, 1975. *Promised Land*, 1976. *The Judas Goat*, 1978. *Looking for Rachel Wallace*, 1980. *A Savage Place*, 1981. *Early Autumn*, 1981. *Ceremony*, 1982. *The Widening Gyre*, 1983. *Valediction*, 1984. *A Catskill Eagle*, 1985. *Taming a Sea Horse*, 1986. *Pale Kings and Princes*, 1987. *Crimson Joy*, 1988. *Playmates*, 1989. *Stardust*, 1990. *Pastime*, 1991.

Uncollected story

'*Surrogate*', 1982

88

CATHERINE AIRD

on

John Putnam Thatcher

To have been invited to write about one of my great detective heroes is a pure delight and indulgence: rather like being allowed to choose any cake on a proffered plate rather than politely having to take the one nearest.

Even in the very first book in the corpus (*Banking On Death*) John Putnam Thatcher appears as a mature man in years and a very mature man—not to say a philosopher—in outlook. Indeed, he gives the reader the distinct feeling that he sprang, like Athena, fully armed from the forehead of Zeus, so little is revealed of his antecedents, and so sure is his outlook on life.

We do know that he hailed from Sunapee, New Hampshire, and that he went to Harvard. An old friend from those days, the rakish Tom Robichaux (of Robichaux and Devane, Investment Bankers), occasionally calls him 'Putt' but nobody else does.

In a time-tested detective tradition John Putnam Thatcher is the male equivalent of a 'femme sole'. He is a widower—his late wife's name is never mentioned—with sons (equally anonymous) and a married daughter, Laura Carlson. All that the reader knows about his wife is that she had a penchant for Oriental rugs—and that her death has not made John Putnam Thatcher footloose and fancy free. All his domestic needs are taken care of by the housekeeper at the Dorchester where he lives.

His real life, though, is centred on the Sloan Guaranty Trust (the third largest bank in the world) whose corporate identity comes across in a way that many professional public relations firms would envy. John Thatcher's activities take place in the field (which is largely unworked in detective fiction) of commercial fraud (as opposed to real life, where it is worked only too often): and the collected works contain the hidden but cheering promise that in the workaday world of office and business there lies the chance of adventure.

Our hero is a true corporate polymath, his field of detective activity ranging over such disparate specialities as cocoa futures, the garment industry, North Sea oilfields, fast food and real estate.

In all of this, Thatcher is the person whom we would all like to be—a man who is capable of putting all his business worries out of his mind when he goes home and then sleeping well; an employee who can humour his ineffable—and quite impossible—employer, Bradford Withers, without losing his temper; and a worker able to function in faraway places . . . notably, amongst others, Puerto Rico, Greece and Great Britain.

As in the real world John Putnam Thatcher, whose wit is dry rather than acerbic, is caught between his hopeless boss and his own underlings, who in fact constitute a cohort of eminently believable colleagues in the working and workman-like setting of the Trust Department. These are mainly the raffish, not to say distinctly hedonistic, Charlie Trinkham, the ebullient Walter Bowman, the prim, narrow Everett Gabler (a man after nobody's heart), young Ken Nicholls and Thatcher's personal secretary, Rose Theresa Corsa.

If Thatcher is *sui generis*, Miss Corsa, as he never fails to call her in his old fashioned Ivy League way, is one of the great characters of the *oeuvre*. She could, I think, be described as more 'Colkitto to your grave Montrose' than Dr Watson to Sherlock Holmes or Archie Goodwin to Nero Wolfe though I swear that the word 'side-kick' never entered my mind—just as I am sure it is not in the vocabulary of Rose Theresa Corsa.

Her higher realism is as much of a joy to the reader as it is to her boss, the Vice-President of the Company and Head of the Trust Department, John Putnam Thatcher, and while his relationships with the police indicate a high level of public-spiritedness and mutual regard, his exchanges with his secretary are of a never-failing delight as far as we are concerned.

Some twenty books have now been published about this character, who has been created by two women authors who themselves met at Harvard University, Mary J. Latsis, who is an economist, and Martha Henissart, who is a lawyer. They have written together for more than twenty-five years under the pseudonym of Emma Lathen. Under another nom-de-plume (that of R.B. Dominic) they are the authors of a series of detective stories set in Washington's political arena with one Congressman Benton Stafford as their hero, but I mustn't go on . . .

THE CASES OF JOHN PUTNAM THATCHER, BY EMMA LATHEN

Banking On Death, 1961. *A Place For Murder*, 1963. *Accounting For Murder*, 1965. *Murder Makes the Wheels Go Round*, 1966. *Death Shall Overcome*, 1967. *Murder Against the Grain*, 1967. *A Stitch In Time*, 1968. *When In Greece*, 1969. *Come to Dust*, 1969. *Murder to Go*, 1970. *Pick Up Sticks*, 1971. *Ashes to Ashes*, 1971. *The Longer the Thread*, 1972. *Murder Without Icing*, 1973. *Sweet and Low*, 1974. *By Hook Or By Crook*, 1975. *Double, Double, Oil and Trouble*, 1978. *Going For the Gold*, 1981. *Green Grow The Dollars*, 1981. *Something in The Air*, 1988.

89

SARAH CAUDWELL

on

Henry and Emmy Tibbett

If Patricia Moyes' wide range of interests includes a fascination with the laborious details of routine policework, she has for many years successfully concealed it from her readers.

We should assume, no doubt, that long periods in the life of her hero, Chief Inspector Henry Tibbett, are spent at his desk in Scotland Yard, in conscientiously orthodox investigation of sordid and commonplace crime; but happily it is not these that she chooses to chronicle. The cases she tells us of are those which Henry encounters, often by chance, far from his usual professional surroundings and in the company of his loyal and resourceful wife Emmy—on holiday, skiing in the Swiss Alps or sailing in the Caribbean, or at a conference of senior policemen in Geneva, or assisting on not-quite-official secondment in a diplomatically sensitive investigation in Washington.

Henry, in short, despite his profession, is firmly in the amateur tradition of detective fiction, and the plotting in these stories is as deft, the touch as light, the cast of suspects as diverse and attractive, as in any of the classics of the 'Golden Age'. In character, however, he is as far removed from Sir John Appleby or Roderick Alleyn as he is from Inspector Dalziel or Inspector Morse. He is not a Great Detective, but a very ordinary man, of undistinguished appearance, with no aristocratic connections, no bizarre eccentricities, not even a superhuman intellect—simply a detective instinct which he modestly refers to as his 'nose'. (He is the only fictional policeman I can think of whom it seems natural to refer to by his Christian name.)

It is Emmy, however, who gives Patricia Moyes' novels their unique place in detective fiction and in the affections of her readers. Even in merely mechanical terms, her role in the story is always a far more active one than that usually played either by the spouse of the detective or by any of the multitudinous constables or sergeants upon whom other fictional police officers depend for support and admiration. It is Emmy, as often as not, who first becomes acquainted with the eventual suspects, she who catches the sinister undertone in some apparently innocent conversation, she who in pursuit of information sometimes finds herself in unexpected danger.

But there is more to it than that: though the stories are told in the third person, they are told largely from Emmy's point of view—it is through her eyes that we see the landscape, observe the interplay between the other characters, and watch the development of events.

She too strikes us at first as a very ordinary person, and in a sense perhaps she is. Kind-hearted, sensible, reliable, attractive without being glamorous, always in danger of putting on a little too much weight, with no particular talents outside the domestic sphere, she is not the kind of woman to make a powerful impact on first acquaintance. She grows on us gradually, like one of those friendships which we go on thinking of as casual until a sudden absence brings home its importance in our lives.

We find that we have become aware of qualities in her which underlie and go beyond the obvious ones. Her capacity for sheer enjoyment, of life, people, and places: few writers equal Ms Moyes in conveying the physical pleasures of being in a particular place—the taste of *raclette* cheese eaten toasted on an Alpine mountainside, the scent of flowers on a warm night in the Caribbean—and it is with Emmy that we share them. Her sceptical intelligence and shrewd sense of the absurd. Her warmth and generosity of spirit—something a good deal tougher than mere good nature. And finally a certain wistfulness, a sense of dreams and illusions not quite painlessly laid aside: sensible, practical, devoted though she is, she is also still the woman whose first love was the doomed fighter pilot of *'Johnny Under Ground'*.

I was tempted, I confess, to name Emmy as my favourite detective, and leave Henry out of it. But Emmy, I know, would not have liked it—it might hurt Henry's feelings, and she would never stand for that.

THE CASES OF HENRY & EMMY TIBBETT, BY PATRICIA MOYES

Dead Men Don't Ski, 1959. *The Sunken Sailor*, 1961. *Death on the Agenda*, 1962. *Murder à la Mode*, 1963. *Falling Star*, 1964. *Johnny Under Ground*, 1965. *Murder Fantastical*, 1967. *Death and the Dutch Uncle*, 1968. *Who Saw Her Die?*, 1970. *Season of Snows and Sins*, 1971. *The Curious Affair of the Third Dog*, 1973. *Black Widower*, 1975. *To Kill a Coconut*, 1977. *Who is Simon Warwick?*, 1978. *Angel Death*, 1980. *A Six-Letter Word for Death*, 1983. *Night Ferry to Death*, 1985. *Black Girl, White Girl*, 1989.

90
ROBERT CAMPBELL
on
Moroni Traveler

The best book. The best automobile. The best restaurant. The best ice-cream cone.

All depend upon time and place and expectation, upon memory and forgetfulness and intellectualization and emotional responses only half understood.

Among marathon runners, golfers and weight-lifters, a phrase is used: personal best.

Every mystery and crime novelist who has ever wrestled the beast knows that there is no best mystery, or best detective, or best novelist. There is only survival. There is only the triumph over the form and the knowledge that the next time the struggle will be just as hard. Sometimes, there is a personal best.

Even award winners are understood to be, in the estimation of a finite group of their peers, the best in a particular year, among a particular group of offerings.

Some of those winners will stand the test of time. In the case of others, future critics and readers will wonder what the judges ever saw in a work so commonplace and undistinguished.

Still other books and writers, never declared winners in such contests of the best, will achieve something as close to immortality as writers ever get.

But the exercise asked of me was to choose a best detective at this moment, in my current frame of mind, and that is no easy task.

I decided to pick someone new, because I assumed that all the great ones like Holmes and Wolf and Poirot would have had many essayists vying for the honor of heaping more honor upon them.

I even failed to consider the modern classics such as Dalgliesh and Joe Leaphorn and the cops of the 87th because they, too, would surely be chosen.

That left me with the new boys and girls on the block. What a crew to choose among.

The tough ladies created by Matera and Paretsky, the curiously diffident New Jersey operative written by Paul Engleman, the marvellous depression figure fashioned by Harold Adams, and a cast of others too numerous (as they say in Hollywood) to mention.

Every one of them a front runner among the detectives I enjoy.

But one of them engages my attention and admiration most because he, like his author, possesses qualities that are admirable. Both character and author are making come-backs of a sort. Both Moroni Traveler, the fictional detective, and Robert Irvine, the writer, are fighting back against a long stretch of just plain bad luck.

And doing it without complaint, self-pity or excuses.

Irvine once offered a character by the name of Christopher in several books, two of which were nominated for Edgars, and then faded away for reasons no-one could quite understand.

Moroni Traveler was a more successful man, a football hero, once upon a time, but now he is a private detective in a kind of dubious battle with Mormon Salt Lake City and the Church of the Latter Day Saints.

I think what impresses me most is that Traveler lives comfortably and authentically in that city and in his skin, accepting the fact that he will probably have to pay penance all his life for an accidental death he caused on the gridiron.

In ways subtle and difficult to pinpoint he exists in that milieu so completely that it's difficult to imagine him operating anywhere else.

He's a fool for women—at least for one woman—but weaves no great philosophies or draws no profound conclusions from his obsession. Traveler is upfront in his feelings for his elusive and neurotic love as he is in his opposition to arbitrary authority, yet there are small flashes of insight that inform us that he has a fiercely guarded interior life worth investigating.

Moroni Traveler is presented to us as a fully matured character, with plenty of warts and rough edges, but there is that hint of potential growth and ongoing revelation that is, I believe, essential to the success of today's fictional detective.

THE CASES OF MORONI TRAVELER, BY ROBERT IRVINE

Baptism for the Dead, 1988. *The Angel's Share*, 1989. *Gone to Glory*, 1990.

91
ALEX AUSWAKS
on
Mark Treasure

'So altogether you've made the best of an appalling situation.'

Molly Treasure

'Well "there's nothing in banking but what you ought to be able to learn in a week or two".'

—Judge Thomas Mellon quoted by Mark Treasure

It used to be said that if anyone had landed from Mars at the turn of the century, the best way to acquaint the new arrival with every aspect of the lives of real people was to take the Martian to La Scala in Milan to see and hear a complete cycle of Verdi operas. In these operas were the mainsprings of human action and their results.

If a Martian were to land in England today, and had to be acquainted with England and the English, the new arrival would, of course, be initially locked up in a hotel room with a complete set of David Williams' Treasure novels.

Mark Treasure does not come on strong. There are no exciting, interesting, extraordinary, uncommon characteristics which other sleuths possess and which may engage the reader, but seldom have anything to do with the mystery and its solution. But because he does not come on strong, wears his many talents lightly ('I rub along' he says when asked how he manages also to be chairman of a pharmaceutical company), the most fascinating array of people congregate round him, not overwhelmed by him, free to be themselves.

And the plots are a treat, too.

His cases begin when he is trying to unravel a financial puzzle and at least one missing piece leads to murder. Often, he begins by merely wanting to prevent grief or scandal. But because he is good *with* people as well as good *about* people, amateur sleuthing isn't just a hobby for him from his staid professional life. It isn't enough to unravel the financial knots, nor bring the criminal to book, nor see justice done (with a small 'j') . . . there must be a greater Justice: victims must be compensated, widows and orphans given a fresh start . . .

THE CASES OF MARK TREASURE, BY DAVID WILLIAMS

Novels

Unholy Writ, 1976. *Treasure Up in Smoke*, 1978. *Murder for Treasure*, 1980. *Copper, Gold and Treasure*, 1982. *Treasure Preserved*, 1983. *Advertise for Treasure*, 1984. *Wedding Treasure*, 1985. *Murder in Advent*, 1985. *Treasure in Roubles*, 1986. *Divided Treasure*, 1987. *Treasure in Oxford*, 1988. *Holy Treasure*, 1989. *Prescription for Murder*, 1990.

Stories

'*Treasure Finds a Mistress*', 1980. '*Uncle's Girl*', 1983. '*The Bully*', 1984. '*Three's a Crowd*', 1986.

92
HAUGHTON MURPHY
on
Perry Trethowan

G iven the wide and imaginative range of settings in which Robert Barnard's crime adventures take place, it would not be credible to have a single detective at the center of them all. Barnard has, however, created one series character who has appeared so far in five novels—Superintendent Perry Trethowan of Scotland Yard. (He is actually Peregrine Leo Trethowan, but is called that at one's peril. The peril is real, too, since Perry is six feet five, weighs seventeen stone and was, at least in younger days, a shotputter and weightlifter.)

Trethowan was introduced in *Sheer Torture*, where it became clear that he is the one stable figure (leaving aside his own wife and child) in 'a large family of lunatics'. The Trethowan clan comes complete with a Hitler-worshipper and mediocre artists of various sorts, all united in a love of publicity; any resemblance to the Mitfords or the Sitwells is, of course, pure coincidence.

At the age of eighteen, Perry joined the army as the only act his family would understand as rebellion. 'If I'd said I wanted to go to ballet school,' he once explained, 'or go to the States and graduate in dope-peddling, they'd probably have patted me on the head, [but] when I said I wanted to join the army, all hell broke loose.' Later he continued his rebellion by becoming a policeman. Disinherited, he remained out of touch with his relatives for fourteen years, until the death of his father, as described in *Sheer Torture*.

In keeping with the Trethowan eccentric tradition, Perry's father died while experimenting with an S&M torture device installed by him at Harpenden House, the 'inconvenient and slightly ludicrous' family mansion in Northumberland. And, for good measure, the father was wearing 'gauzy spangled tights' when he was killed. Fortunately the father's perversions were not visited on his detective son.

In the novels after *Sheer Torture*, Perry's odd relatives recede into the background, with the exception of his sister, Cristobel, to whom he becomes reconciled. A romantic novelist, she entices him to the world convention of romantic writers in Bergen, Norway, that is the setting of *The Cherry Blossom Corpse*. Otherwise Trethowan avoids Harpenden House and its residents as much as possible, living quietly with his studious wife, Jan, and young son, Daniel, in Abbey Road in London.

Barnard has said that he does not plan to use Perry Trethowan in the future. This is a great pity. Readers will miss what Perry himself has called his 'nasty vein of dry facetiousness' and his first-person observations on the world around him (reflecting his creator, perhaps?) such as:

'I have to admit that [academics] have seemed the most snivelling, self-important scraps of humanity you can imagine, and as windy and whiney a bunch as ever demanded special privileges without doing anything to deserve them.' (This from *The Missing Bronte*.)

May one plead for more dry facetiousness from Trethowan/ Barnard, more Trethowan adventures? Young David is surely about to go off to public school, and everyone knows the potential for murder in such a hothouse. And what about wife Jan's newly acquired degree in Arabic? Surely her knowledge of that language can be put to good (and timely) use! Perry Trethowan is still young, much too young to be killed off. Let's have more of him.

THE CASES OF PERRY TRETHOWAN, BY ROBERT BARNARD

Sheer Torture, 1981. *Death and the Princess*, 1982. *The Missing Bronte*, 1983. *Bodies*, 1986. *Death in Purple Prose*, 1987.

93
JAN BITSCH STEFFENSEN
on
Van der Valk

Inspectors in the police novel can be divided into three main categories: *First*, the classical dummy presenting old ways of thinking and exclusively acting as a mirror for the brilliant private investigator—for example, Chief Inspector Japp for Hercule Poirot; *next* there is the intelligent, accepted and therefore often a bit or more boring Inspector; *last*, the most interesting figure: the clever inspector with a special way of doing things, like Simenon's Maigret. Nicolas Freeling's Van der Valk is another of that kind, inspired by Maigret without simply being a copy.

Van der Valk is barely just tolerated by the Dutch police force—only because he solves his cases. From 1962 until his premature death in 1972, Van der Valk struggled through cases of a very different nature. He was engaged in ordinary crime and political intrigues, local crime and international affairs.

Van der Valk is a pessimist, critics have often claimed. I am not so sure that I would agree with that. I will admit, though, that he is grumpy—but in a positive sense. Being grumpy and pessimistic is his way of 'staying alive' and keeping his distance from a system he does not approve of. That he is not very fond of his own town, Amsterdam, and of Holland, is as true as it can get.

At the same time he is cosmopolitan. Apart from his mother tongue, Dutch, he speaks English, French and German, when his cases take him beyond the Dutch border. In *The Lovely Ladies*, he finds the solution in Ireland, and in *Guns before Butter*, a great part of his efforts occur in France and Germany. He has a broader view of the world than the narrow and moralistic values dominating in his native country. Several times in the ten stories he appears in, Van der Valk bitterly criticizes part of the Dutch mentality, culture and way of living. Some critics have marked him as conservative—yes, even a reactionary—but it is true only to a minor extent. It is true that he opposes certain modern achievements and values, but he is not sentimental, and it is never his intention to restore the past. His aim is to advise his fellow countrymen, to reconsider the evolution of modern culture. He has a (bad) habit of being precocious, but in a constructive way, I think.

Although he is often called out when he is off duty he keeps, as others of these unconventional fictional Inspectors, a distance from his job. Van der Valk is married to the French Arlette, whose hostility towards Holland is so strong that it becomes almost incomprehensible why she does live in Holland. The only answer is, of course, that she is married to Piet, which is the inspector's Christian name. Arlette's French origins and her hostility are definitely a major factor in Van der Valk's attitude towards Dutch culture. That Arlette herself has an ambiguous attitude towards Dutch culture is underlined in *The Widow* in which Arlette later returns to Holland.

Van der Valk has over the years been handed several cases of an unsolvable character. In one case, he and his wife, in disguise, are sent to a small country village to solve an old crime. Others have political implications and are assigned to him by his worried superiors.

He does not solve mysteries by collecting technical evidence. He set out to hunt, analyse and understand the various psychological circumstances surrounding the actual events. A theme Freeling occupies himself with in most of his crime novels. Therefore Van der Valk often works by himself—with Arlette playing a more or less important role. In *The Long Silence*, she is directly included in the inspector's crime solving attempts, and after his death in *The Long Silence* she solves the actual case. Later she gets a book of her own.

Van der Valk's most unusual method appeared in Freeling's very first crime novel. In *Love in Amsterdam* Van der Valk directly includes the prime suspect in his investigations, and protects him from attempts made by the district attorney and others to finish off the case with a fast trial and a long jail sentence. They are, of course, wrong and Van der Valk eventually arrests the right criminal.

In 1972 Nicolas Freeling became tired of his hero, and he was killed by a criminal half way through *The Long Silence*. Freeling 'kills' his inspector properly, and it is significant that in this last book we, for the first time, learn a great deal of the Inspector's previous life.

After the 'burial' of Van der Valk, Freeling introduced the French inspector Henri Castang. He is a boring duplicate of Van der Valk. Readers complained, but it seems to me that Van der Valk had completed his job. I am not in favour of reviving deceased detectives, although *Sand Castles* in which Freeling does exactly that, is a better book than the Castang stories. This is perhaps also the justification of Freeling's unusual step. Van der Valk lives again.

THE CASES OF VAN DER VALK, BY NICOLAS FREELING

Love in Amsterdam, 1962. *Because of the Cats*, 1963. *The Lovely Ladies* 1963. *Guns Before Butter*, 1963. *Double-Barrel*, 1964. *Criminal Conversation*, 1965. *The King of The Rainy Country*, 1966. *The Dresden Green*, 1966. *Strike out where not Applicable*, 1967. *Tsing-Boum*, 1969. *Over The High Side*, 1971. *A Long Silence*, 1972. *Sand Castles*, 1989.

94

HELEN ESPER OLMSTED

on

Amos Walker

Amos Walker (Loren D. Estleman's creation) is my kind of gumshoe. He's a sweetheart and a hunk. His 6 ft. 1 in. frame is well padded with muscles in all the right places. He has brown hair and brown eyes. He has a couple of battle scars on his face, which only add to his rugged good looks. He is witty, sometimes sarcastic, but always sincere.

Walker has a B.A. in Sociology, he spent eleven weeks in the Police Cadet training program and is a veteran of Vietnam, which places his age at just this side of forty.

He likes old movies and Angela Lansbury. He is a dog lover. He only likes cats if they are 'dog-like' which poses the question if he ever got a cat would he build a cat house or a dog house that looked like a 'cat house'.

Walker is an avid Scotch drinker and keeps the proverbial bottle in a desk drawer. He smokes Winstons but is polite about it as long as non-smokers don't invade his space.

Walker lives by a strict moral code and has a street language all his own; however, it leaves little doubt in the minds of thugs what he is talking about.

As everyone has a slight crack in his makeup, Amos is no exception. The chink in his armour is his ex-wife, Catherine; against his better judgment he sometimes gets into a love-hate relationship with her. He doesn't want to see her hurt, neither does he want her to become a part of his life again.

Walker is not naïve enough to trust many people, but he will occasionally take a chance if he has a good feeling about them. Generally though, he spends the first twenty-four hours or so of an investigation sorting out truth from fiction. If he catches himself being too trusting, he lets his mind dwell for a few minutes on his murdered partner, Dale Leopold and *voilà*, instant cure!

He is somewhat romantic. He likes most women, but has no illusions about them. He appreciates good-looking, sexy women especially if they have brains. But he dates casually and doesn't hop into bed with them as a way of life.

Walker lives on the edge of Hamtramck in a small but comfy house he once shared with Catherine. He takes care of all the repairs around the house. His love of neatness and his bachelor status have made him a good housekeeper and a good cook. He is a man I'd love to have around the house. I'll bet he could cook me a rack of lamb well done, just the way I like it.

There are only a few people, like Inspector John Alderyce of the Detroit Police Department and Barry Stackpole, a freelance journalist, that Walker calls his friends in a business capacity. I hope I am one of his friends in a more personal way.

In his latest adventure, Walker has more than his share of problems with the broads. His ex-wife, Catherine is involved in the case in as much as she is married to Sahara, one of the bad guys. He also finds out that his lady client, Gail Hope, a sexy, middle-aged ex-movie queen and now owner of the Club Canaveral, is the real criminal in the case. This is when he finds out *Sweet Women Lie*.

I'm sure Amos could be likened to a bloodhound on the scent. When he goes after his suspect, he doesn't let go. But before he goes after him/her, he straps on a shoulder holster that houses a Smith and Wesson .38 caliber. If he figures he's likely to get himself in a situation where he might get patted down, he adds a small gun in an ankle holster to his attire.

Being a native Detroiter, now living in Howell, I can understand why Amos is wary when he walks the 'mean streets' of Detroit, where even in the early hours of the morning, old people are mugged, drug pushers accost ten- and eleven-year olds with their hallucinogenic drugs and small children get in the way of bullets in a drug war that never sleeps. If he can make just one little dent in the crime rate, it makes his day.

Amos Walker is the best. I think I have a crush on him. I wonder sometimes if it's true what they say about younger men liking older women because of their experience and, if it's so, do you think I have a chance with Amos?

THE CASES OF AMOS WALKER, BY LOREN D. ESTLEMAN

Novels

Motor City Blue, 1980. *Angel Eyes*, 1981. *The Midnight Man*, 1982.

The Glass Highway, 1983. *Sugartown*, 1985. *Every Brilliant Eye*, 1986. *Lady Yesterday*, 1987. *Downriver*, 1988. *Silent Thunder*, 1989. *Sweet Women Lie*, 1990.

Story collection
General Murders, 1988.

Uncollected stories
'*Cigarette Shop*', 1990. '*The Man Who Loved Noir*', 1991.

95
LINDA SEMPLE
on
V.I. Warshawski

SURVEILLANCE REPORT

Client: Maxim Jakubowski
Subject: Victoria Iphigenia (V.I.) Warshawski
Age: 'The time when thirty is a fond memory'
Occupation: Private Investigator specialising in financial, insurance and security operations.
Appearance: 5′ 8″ tall; light brown hair: olive skin, which goes gold when tanned; grey eyes; faint knife scar from underneath left eye to jawline. Dresses expensively mainly in silk, linen and cotton, Italian shoes, particularly Bruno Magli pumps.
Background: Parents both deceased. Father was a Polish/American police officer, mother Jewish/Italian. Born on Chicago's South Side, mother died while subject was an adolescent. Assorted cousins and aunts still living, whom she sees infrequently. Played basketball at Senior High School and went to University of Chicago on an Athletic Scholarship. Qualified as a lawyer and spent some time as a public defender before resigning to go private. Member of

the Chicago Bar. Divorced from lawyer Richard Yarborough. No children.

Finances: It seems she makes no more than between $20K–$30K p.a. Rents a scruffy office on the 4th floor of the Pulteney Building in the loop. Has a mortgage on a 3rd floor co-op apparently part paid for by $25K from a mafia boss whom she helped out after her rented flat was burnt down.

Associates: Very few close friends, mostly from college. Closest friend is Dr Charlotte Herschel an Austrian émigré who runs an obstetrics and neo-natal clinic and is a consultant at Beth Israel. Met Herschel and other close friend Agnes Paciorek (killed during subject's investigation into the Catholic Church) while organising an 'abortion underground' at college. Has good relationship with downstairs neighbour Mr Contreras with whom she part-owns a golden labrador, Peppy. Regular but casual romantic attachments with Roger Ferrant, English consultant with Ajax Insurance, and Murray Ryerson, reporter on the Herald-Star. Subject has also been lovers with various men who were later revealed to be implicated in her investigations and were subsequently killed or arrested. Recently, subject seems to have curbed habit of sleeping with suspects.

Observations: Subject is known to her close friends as 'Vic'. Old family friend which she hates such as Bobby Mallory of the Chicago Police call her 'Vicki'. He, and other police connections from her father and her days as public defender, allow reasonable access to privileged information which help with her enquiries.

Subject seems to socialise almost solely with Herschel, Contreras, Ryerson and Ferrant except when on a case when she spends most time with suspects. Subject has a sentimental attachment to objects which belonged to her mother including some jewellery, seven (originally eight) Venetian wine glasses and, in her office, a picture of the Uffizi Gallery and an Olivetti typewriter.

Political allegiances are firmly liberal and strongly feminist. Actively involved in pro-choice work at Herschel's clinic and frequently deals with cases of fraud and corruption in large companies and multinationals (see attached reports on Grafalk Shipping case, Xerxes Chemicals and Corpus Christi). Subject is fiercely loyal and thus can be strong-willed and less careful when cases involve friends and family.

Owns a Smith and Wesson handgun but prefers not to carry it all the time relying instead on wits, physical strength and agility. Hence subject is often hospitalised or otherwise roughed-up in the course of investigations. Has no qualms about using illegal methods such as breaking and entering when investigating a case; has also been known physically to intimidate suspects. Has killed during investigations.

I have no reservations in recommending V.I. Warshawski as the pre-eminent current woman Private Investigator.

Respectfully submitted,
Linda Semple.

THE CASES OF V. I. WARSHAWSKI, BY SARA PARETSKY

Novels

Indemnity Only, 1982. *Deadlock*, 1984. *Killing Orders*, 1985. *Bitter Medicine*, 1987. *Blood Shot*, 1988. *Burn Marks*, 1990.

Uncollected stories

'Three-Dot Po,' 1985. 'Skin Deep', 1986. 'At the Old Swimming Hole', 1986. 'The Case of the Pietro Andromache', 1988. 'The Maltese Cat', 1990.

96

MELODIE JOHNSON HOWE & CATHERINE KENNEY

on

Lord Peter Wimsey

Being an American woman I grew up with guys like Philip Marlowe and Lew Archer. In high school they sulked in the back of the class. They leaned, silent and moody, against their lockers. And they never asked a girl to the prom. If they did ask you for a date you spent the entire evening trying to engage them in conversation. When they chose to respond it was usually with a question like, 'Are you still a virgin?'

I suppose that's why I've always had a secret passion for Lord Peter Wimsey. He was my first introduction to a man who could talk. He used words the way a juggler tosses his plates in the air. He used words to entertain, to take your breath away. He could talk about love, music, and murder all in the same sentence. Of course there were times he did lapse into baby talk and say such things as: 'Ta, Ta, phiffle, burblin', toddle.' But he was a lord, not a loner. He was raised by a nanny in a nursery. The only nursery guys like Marlowe and Archer knew sold plants. And to be honest, the only lord I knew was a drunken red-haired woman who owned the apartment house we lived in and demanded to be called the landlord, not the landlady. A feminist before her time.

I am a woman who admires true style. In fact, I find it sexy. American loners show their disdain for style by wearing one rumpled jacket. Not Lord Peter. He had a jacket to smoke in, to dine in, to hack in. He even had a jacket just to wear in Norfolk. Now that is true style. Of course there was the bathrobe decorated with the peacocks. But only Bunter saw him in that.

American loners thought they were being brave when they punched some guy in the mouth. They didn't know the meaning of

227

the word. Lord Peter was braver than all of them. He dared to ponce without desiring to wear a dress and live in West Hollywood.

Before that sniffy Harriet Vane married him, I longed to toddle down the mean streets of Piccadilly with Lord Peter. I dreamed of going to the symphony with him. I would even restrain myself from humming along and moving my fingers as if I were conducting. I wanted to sit next to him in his Daimler Twin-Six with my hand resting on his thigh. Yes, yes, his thigh. I longed to have dinner with him at the Savoy. I'd even force myself to eat an egg omelet before the main course. Or is it after the main course? Oh God, I longed to look into his eyes over a glass of Montrachet 1908. Then, ever so slowly, reach across the table, grab his ascot, remove his monocle, and ask him, 'Are you still a virgin?'

—MELODIE JOHNSON HOWE

Somewhere in the Middle East
September 25, 1990

Dear Mr Jakubowski:

I write on behalf of my grandfather, Lord Peter Wimsey, who sends his compliments and best wishes for the success of your forthcoming book on Great Detectives. He has asked me to express his regrets that the press of diplomatic duties prevents him from answering your query directly. The recent unpleasantness in the Middle East has moved the Foreign Office to enlist Lord Peter's help once again. Since early August, when he reluctantly abandoned his summer holiday in Scotland, we have been travelling in a region well-known to me from my research at several of its archaeological sites. The promise of my grandfather's conversation is one of the few things that can bring me half-way round the world, and I gladly accepted his invitation to assist him in handling this most delicate situation. We trust your discretion in this matter, and mention it only to explain the tardiness of the reply.

Turning to more pleasant but less weighty subjects, you have asked for details of Lord Peter's detective career. For this, please refer to the well-documented eleven-volume biography by Dorothy L. Sayers who, for some mysterious reason, called the books novels and ornamented them as such. Lord Peter, who is fairly demanding in such matters, finds Miss Sayers' study to be, on the whole, sound, scholarly, and sincere. His personal favorites include the reports of his investigations into death and deception at the old Bellona Club and at Pym's Publicity (*Murder Must Advertise*), as well as the meticulous record of that miserable business at Fenchurch St Paul (*The Nine Tailors*). I might add that, except for my great-aunt Helen, Duchess of Denver, everyone in the family is particularly fascinated with the four-part story of my grandparents' courtship, with *Gaudy Night* and *Busman's Honeymoon* being considered nonpareil. Lord Peter is himself more fond of these later books than his essential modesty allows him to admit, but he once praised them to me as the best example of Miss Sayers's acute understanding of the inexhaustible mysteriousness of human life. He does not care so much for her short stories about his adventures, which tend to the bizarre and deal with less interesting people and situations.

I should think that fans of Lord Peter's earlier detective career will be gratified to learn of his continuing vivacity and good humour. Together with my grandmother, the novelist Dame Harriet Vane, he is the center of our family, an unshakable rock in an increasingly unstable world, and the critic whose approbation all of us most desire. My earliest memories of him include my delight at his insatiable curiosity, his wit, and his infectious love of life. I am happy to report that these qualities still distinguish him.

After abandoning detective work per se, Lord Peter continued to work for the public good, but out of the public eye, functioning as all effective diplomats must do: quietly and without fanfare. Yet the qualities which made him a great detective in those days between the two great wars are the very qualities which have served him well in his second career: wide-ranging knowledge of the world, intellectual acumen, meticulous logic, respect for fact, and a supple, genuinely imaginative mind. Good diplomats, like good detectives, must know not only how to ask questions, but how to listen as well; they must learn to read people and situations as if they were mysterious texts, which, of course, they are. One thing that distinguishes Lord Peter, and indeed most detectives, from the professional diplomat is a love of truth. As he once put it, they call Wimsey to the negotiating table only when they decide they need some common honesty, for a little variety.

My grandfather has acknowledged that he learned his craft from many colleagues, including his late brother-in-law, Chief Inspector Parker of Scotland Yard; his most valued employee at the detective agency, Miss Climpson; Mr Venables, who showed him the value of mistakes in detection; and his partner in life, Harriet Vane Wimsey.

He thinks that any attempt to name the 'world's greatest detective' is both unseemly and unhelpful, but he often remarks about the importance of his mentor, Sherlock Holmes, as well as the detectives portrayed by Wilkie Collins and E.C. Bentley. He remains a great admirer of Agatha Christie's Poirot.

Between wars and insurrections, conflicts and calamities, Lord Peter has enjoyed life at Talboys, cataloguing his collection of incunabula for the Wimsey Bequest to the Bodleian,* editing the *Wimsey Papers*, and campaigning for the restoration of sanity to British architecture. He has entered the computer age, and recently has been investigating the use of computers in counter-terrorism. In short, he continues his life-long resistance to war, haste and violence.

This autumn, Wimseys from around the world will gather to celebrate Lord Peter's 100th birthday. This is reason for celebration indeed, for he is as alive today as ever, and still a delight to us all.

Yours sincerely,
Harriet K. M. Wimsey
as dictated to CATHERINE KENNEY

*Some memorabilia, including the monocle, have been left to Eton.

THE CASES OF LORD PETER WIMSEY, BY DOROTHY L. SAYERS

Novels

Whose Body?, 1923. *Clouds of Witness*, 1926. *Unnatural Death*, 1927. *The Unpleasantness at the Bellona Club*, 1928. *Strong Poison*, 1930. *The Five Red Herrings*, 1931. *Have His Carcase*, 1932. *Murder Must Advertise*, 1933. *The Nine Tailors*, 1934. *Gaudy Night*, 1935. *Busman's Honeymoon*, 1937.

Story collections

Lord Peter Views the Body, 1928 (twelve stories). *Hangman's Holiday*, 1933 (twelve stories, four with Wimsey). *In the Teeth of the Evidence*, 1939 (seventeen stories, two with Wimsey). *In the Teeth of the Evidence*, 1972 (with three additional Wimsey stories). *Lord Peter*, 1972 (American collection gathering all twenty-one Wimsey stories). *Striding Folly*, 1972 (three Wimsey stories).

97

CAROLYN G. HART

on

Leonidas Witherall

E rudite, clever, charming and suave, Leonidas Witherall definitely is my kind of guy.

Also known as Bill Shakespeare because of his uncanny resemblance to library statues of the bard, Witherall is the canny, never-say-die hero of eight zany, tongue-in-cheek mysteries by Phoebe Atwood Taylor writing as Alice Tilton.

The Tilton series, a counterpoint to the Asey Mayo novels by Taylor, provides a sardonic appraisal of American life from the late nineteen thirties to the late nineteen forties, including a marvelous look at the homefront during World War II.

I hate to admit it, but I'm afraid my delight in these books springs from Bill Shakespeare's dismissal of all rules and regulations as unimportant impediments in the path of justice. Bill will do whatever is necessary to solve the crime: move a body, delay reporting a murder, connive in a nefarious fashion to outwit the villain, manufacture evidence, rearrange the scene of a crime—honestly, there are no limits to Bill's creative approach to crime solving. Bill further strikes a chord with this writer because he is, unknown to his scholarly peers and fellow suburbanites, the pseudonymous author of the red-blooded Lieutenant-Haseltine-To-The-Rescue thrillers, episodes of which are broadcast daily on the radio. Haven't we all *wanted* to write those kinds of books, with a villainous Japanese general and missing ruby red necklaces and sinister Russian countesses and perilous, fraught-with-danger, last-minute miraculous rescues of the lovely Lady Alicia?

Believe me, there's a lot to Bill Shakespeare.

The tone of the series can be understood immediately upon reading the title to the first, *Beginning with a Bash*. The humor is irreverent, the implausible situations hilarious, and the cynicism totally satisfying.

I adore each and every one of the eight Tilton books, but I have two favorites, *The Hollow Chest* and *Dead Ernest*.

In *The Hollow Chest*, Witherall, at that time headmaster of an exclusive boys school, is direly in need of a staunch character reference in a particular Boston suburb because the fifth form had victoriously routed a general in a tank, interrupting vital military maneuvers, and the schoolboys were therefore suspected of being possible Fifth Columnists. And, horror of horrors, a fifth former is missing, his grumpy guardian demands an accounting, and Bill discovers that much of his future depends upon the whims of a great white horse. There's a community fund drive, Bill poses as a gravy salesman, and the octopus of fate, a component of all the series, vigorously wiggles its many appendages before all is satisfactorily resolved.

Dead Ernest is a marvelous chase of an itinerant freezer which includes a corpse among its contents. The freezer appears—by mistake?—in Bill's kitchen, and he feels it incumbent upon him to solve the vexing questions the body raises, so that he can finish his next Haseltine opus, which is long overdue.

When the denouement of each book is about the occur, Bill or a companion recalls the brave Lieutenant Haseltine's inveterate reference to the historic battle of Cannae in 216 B.C., when Haseltine is ready to triumph. As Mrs Finger puts it, in *Dead Ernest*, 'After the gallant lieutenant's been buffeted around by fate until he's all but a pulp, he thinks of Cannae, and he just solves everything!'

And so does Leonidas Witherall, aka Bill Shakespeare, to my continuing pleasure and delight.

Let's see, I haven't read *File for Record* recently . . .

THE CASES OF LEONIDAS WITHERALL, BY PHOEBE ATWOOD TAYLOR
Beginning with a Bash, 1937. *The Cut Direct*, 1938. *Cold Steal*, 1939. *The Left Leg*, 1940 *The Hollow Chest*, 1941. *File For Record*, 1943 *Dead Ernest*, 1944 *The Iron Clew*, 1947.

98

PAULA GOSLING

on

Nero Wolfe

I t's envy, really.

Just imagine yourself to be Nero Wolfe on a typical day (I often do). Since the death of Mycroft Holmes, you are the world's most brilliant stationary genius. You are a consulting detective, and you charge outrageous prices for your services. You need to—for your lifestyle is extremely expensive.

You never leave home if you can avoid it. You sleep in canary-yellow silk pyjamas on black silk sheets, then rise to have breakfast served in your room by Fritz Brenner, your own private chef, a brilliant man whose sole purpose in life is to satisfy your every culinary whim. Perhaps today it's *Eggs au Beurre Noir*, *Petit Saucisson* (from the secret recipe of one of Europe's master chefs, confided to you alone in gratitude for detective services rendered), blueberry muffins, and coffee in your special blend.

You bathe and dress—then spend two hours devoting yourself entirely to your favourite hobby—raising rare orchids in the glasshouse on the roof. (Actually, since this is *your* dream, it can be what you like.)

Perforce, this happy interval is followed by two hours dealing with business matters, aided by your private secretary, a lively, witty, and sympathetic person who runs all your errands for you, and protects you from Life's Vicissitudes (including the occasional bullet). Then luncheon (Clam fritters? Chicken Fricassée with dumplings?), a pause for peaceful digestion, and another uninterrupted two hours on the roof.

At six o'clock you come down in your private elevator, and ring for Fritz to bring in a chilled bottle of the beer you like so well. Possibly two. Or three. You open them with a gold bottle opener given to you by a grateful client, and keep track of your consumption by dropping the bottle caps into your desk drawer. Reluctant as one is to admit it, there *is* a weight problem. You now tip the scales at well over a quarter of a ton, and it would be annoying if you had to have yet another chair custom-made to accommodate your bulk. As it is, the one behind your desk is the only one you find truly comfortable. (Visitors sit opposite you in leather chairs—paying clients in the red one, all others in the yellow. On his occasional visits to fish for information, Chief Inspector Cramer also rates the red chair, from which he usually insults you.)

Then comes dinner—definitely *Duck Mondor* with all the trimmings. You may spend the balance of the evening playing billiards in the basement, or reading, or turning the television on and off several times just to confirm your low opinion of it. Then to bed again on those silken sheets. Very satisfactory.

Ummm—about that secretary.

If you are Nero Wolfe, then he is Archie Goodwin, and there are times when he will annoy you. Times, perhaps, when the income tax is due or the bank account is getting low. Then he will start to nag, and invariably force or trick you in some devious way to actually work. The man, for all his savvy and good looks, can be a trial.

If the case you reluctantly undertake is a complex one you might direct Archie to enlist the services of Saul Panzer (an extraordinary investigator in his own right, a master of disguises unequalled in tailing a suspect), Fred Durkin (solid, reliable, and blessedly unimaginative), and Orrie Cather. Archie doesn't like calling in Orrie, who is brash, handsome, and covets Archie's job.

But Archie doesn't have to worry. He is irreplaceable, and —although you bicker with him occasionally—you know it. Of course, there *are* times when Archie's interest in beautiful women can become irksome—but there are other times when his way with a maiden or a madam can be extremely useful, so you tolerate his occasional lapses. Even in the case of Lily Rowan, his socialite friend, who once kissed you thoroughly and repeatedly in the back of a taxi to help you maintain a disguise.

The experience still gives you nightmares.

You, yourself, have no need for or interest in women—not since your youth in Montenegro, fighting in the Resistance, when the one woman above all others . . . ah, well, she is dead and that is in the past, along with your pain. The real truth is you find women tiresome. Under questioning, they tend to cry, forcing you to leave the room and hide in the kitchen until Archie calms them down. You hate unnecessary physical exercise.

So, you continue to live in your old brownstone house on 35th Street in New York City, indulging your taste for shad roe, good beer, and orchids. You have become rich and famous for living exactly as you please, and for solving some of the most fascinating cases on record.

No wonder people envy you.

And admire Rex Stout, the man who created you.

THE CASES OF NERO WOLFE, BY REX STOUT

Fer-de-Lance, 1934. *The League of Frightened Men*, 1935. *The Rubber Band*, 1936. *The Red Box*, 1937. *Too Many Cooks*, 1938. *Some Buried Caesar*, 1938. *Over my Dead Body*, 1940. *Where There's a Will*, 1941. *Black Orchids*, 1943. *Not Quite Dead Enough*, 1944. *The Silent Speaker*, 1946. *Too Many Women*, 1947. *And be a Villain*, 1948. *The Second Confession*, 1949. *Trouble in Triplicate*, 1949. *Three Doors to Death*, 1950. *In the Best Families*, 1950. *Curtains for Three*, 1950. *Murder by the Book*, 1951. *Triple Jeopardy*, 1951. *Prisoner's Base*, 1952. *The Golden Spiders*, 1953. *Three Men Out*, 1954. *The Black Mountain*, 1954. *Before Midnight*, 1955. *Might as Well be Dead*, 1956. *Three Witnesses*, 1956. *Three for the Chair*, 1957. *If Death ever Slept*, 1957. *Champagne for One*, 1958. *And Four to Go*, 1958. *Plot it Yourself*, 1959. *Three at Wolfe's Door*, 1960. *Too Many Clients*, 1960. *The Final Deduction*, 1961. *Gambit*, 1962. *Homicide Trinity*, 1962. *The Mother Hunt*, 1963. *Trio for Blunt Instruments*, 1964. *A Right to Die*, 1964. *The Doorbell Rang*, 1965. *Death of a Doxy*, 1966. *The Father Hunt*, 1968. *Death of a Dude*, 1970. *Please Pass the Guilt*, 1973. *A Family Affair*, 1975. *Death Times Three*, 1985 (by Robert Goldsborough). *Murder in E Minor*, 1986. *Death on Deadline*, 1987. *The Bloodied Ivy*, 1988. *The Last Coincidence*, 1989. *Fade to Black*, 1990.

99

BRIAN STABLEFORD

on

Prince Zaleski

---

*P*rince Zaleski, a collection of three novelettes by M.P. Shiel, was the seventh volume of John Lane's 'Keynotes' series, issued in March 1895. The eponymous hero of the stories is the most bizarre of all English detectives, and the mysteries which confront him are no less grotesque; yet his creator regarded him, with reason, as a 'legitimate son' of Poe's Dupin while damning Sherlock Holmes as a mere bastard. We may agree with him, if we follow a line of descent through Poe's French translator Baudelaire, the inspiration of the Decadent Movement which flourished in Paris in the 1880s and was imported into England by Arthur Symons in 1893.

The Decadent Movement consisted of writers who accepted that modern civilization was in irreversible decline, its essential vitality having been sapped by the luxury and comfort which had enervated its ruling classes. Unlike the Romantics, however, the Decadents saw no virtue in rebellion against this state of affairs; they set out instead to become connoisseurs of perversity, praising the use of psychotropic drugs in the search for 'artificial paradises', and complimenting the excesses of exotic lifestyles. In the meantime, they accepted that the unavoidable lot of the neurotic genius—especially those whose aristocratic ancestry made them victim to hereditary neurasthenia—was to labour under the triple curse of *ennui*, *spleen* and *impuissance*.

Zaleski is a perfect portrait of the Decadent genius. He lives alone, surrounded by ludicrous Orientalia, permanently stoned. He solves the first two mysteries which confront him without rising from the couch where he languishes. The first of them, though it takes the form of a vexing locked-room puzzle, yields very easily to his practised eye because its plot hinges on a typical Decadent syndrome; it involves an aristocrat driven to extraordinary extremes by the treacherous disease which infected the art of so many Decadents while it slowly destroyed them in mind and body: syphilis. That same ailment plays a minor but crucial role in the second story, causing confusion to arise in the matter of the apparent theft of a quasi-magical jewel—whose properties, we are specifically told, may be taken to symbolise an 'inborn perverseness and whimsicality in Nature' whose effects are destined to become ever clearer.

It is the third story in the book which has attracted most attention in modern times, featuring as it does the eugenically-inclined Society of Sparta, which represents itself—in a manner which has seemed to many readers ironically prophetic—as 'The S.S.' Shiel, like so many writers who flirted with Decadence, eventually found it too nihilistic a creed, and reinvested his faith in the philosophy of progress; in his case the philosophy was an un-Marxian brand of socialism curiously alloyed with quasi-Nietzschean ideas regarding the virtues of the *übermensch*; that reinvestment is foreshadowed, in an admittedly curious fashion, in the story. In the Society of Sparta Shiel describes a company of visionaries who have discovered the idea of the overman, but have an entirely mistaken notion of the methods required to bring about his advent—and one might indeed be able to discover in this a prophetic comment on the glamour of fascism. Zaleski, who is emphatically not an overman (though his successor in Shiel's work, Cummings King Monk, might be reckoned one) reveals his limitations in coping with their threat, not because he is unable to counter the menace successfully, *but because he has to rise from his couch to do so*; in this necessity we find the crucial failure of the Decadent Detective.

John Lane, the publisher of *Prince Zaleski*, was host to some of the most significant products of the English Decadent Movement. *The Yellow Book*, whose art editor Aubrey Beardsley also decorated the Keynotes series, was his, and he also published Murray Gilchrist's *The Stone Dragon* and Arthur Machen's *The Great God Pan*, as well as Shiel's second and even more gorgeously Decadent collection *Shapes in the Fire*. By the time the latter appeared, though, the English Decadent Movement was dead—ritually assassinated by the trial and crucifixion of Oscar Wilde—and the word had been expunged from the Victorian literary vocabulary. Shiel went on to other, and better, things—but Prince Zaleski still exists, perhaps the most extraordinary and absurd of all the monuments to the divine insanity which was Decadence.

THE CASES OF PRINCE ZALESKI, BY M. P. SHIEL
Prince Zaleski, 1895 (short-story collection).

100
FRANCES FYFIELD
on
Aurelio Zen

' B ut I don't understand. Surely you're not a real policeman? I mean you work for the Ministry, don't you?'

A complex character, this Commissioner Zen. He may once have peopled his youthful imagination with any number of heroes, none of whom he ever managed to emulate. Unlike the privileged and pedigree hero, Zen would have sprawled at the second fence instead of reaching that winning post which his life has made into a myth. If there was ever a role model for Inspector Zen, he has long since defied it: whatever dreams he has are controlled by inertia or circumstance; whatever good he does has every chance of being obfuscated by accident, corruption and disbelief, all expediencies to which he bows if not with grace, at least with dignity, growing, meantime, another skin. And for all that, remains honest. No one takes bets on Aurelio Zen. Not even his mother.

There may well be an ambiguity in the creation of an Italian detective by an Englishman born in Belfast, but put that out of your mind. Michael Dibdin writes with the instinctive appreciation born of love for his second environment and native Italians read him by the bucketload. Besides, Aurelio himself is a rank outsider in his own fragmented and tribal race. A middle-aged man prone to every temptation under his debilitating sun, succumbing to many of the lures while wondering why he cannot fall prey to more; accepting the corruption of his establishment by bowing halfway. When Zen is in favour, he suffers a temporary love affair with that strange and alien state of being accepted by his peers, looks wistfully at the pleasant sensation and knows it will pass.

Despite the author's alarming skill for the visual, Zen's physical presence remains elusive. He huffs and puffs a bit, is clumsy in a motor car and may be even worse in a fight. He isn't even polite. Acting as if he has sold his soul to the devil without being bothered to argue the price, he remains the cynic who has not yet rid himself of hope, and in the meantime it is entirely credible that the beautiful girl in the office would like to take him home for bed as well as pasta. She would too, if only he could say the right words. Which, of course he can't. There may be poetry in his soul, but rarely on his lips.

His life is a prolonged accident in slow motion. For instance, when Aurelio is sent out to frame an innocent man for the purpose of saving a political villain, he unearths a convenient truth which serves the same purpose. In the habit of criminal intelligence, fact is less complex than anyone imagined, but none of Zen's contemporaries even consider the possibility of his knowledge being honestly acquired at the risk of his own life. Zen merely shrugs and accepts the accolades for being false. He is not there to change the world, and a favour owed 'is better than money in the bank', boy. Better than money in the bank.

To laugh and cry with Zen (frequently the former), is to rejoice in the discovery of an adorable and admirable realist whose life is to be prized beyond millions of lira. Long may he survive, intact with his dreadful knowledge of the world and his wily compassion.

Better far, than money in the bank.

THE CASES OF AURELIO ZEN, BY MICHAEL DIBDIN

Ratking, 1988. *Vendetta*, 1990.

THE CONTRIBUTORS

HAROLD ADAMS is the creator of the Carl Wilcox series, which so far includes eight novels. *The Naked Liar* was nominated for the Shamus Award for Best Novel of 1985 by the Private Eye Writers of America. He would have written on Poppy Ott or anything at all written by Leo Edwards but his own copies were given away by his father when he was in service during WWII. He lives near Minneapolis, Minnesota.

ROBERT ADEY has been a devotee of locked room mysteries and other impossible crimes since an early age, and over thirty years has built up perhaps the finest collection in the world. His bibliography *Locked-Room Murders*, being reissued in 1991, is the definite work on the subject. He is also the co-editor of *The Art of the Impossible*.

JACK ADRIAN is a writer and editor specializing in popular and genre fiction. He has written stories and comic strips under a variety of pseudonyms, and has edited many books, including collections of stories by E.F. Benson, Dornford Yates and Edgar Wallace. He is co-editor of *The Art of the Impossible*.

CATHERINE AIRD is a past Chairman of the Crime Writers' Association. Her police procedural series featuring Inspector C.D. Sloan, set in the imaginary county of Calleshire, are perennially popular for their wit and their endearing characters. She lives in Canterbury.

NIGEL ALGAR is a major collector of American crime fiction. A film expert, he has worked for many years as Head of Marketing for the distribution arm of the British Film Institute. He has also organized a Jim Thompson season at London's National Film Theatre.

ALEX AUSWAKS is a member of the Crime Writers' Association who has for the last few years been living in Israel, where many of his short stories are set.

ADAM BARNETT-FOSTER is a pseudonym and has represented the imaginary country of San Serriffe in an anthology of international science-fiction. The fact that he doesn't exist doesn't appear to bother him unduly.

MARCEL BERLINS is the legal correspondent and crime reviewer for THE TIMES. He is a member of the jury for the Crime Writers' Association Gold and Silver Dagger Awards. He lives in London and is also a contributing editor to ESQUIRE.

BOB BIDERMAN recently moved from Portland, Oregon back to London. Born and educated in America, he divides his time between Britain, France and the USA. He has published six novels including his Joseph Radkin mystery series: *Strange Inheritance, Judgement of Death*, and *The Genesis Files*, which was selected by THE GUARDIAN as one of the top ten crime novels of 1988. His latest Radkin mystery, *Paper Cuts*, concerning the conflict between environmentalists and the lumber industry, is set in America's Pacific Northwest.

SIMON BRETT was President of the Oxford Union Dramatic Society, a Producer of Light Entertainment for BBC Radio and later for London Weekend Television before becoming a full-time writer. He has created the highly popular *After Henry* television and radio series, and is known for his witty crime novels featuring down-on-his-luck actor Charles Paris and the indomitable Mrs Pargeter. His novel *A Shock to the System* was recently filmed, featuring Michael Caine.

PAUL BUCK is known for his avant-garde poetry, his translations of lyrics by Jacques Brel for singer Marc Almond and his novel of the cult film *The Honeymoon Killers*.

GWENDOLINE BUTLER is the author of more than fifty books. She has received a Silver Dagger Award in 1974 for *Coffin for Pandora*, an award for Best Romantic Novel of the Year in 1981, and an Ellery Queen Short Story Award. Her staple character is John Coffin. She also writes as Jennie Melville, featuring woman detective Charmian Daniels in many of her books.

ROBERT CAMPBELL has enjoyed a long career as a writer of

novels, television plays and screenplays. His books include *The Junkyard Dog* which won the Edgar Award, seven other Jimmy Flannery mysteries and the *La La Land* series. His screenwriting credits include *The Masque of the Red Death, Machine Gun Kelly* and *Man of a Thousand Faces* for which he received an Oscar nomination.

SARAH CAUDWELL has, with her first three Hilary Tamar novels, established herself as one the crime field's major authors. *The Sirens Sang of Murder* won the Anthony at the 1990 Bouchercon. She is the daughter of Claud Cockburn and her mother was the real-life model for Isherwood's Sally Bowles. Until recently a practicing barrister, she now writes full-time and lives in London.

JOHN CONQUEST, son of British writer Robert Conquest, was for many years the mainstay of the agitprop section of London's weekly magazine TIME OUT. An enthusiastic lover of all things noir and progressive country and western music, he moved to Austin, Texas, a few years back where he is deeply involved with the local music scene. He is the author of one of the definitive books on private eyes, *Trouble is Their Business*, which has won an Edgar.

SCOTT A. CUPP was born in Oklahoma and lives in Texas. He is a regular reviewer for MYSTERY SCENE magazine and has written 'alternative western' short stories.

CELIA DALE's first novel was published in 1943. She has since written ten others, *Sheep's Clothing* being her most recent. Her story 'Lines of Communication' won the 1986 Crime Writers' Association Veuve Clicquot Short Story Award. Many of her stories have been adapted for radio and television. She lives in North London.

P.C. DOHERTY was born in Middlesbrough and studied at Oxford where he obtained his doctorate. He is a prolific author of historical mysteries featuring English Chancery clerk Hugh Corbett and has begun a new series as Paul Harding. He is the headmaster of a school in North-East London.

WAYNE D. DUNDEE is the founder and editor of the admired small press mystery magazine HARDBOILED. He is the author of four Joe Hannibal novels and a clutch of stories, including

'Body Count' which was nominated for the Edgar. He lives in Illinois.

SUSAN DUNLAP is a founder member and current President of Sisters in Crime. She has three categories of mystery protagonists: California Homicide Detective Jill Smith, forensic pathologist turned private investigator Kiernan O'Shaughnessy, and amateur Sleuth cum public utility meter reader Vejay Haskell. She lives in Albany, California.

MICHAEL EATON is a British scriptwriter. His screenplay for *Fellow Traveller* was nominated for a BAFTA Award, and he has been responsible for a variety of a major television features, including the recent, controversial film on the Lockerbie air disaster.

MARTIN EDWARDS is a Liverpool solicitor. He is the author of five non-fiction books, over 250 articles which have appeared in publications as diverse as THE TIMES, GOOD HOUSEKEEPING and CADS. He reviews crime fiction for THE CRIMINOLO-GIST. He has recently completed his first crime novel, which features a solicitor-detective but which, he hopes, is not in any way autobiographical.

AARON ELKIN's Gideon Oliver mysteries are noted for their combination of traditional whodunit detecting, dry wit and fast action. A sometime boxer, anthropologist and business admini-stration professor, Elkins is now a full-time novelist and technical advisor to the television series adapted from his books. *Old Bones* won the Edgar award. He lives on an island off Washington's Olympic Peninsula.

LOREN D. ESTLEMAN is a three-time winner of the Private Eye Writers of America Shamus Award. An authority on criminal history and the American West, he is best known for his acclaimed Amos Walker private eye mystery novels. He is also one of the major contemporary author of western novels. His most recent books are *Peeper* and the first in his Detroit trilogy *Whiskey River*. He lives in Whitmore Lake, Michigan.

BARRY FANTONI is well-known in England for his cartoons in the satirical magazine PRIVATE EYE, his popular books on astrology and his tongue-in-cheek private eye Mike Dime, who has appeared in two novels and several short stories. He lives in London.

SOEUR VAN FOLLY is the author of the Benny Dickteen mysteries, *Dirty Abbots, Kick the Abbot, The Abbey Habit and Mother Inferior*, soon to be a major series on the Wishaw Cable Television Network. Also gaining wider currency are her Mother Brown stories, especially *Knees Up!*

FRANCES FYFIELD is a pen name for Frances Hegarty, a criminal lawyer, practicing and living in Central London. She has written three novels, *A Question of Guilt, Shadows on the Mirror* and *Trial by Fire*, and, under her own name, *The Playroom*.

NEIL GAIMAN collaborated with Terry Pratchett on the best-selling comedy novel *Good Omens*, and has been acclaimed for his scriptwriting for groundbreaking comics like *Black Orchid, Sandman, Hellblazer, Violent Cases* and *The Books of Magic*.

STEPHEN GALLAGHER is currently one of the biggest names in the horror writing field. He worked in television before becoming a full-time writer. His novels include *Chimera* (recently adapted for the screen by himself), *Follower, Valley of Lights, Oktober, Down River, Rain* and *The Boat House*.

MICHAEL GILBERT is synonymous with classic English crime writing. His first novel, *Close Quarters* appeared in 1947 and his latest is *The Queen Against Karl Mullen*. He is a founder member of the Crime Writers' Association and was awarded the C.B.E. in 1980 in recognition of his legal and writing careers.

JOE GORES, a past President of Mystery Writers of America, has received three Edgars, for best first novel, best short story and best one-hour teleplay. For many years, he was a private detective, has written nine novels, including *Hammett*, filmed by Wim Wenders, and been heavily involved with television (*Columbo, B.L. Stryker, Kojak, Magnum P.I., Mike Hammer* and *Remington Steele* being well-known series to which he has contributed. He lives near San Francisco.

ED GORMAN is the founder and editor of MYSTERY SCENE,

the crime field's indispensible magazine. He is also a prolific author in the crime, horror and western field, in addition to editing the two *Black Lizard Anthologies of Crime Fiction*. His story 'Prisoners' was nominated for the Edgar. He lives in Cedar Rapids, Iowa and is the invisible man of crime fiction, who communicates freely by phone but hasn't been seen by anyone in the crime community for years. He is not Thomas Pynchon, though.

PAULA GOSLING was born in the USA but moved to England in 1964. She worked in advertising before switching to full-time writing. Her first novel won the John Creasey Award and was filmed, alas, with Sylvester Stallone. Lt. Jack Stryker and Inspector Luke Abbott are her two main sleuths. She served as Chairman of the Crime Writers' Association in 1988–89. The OBSERVER described her as 'the deadliest import since they found a black mamba in a crate of oranges at Covent Garden'.

LESLEY GRANT-ADAMSON has been hailed as one the brightest rising stars of British crime fiction. She lives in London and has written seven mystery novels. Her latest, *Flynn* introduces her new series character, gutsy, streetwise private detective Laura Flynn.

COLIN GREENLAND is a young British author and critic. His novel *Take Back Plenty* was presented with the 1991 Arthur C. Clarke Award. He is the reviews editor of FOUNDATION and contributes to THE FACE, THE TLS, and the SUNDAY TIMES, amongst others.

WENDY M. GROSSMAN is a writer and folksinger living in London. She founded THE BRITISH AND IRISH SKEPTIC, now simply THE SKEPTIC, which she edited for two years. Forensic evidence suggests that she first made Miss Marple's acquaintance at the age of eleven or twelve, sandwiched in-between reading Nancy Drew and re-reading Sherlock Holmes.

PHILIP HARBOTTLE is a British literary agent and pulp expert, and probably the world's foremost authority on the works of John Russell Fearn.

ANNE HART lives in St. John's Newfoundland where she is a librarian at Memorial University of Newfoundland and the author of a number of short stories, poems and plays. She has written *The Life and Times of Miss Marple* and *The Life and Times of Hercule Poirot*.

CAROLYN G. HART is the author of the award-winning Annie Laurance series. Annie owns a mystery bookstore, Death on Demand, on an island off the coast of South Carolina. Somehow, together with boyfriend, and later husband, Max Darling, she always ends getting involved with murders. Carolyn who has won both the Agatha and the Anthony awards, lives in Oklahoma.

SCOTT HERBERTSON is an American crime and mystery fan and reader.

REGINALD HILL was a school teacher and lecturer until 1980 when his writing allowed him to go full-time freelance. He has written over thirty novels, including the acclaimed Dalziel and Pascoe series, the last volume of which, *Bones and Silence* won the Gold Dagger Award and was shortlisted for the Edgar. He also writes as Dick Morland, Charles Underhill and Patrick Ruell.

EDWARD D. HOCH, a past President of the Mystery Writers of America was born in Rochester, New York in 1930 and he has lived most of his life there. Following a brief career in advertising, he has been a full-time writer since 1968; the author of over 750 short stories and thirty books. He is an Edgar-winner for his story *The Oblong Room*, currently edits THE YEAR'S BEST MYSTERY AND SUSPENSE STORIES and his stories have appeared in every single issue of ELLERY QUEEN'S MYSTERY MAGAZINE since May 1973.

MELODIE JOHNSON HOWE who lives in Los Angeles, was an actress under contract to Universal Studios in the 1960s and appeared in numerous movies, television shows and commercials. She is married to the Head of Music at Columbia Pictures. Her first novel is *The Mother Shadow*.

JIM HUANG lives in Boston where he runs Spenser's Mystery Bookstore and publishes and edits THE DROOD REVIEW and THE MYSTERY YEARBOOK.

MAXIM JAKUBOWSKI edited this here volume. Born in England and educated in France, he followed a career in the food industry with a long spell in the editorial clouds of the publishing world, before opening the world's largest mystery bookstore MURDER ONE on London's Charing Cross Road. He also edits the Blue Murder imprint, the annual NEW CRIMES anthology and still finds the time to pen even more books when a 25th hour or more intervenes on odd days.

RUSSELL JAMES had seven years of military education before opting out to see the world. Amongst other joys, his favourites include the dawn shift on a Mediterranean radio station and backstage work at the Old Vic. He later became a systems analyst with IBM before setting up his own business consultancy. His first two novels are *Underground* and *Daylight*.

H.R.F. KEATING is the creator of Inspector Ghote, one of crime and mystery's most popular investigators. He has been a Chairman of the Crime Writers' Association and the Society of Authors, President of the Detection Club, and twice a winner of the Gold Dagger Award. He was the crime books reviewer of the TIMES for fifteen years and is a regular broadcaster.

CATHERINE KENNEY was for many years Chairman of the English Department at Chicago's Mundelein College. She is the author of *The Remarkable Case of Dorothy L. Sayers* in addition to a book on James Thurber.

JERRY KENNEALLY is himself a private investigator, living and working in the San Francisco Bay area. He is the author of the Nick Polo mystery series.

PHILIP KERR was born in Edinburgh and lives in London. As a freelance journalist, he has written for a number of newspapers and magazines, and reviews crime for TIME OUT. He has published three novels featuring pre (and post) war Berlin P.I. Bernie Gunther: *March Violets, The Pale Criminal* and *A German Requiem* He has also edited *The Penguin Book of Lies*.

DANIEL PATRICK KING is a regular reviewer for WORLD LITERATURE TODAY and contributes articles on criminal law and criminology to international journals. A professor and writer, he has contributed to 20TH CENTURY CRIME WRITERS.

DAVID LANGFORD is the winner of innumerable Hugo awards in the science fiction field. A keen collector of golden age crime, he is the author of several novels, including *The Space Eater* and non-fiction books, often of a humourous nature. He lives in Reading.

ANTHONY LEJEUNE is one of Britain's major crime reviewers, covering the genre in his DAILY TELEGRAPH column. He is also the author of several novels in the field and the definitive book on London clubs.

MICHAEL Z. LEWIN was born and educated in the USA but now lives in Somerset, England. He is the creator of private eye Albert Samson and police lieutenant Leroy Powder. He has twice been nominated for Edgars. The 'Z' stands for Zinn, which is his mother's maiden name.

MARGARET LEWIS was born in Northern Ireland, and brought up and educated in Western Canada. She teaches Shakespeare for the Open University and works for the Public Relations Department of the University of Newcastle upon Tyne. Her authorised biography of Ngaio Marsh appeared in 1991.

PETER LOVESEY is currently Chairman of the Crime Writers' Association. He is the creator of Victorian detective Sergeant Cribb who appears in eight novels and two television series. He has also written two novels featuring the sleuthing of Queen Victoria's son, Albert, Prince of Wales. He has won both the Gold and Silver Dagger awards, the Veuve Clicquot short story prize, the French Grand Prix de Littérature Policiere and been nominated for the Edgar.

RICHARD A. LUPOFF is well-known in the science fiction field for his many novels, but he has also written acclaimed critical books on Edgar Rice Burroughs and the comics genre. A short film based on a short story of his was nominated for the Oscar, and he hosts his own radio show in San Francisco. His last novel was *The Comic Book Killer*.

SHARYN McCRUMB won the Edgar in 1988 for her tongue in cheek mystery *Bimbos of the Death Sun*. She has been nominated three times for the Anthony, and twice for the Agathas, winning the award for her short story 'A Wee Doch and Doris'.

JILL McGOWN was born in Scotland, but has lived in Corby, Northants since she was ten. While she was working for the British Steel Corporation, she won a BBC short story competition and turned to full-time writing when she was made redundant. She has now published eight crime novels to much acclaim in Britain and the USA, the latest being *The Murders of Mrs Austin and Mrs Beale*.

JONATHAN MAIN was until recently the Central London representative for a major British publisher. He has now returned to the book trade whence he initially came.

JOHN MALCOLM is very popular with his eight Tim Simpson mysteries set in the art world. The latest in *Sheep, Goats and Soap*. He lives in Sussex.

MARGARET MARON is the creator of Lt. Sigrid Harald, NYPD and of Judge Deborah Knott, Colleton Co., NC. She is a past President of Sisters in Crime and serves on the Mystery Writers of America board of directors.

JAMES MELVILLE was born in London and worked for many years as a cultural diplomat with the British council in Indonesia, Hungary and Japan. His series character Superintendent Tetsuo Otani of Kobe first appeared in *The Wages of Zen* in 1979. Since, he has published eleven more Otani novels and two thrillers based on actual events in 20th century Japanese history.

BARBARA MERTZ is also Barbara Michaels who is also Elizabeth Peters. As Barbara Mertz, she is the author of definitive books on Egyptian history; as Barbara Michaels, she is generally recognized as the queen of romantic suspense, and as Elizabeth Peters she is known for her delightful thriller romances with exotic settings, making use of her own archaeological background. She collects great hats and lives in Maryland.

ION MILLS is the creator and publisher of Britain's innovative hardboiled reprint list No Exit Press. He lives in Hertsfordshire and also has a passion for gaming and racing greyhound dogs.

SUSAN MOODY was born and educated in Oxford. After spending ten years in the US, she returned to England and now lives in Bedford. She is the creator of the indomitable heroine Penny Wanawake, who has so far appeared in seven novels. She is a past Chairman of the Crime Writers' Association.

MICHAEL MOORCOCK is one of the major personalities in the science fiction and fantasy field, the prolific author of countless novels and entertainments, in addition to his editing of NEW WORLDS magazine in the 1960s which is generally recognized as having instigated new levels of quality in the genre. He is a winner of the Nebula award and a list of his titles would add another twenty pages to this book, but they are all well worth reading, and so say I.

PATRICIA MOYES won the Edgar in 1971 and was for six years Assistant Editor of VOGUE. She now lives in the British Virgin Islands and is the creator of perennial favourites Henry and Emmy Tibbett, who appear in seventeen novels, the last being *Black Girl, White Girl.*

HAUGHTON MURPHY is the author of the Reuben Frost novels, most recently *Murder Saves Face*. He lives in New York City, where he practiced law before becoming a full-time writer in 1989.

KIM NEWMAN is a British writer and film critic. A prolific author, he has published half a dozen novels in the sf and fantasy field (as himself and alter-ego Jack Yeovil), reviews in a variety of British newspapers and magazines and on television, and has written books on horror films and the western.

VICTORIA NICHOLS and SUSAN THOMPSON both live in California. They are the authors of *Silk Stalkings: When Women Write of Murder*, the first comprehensive book on series characters created by women authors in crime and mystery fiction. It was nominated for the Edgar.

FREDERICK NOLAN is a leading British spy thriller writer. His *The Oshawa Project* was filmed as *Brass Target*. He has also written biographies of Rodgers and Hammerstein and Jay J. Armes, detective. An expert on westerns and the old West, he has written a definitive study of the Lincoln County War of 1978 and pens a regular column for THE BOOKSELLER.

HELEN ESPER OLMSTED is a scriptwriter and co-producer for Homicide Host Productions. She is the creator of Lt. Alfredo Raconni and her interactive plays have been produced throughout the USA and Canada. She lives in Howell, Michigan.

RALPH H. PECK has published his first mystery novel, *Murder on a Quiet Street*. He first broke into print in OPEN ROAD FOR BOYS when he was twelve. He has worked as a copywriter and for THE NEW YORK TIMES. He is better known as a travel writer and forests blame him for 36 books. He lives near Buffalo, NY.

MIKE PHILLIPS was born in Guyana and came to Britain in 1955. He has been a teacher, has worked in journalism and broadcasting and currently lectures on media studies at Central London Polytechnic. His Sam Dean novels have been wonderfully received in Britain, with the second volume *The Late Candidate*, winning the Silver Dagger, and the first *Blood Rights*, made into a popular TV series.

BILL PRONZINI has published over forty novels, three non-fiction books, four collections of short stories and some 275 uncollected stories and other pieces. He has also edited or co-edited upwards of sixty anthologies in a variety of different fields. He has written 18 novels in the 'Nameless' series and received two Shamus awards and the Lifetime Achievement Award from the Private Eye Writers of America, and five Edgar nominations.

B.J. RAHN is a professor in the English Department at Hunter College, City University of New York. She has been researching, writing and teaching about the modern crime novel for the past ten years, and contributed to THE ARMCHAIR DETECTIVE and TWENTIETH CENTURY CRIME WRITERS.

JERRY RAINE was born in Yorkshire, brought up in East Africa and has also lived in Australia. In 1986, he was a winner of THE

MAIL ON SUNDAY's fiction competition. He is Deputy Manager of London's specialist bookstore, MURDER ONE.

MIKE RIPLEY is the creator of cab-driving sleuth Fitzroy Maclean Angel, who has now appeared in four novels. He is the crime reviewer for THE SUNDAY TELEGRAPH and, in civilian life, head of Public Relations for the Brewers Society which often affords him the opportunity to sample beer. *Angel Touch* won the Crime Writers' Last Laugh Award for best humourous novel of 1990.

PETER ROBINSON was born in Yorkshire but now lives in Toronto. His first Inspector Banks novel, *Gallows View*, was short-listed for the John Creasey Award and he has since added three more to the series. His latest book is his first not to feature Banks, *Caedmon's Song*, but there is another Banks, *Past Reason Hated* in the pipeline.

MARK SCHORR is the author of the criminally out-of-print Red Diamond Private Eye series, the first of which was nominated for the Edgar. He has written nine novels, spanning the private eye genre, historical mysteries, spy fiction, police thrillers and action adventure. He lives in Portland, Oregon.

BENJAMIN M. SCHUTZ is a forensic psychologist who specializes in matters of child sexual abuse and custody and visitation disputes. His first Leo Haggerty novel, *Embrace the Wolf*, was nominated for the Shamus award but his third in the series *A Tax in Blood*, actually won the award. There are now five volumes in the series.

PHILIP L. SCOWCROFT is a British mystery fiction expert and regular contributor to CADS, one of the field's most learned magazines.

LINDA SEMPLE was the co-editor for the ground-breaking feminist crime imprint at Pandora. She has written for many women's magazines and works at London's feminist bookstore, SILVER MOON.

IAIN SINCLAIR's first novel *White Chappell, Scarlet Tracings* was runner-up for the prestigious Guardian Fiction Prize in 1987.

His second, *Downriver* has been hailed by Peter Ackroyd as 'a confirmation of the fact that Iain Sinclair is the most inventive novelist of his generation'. Iain Sinclair lives in London where, when not writing, he is a bookdealer specializing in the work of the Beat authors and writers of noir pulp fiction.

RALPH SPURRIER worked for many years in bookselling and publishing before setting up POSTMORTEM BOOKS, Britain's leading crime and mystery mail order company. He has for two years running sponsored the Crime Writers' Association Gold and Silver Dagger awards.

BRIAN STABLEFORD is the author of many books in the science fiction and critical field, including *The Sociology of Science Fiction*. He is a specialist in 19th century and early 20th century literature and a frequent reviewer. His novel *The Empire of Fear* was short-listed for the Arthur C. Clarke Award and his latest collection of stories is *Sexual Chemistry*.

JAN BITSCH STEFFENSEN is the editor of PINKERTON, the only Danish periodical devoted to crime fiction.

JULIAN SYMONS has been showered with virtually every award, prize or distinction the crime field can offer. In addition to his acclaimed novels of mystery, he has also written a history of the genre, *Bloody Murder* and biographies of Dickens, Conan Doyle, Carlyle and Poe. He lives in Kent, near the sea and is still a regular reviewer of mystery fiction.

MARK TIMLIN is a South London author who has made a strong impact on British crime and mystery fiction with the first four of his hardboiled Nick Sharman, ex-cop and doper sleuth.

DUNCAN TORRENS is a pseudonym and can be found in the LONDON A–Z.

DEBORAH VALENTINE is an American author currently living in London and much enjoying her research in local jazz clubs. Her sleuth is ex-policeman Kevin Bryce. She used to live in a small port town located between San Francisco and the Napa Valley, where she pursued her interest in wine and gardening. London must have changed all that.

CAN VAN ASH is the co-author (with Elizabeth Sax Rohmer) of Fu-Manchu creator Sax Rohmer's biography *Master of Villainy*. He is also literary executor for the Rohmer estate and the author of two pastiche novels, involving both Fu-Manchu and Sherlock Holmes.

ROBERT WALLACE was born in Melbourne and lives in the mountains of the eastern seaboard of New South Wales. He has written four thrillers featuring art sleuth Essington Holt as well as a nastly little thriller, *Payday*, and three nice novels in which the thrills are fewer and more widely spaced.

DAVID WILLIAMS is Welsh. After Oxford and the Navy, he turned to full-time writing after a career in the advertising industry. He is the creator of Mark Treasure who figures in all of his fifteen ingenious and witty whodunnits. He lives in Wentworth in Surrey and always wears cream-white ties and a red flower in his button-hole.

JOHN WILLIAMS was born in Wales and now lives in London. A journalist and reviewer for NME, MARIE CLAIRE, THE FACE and ARENA, amongst others, he has just published a book of travel and interviews with many of the leading American crime and mystery writers, *Into the Badlands*. He has survived a drinking binge with James Crumley.

BARBARA WILSON is a co-founder of the influential feminist publishing house The Seal Press. Her feminist mysteries feature sleuth Pam Nilsen who has appeared in three books so far, including her latest, *The Dog Collar Murders*. She has also published collections of short stories and is an award-winning translator.

ADRIAN WOOTTON is a British film expert and a director of the Nottingham Broadway Media Center, where he has organized the Shots in the Dark mystery Festival.

ERIC WRIGHT left England in 1951, still wet behind the ears, He dried out on the Canadian prairies, mostly at the University of Manitoba. He lives in Toronto, where for thirty years he tought English literature at Ryerson Polytechnical Insitute. He has written eight Charlie Salter novels, the first of which, *The Night the Gods Smiled*, won the John Creasey Award.

DOUGLAS WYNN worked for many years as a research chemist and a technical college lecturer. He retired early to concentrate on writing and his interest in criminology. He has written several books on true murder cases and lives in Lincolnshire.